Jossey-Bass Teacher

Jossey-Bass Teacher provides educators with practical knowledge and tools to create a positive and lifelong impact on student learning. We offer classroom-tested and research-based teaching resources for a variety of grade levels and subject areas. Whether you are an aspiring, new, or veteran teacher, we want to help you make every teaching day your best.

From ready-to-use classroom activities to the latest teaching framework, our value-packed books provide insightful, practical, and comprehensive materials on the topics that matter most to K–12 teachers. We hope to become your trusted source for the best ideas from the most experienced and respected experts in the field.

Mega-Fun Math Games and Puzzles for the Elementary Grades

Over 125 Activities That Teach Math
Facts, Concepts, and Thinking Skills

Michael S. Schiro

JOSSEY-BASS
A Wiley Imprint
www.josseybass.com

Published by Jossey-Bass
A Wiley Imprint
989 Market Street, San Francisco, CA 94103-1741—www.josseybass.com

Jossey-Bass books and products are available through most bookstores. To contact Jossey-Bass directly call our Customer Care Department within the U.S. at 800-956-7739, outside the U.S. at 317-572-3986, or fax 317-572-4002.

Jossey-Bass also publishes its books in a variety of electronic formats. Some content that appears in print may not be available in electronic books.

ISBN: 978-0-470-34475-0
Printed in the United States of America

FIRST EDITION

PB Printing   10 9 8 7 6 5 4 3 2

About This Book

This book has two parts. The first part consists of games that are designed primarily to help elementary school children learn, remember, and practice basic arithmetic facts, skills, and concepts by participating in enjoyable activities. The second part consists of games and puzzles that focus on helping elementary school children learn algebra, geometry, measurement, and probability and data analysis. Both parts of the book are also concerned with providing teachers and parents with activities that help children learn the mathematics process skills of problem solving, reasoning and proof, communication, representation, and connections.

The games and puzzles in both parts of this book are built around what we know about how children best learn mathematics: through the use of physical manipulatives and visual images within the context of developmentally appropriate practice, where cooperative groups allow for enjoyable social interactions that aid the learner in the construction of meaning through mathematical communication and connections.

The arithmetic games in the first part of this book are built around inexpensive and readily available materials: egg cartons, paper and pencils, tongue depressors, blank cards (or index cards), wood cubes (or dice), and paperboard. They are easy to make and will take little time or skill to construct. The games are grouped by the materials used to make them. These games deal with a wide range of arithmetic topics: from mastering basic addition and multiplication facts to using the long division algorithm, from learning place value concepts to learning to factor numbers, from using whole numbers to working with fractions and decimals. They also contain activities on other areas of mathematics, such as probability, algebra, and measurement. A Game Grade Level and NCTM Content Area Reference Chart that accompanies this book makes it easy to locate games related to particular content areas. Note that although the main game that is described may provide children with practice in one content area (for example, whole number addition), the variations of the game may describe ways in which it can be altered to focus on other areas of mathematics (such as multiplication of fractions).

The games and puzzles in the second part of this book introduce children to many areas of study, including algebra, logic, geometry, graph theory, number theory, knot theory, game theory, topology, and transformational geometry. In doing so, they offer students insight into the wide range of topics that mathematicians deal with. These games and puzzles use a variety of instructional media, including visual images (in bridge crossing puzzles), physical manipulatives (in crayon digits), and children's physical movements (in people puzzles). All the games and puzzles are easy to construct, and use inexpensive materials that already exist in most schools and homes or that can be easily obtained from a stationery or hardware store. Part Two of this book also focuses more on the process standards of mathematics: on helping children learn the skills and processes involved in mathematical problem solving, reasoning and proof, communication, representation, and connections.

The games and puzzles in both parts of this book help children acquire many skills that would not normally be classified as solely mathematical in nature. For example, they foster language skills. As children play the games and solve the puzzles, they also further develop their hand-eye coordination, their concentration and mental alertness, and their senses of spatial orientation, visual discrimination, memory, and timing. The activities in this book also cultivate children's ability to listen carefully, speak and write precisely, and think clearly, as students express mathematical ideas to their peers, remind each other of rules and directions, interact in the social patterns that gaming and puzzle conventions establish, and teach each other the reasons why certain answers, algorithms, or mathematical meanings are or are not correct.

About the Author

Michael Stephen Schiro was born and raised in Washington DC. He majored in mathematics at Tufts University, with minors in philosophy and English. He taught at the high school, middle school, and elementary school levels in Massachusetts, North Carolina, Pennsylvania, and Iran. He received his master's and doctorate from Harvard University in curriculum and instruction. He has taught courses on curriculum theory and mathematics education at Boston College for the last thirty years. He has published four books that explore ways of enriching the teaching of mathematics. The books present ways of using games and puzzles during mathematics instruction, ways of integrating mathematics and children's literature in the classroom, and ways of using oral storytelling during mathematics instruction. He resides in Newton, Massachusetts, and Mendocino, California. He has two children, Stephanie and Arthur. His current hobbies include writing children's novels that involve children using mathematics in different cultures, collecting puzzles that can be used in the teaching of mathematics, and walking in forests and beside the ocean.

Acknowledgments

I thank Rainy Cotti for her continued support of my work on this book and for writing up the following puzzles: Mirror Puzzlers, Crayon Digits, Crayon Constructions, Triangle Trouble, the Magic Tile, Coin Challenges, and Mystery Monsters.

I thank Doris Lawson for her continued support of my work in creating math games and puzzles and for trying out so many of them in her classroom.

I thank my many university colleagues, and in particular Pam Halpern and Lillie Albert, for their encouragement and the feedback they have given me when their students have used my creations.

And I thank the many creators of games and puzzles who have come before me, and upon whose work the ideas in this book build. In particular I thank Stewart Coffin, the master creator of wood puzzles, for his encouragement in creating the scissors and rope puzzles (which were originally constructed out of leather); Marion Walter, whose work at Education Development Corporation on such materials as Mirror Cards and Chip Trading were an inspiration to me; Martin Gardner, whose articles on math games and puzzles in *Scientific American* inspired many lovers of games and puzzles during the middle of the last century; and Sam Lloyd, whose books on puzzles, which were written over a hundred years ago (many of which are now on the Internet in his *Cyclopedia of Puzzles*), continue to inspire all of us who are interested in puzzles.

For my children, Arthur and Stephanie,
who have always enjoyed the games, puzzles, and stories that
I collect, invent, and adapt

and

For Rainy Cotti, Doris Lawson, Lillie Albert, Pam Halpern,
and everyone else who has encouraged me to continue my
work with instructional games, puzzles, and stories

Contents

Part Two: Problem-Solving Mathematics Puzzles   175

Game Grade Level and NCTM Content Area Reference Chart

Part 1

X = shows skill emphasis of main game / 0 = shows skill emphasis of variations	Page	Grades of Main Game	Grades of Variation	Addition	Subtraction	Multiplication	Division	Place Value	Fractions	Inequalities	Multiples and Factors	Algebra	Geometry	Measurement	Data Analysis and Probability	Problem Solving	Reasoning and Proof	Communication	Connections	Representation
Count	25	1–5	3–5					X	0							X	X	X		X
Capture the Fort	26	1–5				X				X					X	X		X	X	
Foreheaded	27	1–5						X								X	X	X		
Googol	29	1–5								X								X		X
Number-Tac-Toe	30	1–5		X		X											X	X	X	
Ask and Give	33	3–5		X	X			X										X		
Hangmath	34	3–5		X	X	X	X	X								X		X		
Factors	35	3–5		X		X	X				X					X		X		
Get One	38	3–5			X						X							X		
Write It	38	3–5		X		X	X				X				X			X		
Coordinate Tic-Tac-Toe	39	2–5											X		X			X		X
Egg-O	42	1–5	3–5	X	X	X		0	0									X		
Egg Race	44	1–3	3–5	X		0												X		
More or Less	46	3–5	1–3	0		X				X					X			X		
Egg Bump	48	1–3		X	X													X		
Egg-a-Round	49	1–3	3–5	X					0	0								X		
Place-an-Egg Value	50	1–4		X				X		X								X		X
Bing-Egg-O	51	3–5	4–5	0		X				0								X		
Three Hundred	53	2–5		X	X			X							X	X		X		
Egg Throw	56	3–5	1–4	X		X		0						0				X		
Divide and Move	58	3–5					X											X		
Egg-Cala	59	1–5														X		X		
Nines	62	1–4		X	X										X	X		X	X	
Roll It	63	1–5	1–5	X	0	0	0									X		X		
Cardinal-Ordinal	64	1–2		X														X	X	
Product Shot	67	3–5	1–3	X	0	X									X	X		X		
Rectangles	69	3–5				X							X			X		X	X	

	Page	Grades of Main Game	Grades of Variation	Addition	Subtraction	Multiplication	Division	Place Value	Fractions	Inequalities	Multiples/Factors	Algebra	Geometry	Measurement	Data Analysis & Probability	Problem Solving	Reasoning & Proof	Communication	Connections	Representation
Drop the Die on the Donkey	146	3–5	1–2	0		X												X		
Divi	148	1–5	1–3				X	0										X		
Race	151	1–5	3–5	X	X	X	X		0		0			0				X		
Coordinate Submarine	153	2–5											X		X			X		
Off the Grid	154	2–5											X		X			X		
Jump the Answer	156	1–5		X	X	X	X											X		
Math Ball	158	1–2	2–4					X	0		0							X		
Simon Says Math	159	1–5	3–5	X	X	X	X	0										X	X	
Number Calisthenics	160	1–4						X										X	X	
Fingers	161	1–2	3–4	X		0								X				X		
Hands In	162	1–3		X										X				X		
Twist-'em	163	1–5	2–5	0	0			X										X	X	
Math Rover	164	1–3	3–5	X	X			0			0	0						X	X	
Operation Hopscotch	165	3–5	2–4	0		X												X	X	
Bean Bag Toss	167	3–5	1–5	0		X	0											X		
Math Jacks	168	3–5				X												X	X	
Math Marbles	169	1–3	3–5	X		0												X	X	
Bounce	171	1–4	3–5	X	X	0									X			X		
Number Race	172	1–5	2–5	X	X	X	X	0										X		

Part 2

X = shows skill emphasis of main game 0 = shows skill emphasis of variations	Page	Grades of Main Game	Grades of Variation	Addition	Subtraction	Multiplication	Division	Place Value	Fractions	Inequalities	Multiples/Factors	Algebra	Geometry	Measurement	Data Analysis & Probability	Problem Solving	Reasoning & Proof	Communication	Connections	Representation
Magic Circles	180	1–5		X								X				X	X			
Magic Squares	182	1–5		X								X				X	X			
Hundreds Chart Explorations	184	1–5						X				X	X			X	X	X	X	X
Hundreds Chart Discoveries	187	2–5		X		X		X				X				X	X	X	X	X
Mystery Monsters	197	1–5											X			X	X	X	X	X
Pockets Full of Pennies	200	1–5		X	X							X				X	X	X	X	X
More Pockets, More Pennies	202	1–5		X	X	X						X				X	X	X	X	X
Magical Math!	204	2–5		X	X	X						X		X		X	X	X	X	X
More Magical Math!	208	3–5		X	X	X	X					X				X	X	X	X	X
Visual Estimation	217	1–5											X	X		X	X	X	X	X
Line Designs	221	2–5											X	X		X		X	X	X
Shape Designs	225	2–5											X	X		X		X	X	X
Triangle Trouble!	231	1–5											X			X		X	X	X
The Magic Tile	234	1–5											X			X			X	X
Crayon Digits	242	1–5											X			X			X	X
Crayon Constructions	245	1–5											X			X	X	X	X	X

X = shows skill emphasis of main game 0 = shows skill emphasis of variations	Page	Grades of Main Game	Grades of Variation	Addition	Subtraction	Multiplication	Division	Place Value	Fractions	Inequalities	Multiples/ Factors	Algebra	Geometry	Measurement	Data Analysis & Probability	Problem Solving	Reasoning & Proof	Communication	Connections	Representation
Coin Challenges	248	1–5											X			X	X	X	X	X
Mirror Puzzlers	251	1–5											X			X	X	X	X	X
Count Up	260	1–5		X							X	X				X	X	X	X	X
Dicey Count Up	260	1–5		X							X	X				X	X	X	X	X
Fill Up	261	1–5		X							X	X				X	X	X	X	X
Pick Up	261	1–5		X							X	X				X	X	X	X	X
Run the Track	262	1–5		X							X	X				X	X	X	X	X
Calculator Countdown	262	1–5		X							X	X				X	X	X	X	X
Odds	263	1–5		X							X	X				X	X	X	X	X
I'll Cross That Bridge When I Get to It	271	1–5											X			X	X	X	X	X
More Bridge Crossing Puzzles	274	1–5											X			X	X	X	X	X
Bug Problems	276	1–5											X			X	X	X	X	X
Tracing Puzzles	280	1–5											X			X	X	X	X	X
Geometric Travels	282	1–5											X			X	X	X	X	X
Line Crossing Puzzles	284	1–5											X			X	X	X	X	X
People Puzzles	294	1–5											X			X	X	X	X	
Scissors Puzzles	297	1–5											X			X	X	X	X	
Household Puzzles	299	1–5											X			X	X	X	X	

Introduction

As an introduction to this book, we will first look at the reasons for using games and puzzles during mathematics instruction, then discuss the mathematics content and process standards, and finally turn to practical considerations about how to use games and puzzles in the classroom.

Mathematics Games and Puzzles: Why Use Them?

In this introduction, I will use the word "game" to include both games and puzzles. In general, the distinction between games and puzzles is that in games, two or more players compete against each other to try to reach some goal (usually winning the game), whereas in puzzles, one or more players cooperate with each other to try to reach a goal. Mathematics games (both games and puzzles) are structured activities designed to help children learn both the content and processes of mathematics; children use mathematics manipulatives, visuals, or symbols to accomplish a competitive or cooperative goal, which requires mathematical communication that is directed toward maintaining the activity as participants monitor each other's decisions, moves, reasons, and answers while helping each other learn and understand mathematics. Puzzles offer the opportunity for children to work by themselves; however, it is assumed that children will share with others their solutions and their reasons why their solutions work—and thus the individual struggle to solve a problem becomes a cooperative activity in which children work together to understand mathematics.

When games are used to help children learn mathematics, many parents and teachers inevitably ask, "Why are children playing games, and what are they learning?" Many parents have never thought about using games as a teaching tool, and their questions about why children are "playing games" during math time deserve to be answered, to help them become comfortable with and supportive of their child's educational experiences. Most teachers know that games provide a fun way of learning mathematics. But there are also other reasons for using math games, sixteen of which I briefly present in the following paragraphs. Keeping these reasons in mind when using math games with children can help you maximize the benefits of the games. Keeping these reasons in mind when you speak with other adults (whether parents, teachers, or school administrators) about why your students are playing math games can help them understand their instructional value and become supporters of using games in children's education.

1

1. **Games can make mathematics enjoyable and fun.** Many children think that mathematics is not fun, but it can be an enjoyable endeavor if we ask children to do mathematics in a fun context. Math games are fun to play. They can help children learn to enjoy doing mathematics by associating it with something that they enjoy doing. Children who balk at doing ten problems on a worksheet will frequently enjoy doing fifty problems while playing a game. When children are having fun playing math games, let them know how much they are enjoying mathematics.

2. **Games can help children perceive mathematics as part of our everyday world.** Many children think that mathematics is an activity that takes place only during mathematics time in school. Helping children see how mathematics is part of their everyday world and how it can be found in many of their endeavors is an important part of helping children see the power that mathematics has for them in their lives. Many math games are variations on games that children already know. For example, Operations War is simply a variation of the card game of War. Help children see the link between math games and the everyday games they normally play. It helps them see how mathematics can be relevant to their daily endeavors.

3. **Games can help children view mathematics as a human endeavor, as something that people create.** Mathematics was not given to mankind by the gods, but created by people for their own use and pleasure. Unfortunately, many children think that mathematics is not a human endeavor, in the sense that the problems they are given and the numbers they must deal with come from some unknown source, frequently either a textbook or a photocopying machine. This is not the way things have to be. Many math games put children in charge of generating the numbers they use and thus the problems they solve—frequently by giving children control of number-generating devices, such as dice. In doing so, games help children see mathematics as a human endeavor in which they can participate. This is important for children to learn if they are to become autonomous creators and users of mathematics. To promote this, allow children to alter math games—by changing their rules, the numbers used within them, or their goals—to accomplish their own purposes.

4. **Games can help mathematics be a social activity.** Frequently mathematics is viewed as an endeavor individuals engage in by themselves. This need not be the case. Professional mathematicians often work together. Children who play math games learn together in social groups. There are many advantages to learning in social groups: people enjoy social interactions; social interactions often motivate people to do things they might not otherwise do; learning from a peer who explains things in childlike terms frequently facilitates learning; and teaching a peer who does not understand something can increase both a child's self-esteem and his or her own understanding of the material being taught. The social nature of games can also create a structured environment

in which children learn to interact socially, particularly if a sensitive adult acts as a facilitator of social interactions.

5. **Games can help children test the adequacy of their mathematical concepts and algorithms and revise inefficient, inadequate, or erroneous ones.** The immediate feedback children receive from their peers while playing math games can help them evaluate their mathematical concepts and algorithms and revise inefficient, inadequate, or erroneous ones. This can occur if children must evaluate the adequacy of their concepts and algorithms during a game when peers challenge their behavior, and if they must attempt to justify and communicate the decisions they make during a game using mathematical reasoning and proof. As children justify their decisions, thoughts, and thought processes, they can be challenged by peers and confronted with alternatives, alternatives that can lead them to evaluate and revise their decision-making processes, meanings, or algorithms. In addition, a game serves as an ideal testing ground for newly formulated meanings.

6. **Mathematical games can help children create mathematical meanings over and over again for themselves until the meanings become well established.** Children cannot acquire a full understanding and mastery of mathematical meanings, skills, and concepts after one exposure. They frequently have to encounter mathematical experiences many times and rediscover or reinvent the same meaning repeatedly before they sufficiently understand it and retain it in their consciousness in such a way that they can use it productively. The repetitive nature of math games allows children to repeatedly confront experiences that form concepts and to continually reinvent or rediscover meanings, facts, skills, and concepts. Math games also create a context in which children can repeatedly explain mathematics to each other and, by so doing, help one another construct meanings by rethinking partially developed thoughts. The repetitive nature of math games also allows children to repeatedly use the same problem-solving strategies, use similar types of mathematical reasoning and proof, and practice the use of mathematical language, representations, and communication.

7. **Games can help children view mathematics as understandable.** Many children do not understand the mathematics they use. They simply know how to find answers to problems by rote application of algorithms. It is important for children to realize that they can understand mathematics, that it is not magic. Most math games, in and of themselves, do not attempt to provide children with mathematical meanings. Children must construct mathematical meanings for themselves. What math games can provide is an enjoyable social context in which children can question and share mathematical meanings. During games, encourage children to question answers, concepts, algorithms, and meanings. Encourage peers (as well as adults) to try to answer questions and to partake in the social construction and reconstruction of mathematical meanings that benefit all involved in the process of communicating. Through such endeavors

of making mathematics meaningful, children discover that they can understand it.

8. **Games can help children learn mathematics in a variety of ways.** For many children, learning mathematics involves only the two activities of listening to teachers and solving problems with paper and pencil. The discoveries of psychology indicate that other types of learning activities are also important: large motor activities, in which children learn through the movement of their bodies; the use of manipulative materials, which facilitate learning by letting children do things with their hands; the use of visual images, which assist learning by letting children "see" how and why things work; and the use of social activities, which aid learning by letting children share meaning by communicating with each other. Math games offer children a wide variety of learning activities: most games involve social interactions; physical education games involve large motor skills; board games can be decorated to encourage fantasy; dice and egg carton games capitalize on the music that results from manipulating the gaming materials; and most games are played by manipulating physical materials.

9. **Games can help children discover that there is more than one way of doing mathematics.** Frequently children believe that there is only one correct way of carrying out a mathematical operation or understanding a mathematical concept. This can inhibit learning. Listening to each other describe their algorithms and meanings, in a setting where there is a real need to understand others' justifications, can lead children to understand that there are different ways of conceptualizing mathematics, some of which are more effective than others. This understanding can open up a child's appreciation of his or her own unique meanings, receptivity to new ways of doing things, and inclination to compare different conceptualizations for their efficiency, effectiveness, or meaning.

10. **Games can help children develop their self-confidence as learners and users of mathematics.** Children's self-confidence can increase when they are put in enjoyable and challenging situations where they must make decisions about mathematical issues, determine the adequacy of each other's mathematical decisions and answers, figure out how they arrived at answers and explain their thinking to others in a comprehensible way, debate the truth of each other's mathematical explanations, police the rules of math games, or jointly reach consensus about how to alter the rules of a game. If we give children the responsibility to act as autonomous decision makers and as responsible supervisors of their own and others' learning, we can help them increase their self-confidence as mathematicians.

11. **In mathematics games, a child's mistakes offer opportunities for learning.** Children's mistakes help us and them comprehend what they do not understand. In the context of a game, the mistakes provide a unique teachable

moment—the ability to teach a child concepts at the time and in the situation in which the child needs to understand those concepts. Peers, a teacher, or a parent can help children learn when an error occurs. What we need to emphasize is that when playing a game, the person who makes an error is not "bad," that we learn by making mistakes, and that we all have a responsibility for helping each other play the game—and that this includes helping each other understand the mathematics necessary to play the game. If children make mathematical errors, it is because they can think and have constructed inadequate meanings. Encourage children to think during a game, to share their thoughts, and to try to convince each other using mathematical reasoning and proof of their answers to problems and their reasons for believing those answers to be correct. By verbally justifying their reasons for believing something, children verbalize their meanings, expose those meanings to others to examine for errors, and reconstruct those meanings for themselves. Both the "teacher" and the learner have an opportunity to learn when an error is discovered.

12. **Mathematics games can help children memorize number facts.** Number facts are often best memorized in contexts that create a need for them to be memorized, provide for ample repetitive recall of what was memorized, supply both immediate and desirable rewards for memorizing the facts, and allow children to meaningfully comprehend facts while memorizing them. Mathematics games can provide this context.

13. **Games can help children maintain mathematical facts and concepts that they have just learned.** We often forget things that we do not regularly use. If a child learns multiplication facts in September and then does not practice them for months, he or she is likely to forget what was learned. If a child forgets because learning was not maintained, he or she must relearn the number facts. This is neither efficient nor supportive of a child's self-concept. Playing math games is an excellent way to maintain concepts, skills, and algorithms by providing children with regular practice using what they have learned. Games are an excellent maintenance activity because children love to play them, even if they require the repetitive recalling of math facts, repeated use of arithmetic algorithms, and repeated presentation of mathematical concepts.

14. **Games can help children see mathematics as involving the use of reasoning, thinking, problem solving, and communication.** Mathematics is not in its essence an activity in which one simply memorizes rules and algorithms and then replicates them for some authority, as many children believe. Mathematics is an endeavor concerned with the solving of problems through the use of thought and reason, and communicating one's solutions, thoughts, and reasons to others. One type of problem that children will encounter as they play math games involves finding the best strategy to use during a game. Another type of problem involves understanding the meaning of the

mathematics used in the games. As children solve problems such as these in social groups, they naturally use reasoning, logic, reflection, thought, and communication, and begin to see them as part of mathematics.

15. **Games can help children see mathematics as part of normal human communication.** Most children do not believe that mathematics is something that normal children would naturally talk to each other about. We can encourage natural mathematical communication by asking children to play math games, where the subject of the playful interpersonal interactions is the mathematics of the game. By making mathematical communication a normal and natural part of children's lives, we encourage children to see mathematics as a natural activity that is relevant to their lives. Mathematical communication is also important because it helps children clarify their thoughts for both themselves and others and, by so doing, socially construct and reconstruct mathematical meaning.

16. **Watching children play mathematical games can help us diagnose a wide variety of their mathematical strengths and weaknesses.** Some of the types of mathematical skills that we might observe children using while playing games include arithmetic calculation skills, mathematical reasoning and problem-solving skills, spatial relations skills, and part-whole skills. As children play games, teachers and parents can observe them to determine which types of materials and activities they enjoy most and learn from most effectively. These adults can then use their observations to plan future activities that are tailored to meet the children's needs.

Educators have widely discussed these reasons for using games to help children learn mathematics. They have discussed them in policy documents, such as *Principles and Standards for School Mathematics,* by the National Council of Teachers of Mathematics (2000); in the research literature, such as the writings of Bright, Harvey, and Wheeler (1987) and Kamii and Houseman (2000); in books that describe how to use math games, such as *Mega-Fun Math Games* (Schiro, 1995) and *Games for Math* (Kaye, 1987); and in almost every issue of the journals *Teaching Children Mathematics* and *Teaching Mathematics in the Middle School,* published by the National Council of Teachers of Mathematics.

What does research say about the effectiveness of instructional games in helping children learn mathematics? Basically it seems to say four things, assuming that appropriate games are used in appropriate ways. First, it seems to indicate that games can facilitate children's construction of mathematical understanding and meaning (Kamii and Livingston, 1994; Kamii and Houseman, 2000; Kamii, Rummelsburg, and Kari, 2005). Second, it seems to indicate that games are useful in helping children understand mathematics at different times during instruction: when introducing new mathematical ideas and skills; at the time when new mathematical ideas and skills are being developed; immediately after instruction, when children practice using newly acquired mathematical understandings and skills; and after instruction, over the long haul, to maintain mathematical understanding and skills (Bright, Harvey, and Wheeler, 1985). Third, it seems to indicate that games can help children learn mathematics at basic levels of functioning, such as memorizing facts where problems and answers are associated with each other; at more advanced levels of understanding where children give meaning to mathematical concepts and algorithms; and at higher levels of mathematical functioning where children learn to problem-solve, create, and analyze mathematical proofs (1985). Fourth, research seems to indicate that mathematics games that are sent home with children to be played with parents can create a rich, enjoyable, shared mathematical experience for families, in which parents believe that children learn from the games and enjoy observing and participating in their children's learning (Kliman, 2006).

Mathematics Content and Process Standards

In *Principles and Standards for School Mathematics* (2000), the National Council of Teachers of Mathematics recommends that we teach children both mathematical content and processes—both mathematical ideas and mathematical ways of thinking. Mathematical content includes the ideas, concepts, facts, skills, and algorithms that children learn in the areas of number and operations (arithmetic), algebra, geometry, measurement, and probability and data analysis. Mathematical processes include mathematical skills and ways of thinking that involve problem solving, reasoning and proof, communication, connections, and representation.

Part One of this book focuses most, but not exclusively, on the mathematical content of number and operation (arithmetic) and probability and data analysis. Part Two focuses most, but not exclusively, on the content areas of algebra, geometry, and measurement. Both parts of this book integrate the learning of mathematical content with mathematical thinking processes. The content and process standards are described in detail at the National Council of Teachers of Mathematics Web site http://my.nctm.org/standards/document/index.htm.

Because the mathematical process standards relating to problem solving, reasoning and proof, communication, connections, and representation are so important to children who are learning mathematics, so central to this book, and so frequently ignored when mathematics is taught, I briefly discuss each of these process skills in the following sections.

Problem Solving

Being able to solve problems is critical to children's success in mathematics and in life. In general, mathematical problem solving includes the ability to construct new mathematical understanding, skills, meanings, and values while solving problems;

developing an inclination and ability to identify and solve problems in a variety of settings both in and outside of school; being able to flexibly apply and revise a variety of problem-solving strategies while solving a problem and having the personal confidence and persistence to persevere in solving difficult problems; and developing the ability and inclination to reflect on one's own process of problem solving.

The basic model of mathematical problem solving was first proposed by Polya (1957) and recently extended by Schiro (2004). It includes five stages (or phases): understanding the problem to be solved, devising a plan to solve it, carrying out the plan, looking back to see the effectiveness of the plan and looking forward to see how the plan might be used in the future, and uncovering new problems to solve while exploring existing ones. These steps frequently overlap, and the individual repeats them as failed plans allow him or her to look back at a problem and better understand it in such a way that he or she can devise new plans, and as feedback from endeavors at one stage of problem solving inform activity at other stages. This cyclic model for mathematical problem solving is presented in the following illustration, in which solid arrows show the general direction of action during problem solving and broken arrows show feedback from one type of activity to another.

This model describes only the basics of a theory of mathematical problem solving. A more comprehensive model, such as the one I describe in *Oral Storytelling and Teaching Mathematics* (2004), includes accounting for such things as information about children's knowledge base, children's cultural orientation to problem solving and their learning and thinking styles, and the effects of social interaction during problem solving and learning.

Many strategies exist that can aid children in devising plans for solving problems, including the following: brainstorming, looking for patterns, guessing and checking, using logical reasoning, working backwards, acting out the problem, using objects to simulate the problem, making a diagram, making a model, drawing a picture, making an organized list, writing an equation, constructing a table or chart of information, solving a simpler problem, and examining a similar problem that is familiar. The traditional approach to teaching these strategies is to describe them and then have children practice them. Because children seem to naturally use almost all the problem-solving strategies if they are simply allowed to solve a wide range of rich mathematical problems, I suggest another approach:

1. Have children work on the games and puzzles. While this is occurring, carefully observe which strategies they use.

2. After children successfully play a game or solve a puzzle, discuss as a class how they solved it. As children describe their strategies, elaborate on each by reference to what others in the class have done, name the strategies, and display a list of the strategies for future reference.

3. As you present more games and puzzles and as children work on them, children should identify the strategies they use on the class list, add new strategies to the list, and further elaborate on what each strategy means—in light of their personal experiences.

In general, as children solve puzzles and build gaming strategies while working on activities in this book, help them observe and learn problem-solving strategies that they and their peers use naturally. If you take this approach, children feel greater ownership of strategies; better comprehend the strategies; and better understand that many strategies exist, that there is no one best strategy, and that there are usually different ways to develop gaming strategies and to solve mathematical problems.

Reasoning and Proof

Two skills that children need to acquire are the abilities to use mathematical reasoning and to "prove" to others that their answers to problems, their gaming strategies, and their solutions to puzzles are correct. Mathematical reasoning and proof include the ability to pose, analyze, and explore mathematical hypotheses; the ability to develop mathematical arguments and evaluate the mathematical proofs of others; the ability to use different types of reasoning and proof to convince others that your ideas are correct; the ability to respond to other people's challenges to your reasons and proofs and if necessary restate, revise, or abandon those reasons if they are poorly stated or incorrect; and both an understanding that providing reasons for conjectures is important as well as the inclination to do so.

What we want from children who play the games in this book is for them to construct insights into the games, create mathematical strategies for winning the games, explain those insights and strategies to others in their own words, have good reasons for believing in their insights and that their strategies work, and respond appropriately to challenges to the adequacy of those reasons and strategies. These are important skills to acquire not only in mathematics but also in life in general.

Children should be allowed to express their reasoning and explain their observations in a variety of ways. Some will offer verbal reasons for their beliefs, others will use intuitive logic to justify their ideas, others will use manipulatives to demonstrate what they understand, and still others will draw pictures or make graphs that illustrate their beliefs. But they should always anticipate that an adult or peer might ask them, "Why?" and that they might have to support their beliefs with evidence. In addition, children need to learn to ask each other "Why?" when one of them makes an assertion, listen carefully to what is said in response, and develop the inclination to refute another's reasoning when they believe those reasons to be incorrect, inadequate, or poorly stated.

Communication

Communication is essential to learning and doing mathematics. It is both a way of clarifying meanings and a way of sharing those meanings. When children try to put into words what they have learned at an intuitive level, their intuitive understandings become things that they can more objectively examine, reflect on, refine, and revise. Communicating helps them build more solid mathematical ideas that they can remember and reflect on more easily. In addition, ideas that have been put into a verbal, written, enacted, or diagrammatic form can be challenged by adults or peers. When a child's ideas are challenged, he or she can revise incorrect ideas, amend and revise partially formed ideas, rephrase poorly phrased ideas, and learn to express his or her thoughts in clearer and more convincing language. In addition, by expressing mathematical ideas in a variety of oral, written, and diagrammatic forms, children gain multiple perspectives on a single mathematical idea and thus enrich their understanding of that idea.

The games and puzzles in this book offer children the opportunity to communicate about mathematical ideas—if they are asked to work in cooperative social groups first to play, then to understand and then explain to others their understanding of the games and puzzles, using language that their group agrees on and can understand. In doing so, children can learn not only to express themselves but also to organize their ideas ever more effectively and to express and record their mathematical thoughts and reasons ever more precisely in spoken, written, diagrammatic, enacted, and other forms of mathematical communication.

Connections

Mathematics is not a set of isolated bits of information and algorithms, as many children believe. It is a body of interconnected ideas that relate both to other academic fields of study and to the everyday world that children experience.

Children need to understand, for example, that within mathematics, addition relates to subtraction, and the study of the area of rectangles in geometry relates to the study of multiplication in arithmetic. Children need to be able to see and use these types of mathematical connections.

Beyond this, children need to understand that mathematics is related to other fields of knowledge and to their real everyday world. They need to sense that knowledge of mathematics can help them understand other fields of study, such as science and history. They need to see that knowledge of mathematics can also help them better understand and function in "real life." For example, as discussed in Chapter Thirteen, children need to see that network theory originated in a real bridge crossing (transportation) problem that people struggled to solve, and that the information in this field of study can relate to their everyday real and fantasy worlds. The connections that children can make to their daily lives also add richness, relevance, and motivation to the subject of mathematics.

Representation

Mathematics contains powerful symbol systems that allow us to construct models of both theoretical and everyday phenomena in a variety of ways. Learning the nature of these symbol systems, how to use them, and how they relate to each other can provide children with increased understanding of and control over their world. For example, children benefit greatly when they understand how to use tables of numerical data, graphs, and algebraic equations; are able to use these different symbol systems to help them understand and function in their everyday world; are able to see how these symbol systems relate to each other; and are able to transfer data from one of these symbol systems to another. Children are given experience with this in Chapter Ten, for example, when they explore how numerical tables and algebraic equations can produce graphs that contain geometrical designs in which straight lines produce images that appear to be curved.

If children can use several different symbol systems (whether words, equations, diagrams, or manipulations of concrete materials) to describe the meaning of an insight they have into a mathematical or real-world experience, each symbol system will give them a different perspective on that insight, and the multiple perspectives can increase and enrich their understanding. The multiple representations of an idea can also allow children to better communicate their ideas to others, and can provide others with multiple ways of understanding and commenting on children's ideas.

Practical Considerations

Let's look at some practical considerations that help make the use of games and puzzles successful learning experiences for children.

Who Goes First

The first player in a game often has an advantage. A fair way to pick the first player is with a "starting game." Common starting games involve flipping a coin, tossing dice, using counting-out rhymes, drawing straws, spinning a bottle, picking note cards with playing order out of a hat, or cutting a deck of cards. Besides choosing the first player (and if necessary, the second, third, and so on), starting games can be used to divide players into teams and to award any prized position in a game, such as team captain, dealer, or banker.

Parents

Informing parents about why you use math games is a great idea. Doing so can allay doubts that may arise when children come home and describe how they "played with games, puzzles, and magic tricks during math class." The following is a sample of a short note you can send to parents:

> Over the next several months we will be memorizing math facts, practicing algorithms, and working on problem solving during mathematics. Your child will be memorizing math facts and practicing arithmetic algorithms by playing math games. These will involve the use of board games, card games, paper-and-pencil games, and egg carton games. If your child comes home and wants to play a math game with you, try to be accommodating.
>
> Your child will also be learning how to understand a mathematics problem, plan a solution to it, execute the plan, and then look back to determine the adequacy of the solution and its relationship to other mathematical problems by playing math games and working on math puzzles. The problems your child will be working on come from arithmetic, geometry, algebra, and number theory. They will mostly be in the form of puzzles, games, and even magic tricks. If your child wants to play a math magic trick on you, have fun with the trick.
>
> As a result of engaging in this program, your child should acquire the ability to recall number facts quickly, perform mathematics algorithms skillfully, and learn how to create and solve a wide range of mathematical problems of his or her own.

Sending a game home with children to play with their parents and siblings as part of homework is also useful. When doing so, also send a recording sheet home that is to be returned the next day. Related to this idea, you can send home the recording sheets that children create while playing games at school, asking parents to sign and return them to you. By showing the mathematical work children have done while playing a game, these recording sheets are often quite helpful in letting parents know how math games can contribute to children's learning.

A number of books and articles describe how to host a "family math night" for parents, where they and their children can play math games together (as well as do other types of mathematics activities) during an evening or after school, so that parents can both get to know a school's mathematics program and get a sense of what children can learn from mathematics manipulatives and activities that are not based on textbooks or worksheets. You can host a family math night where parents work problems, solve puzzles, and play games with their children. To do so, set up four to six different learning stations, each of which centers on a mathematics manipulative, game, or puzzle. Children can run each station and organize parents to do such things as perform magic tricks or play games. Later, children can teach parents the underlying math. The night can end with a talk about your math program.

Storing Games

It is advisable to store math games in a single place in a systematic manner, so that children know where to find and return them. You can store individual games in cardboard boxes (shoe boxes or pizza boxes work well). Label boxes with the name of the game (and decorate them, if desired). You can rewrite relevant parts of the game instructions from this book and glue them to the inside top of the box, with a list of the materials used in the game. Boxes can be encircled with a rubber band to keep them closed. Groups of about a dozen boxed games can be stored in large cardboard cartons.

Many other methods of systematically storing games exist. Games can be put in zippered plastic bags that are in turn stored in file folders in large cardboard boxes. Putting games stored in zippered plastic bags in hanging shoe bags also works well (see the illustration).

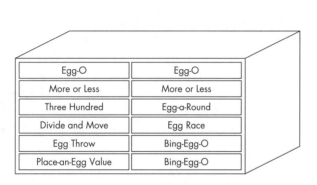
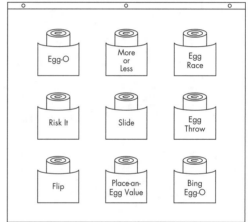

Above all, have a systematic way of storing a single game in a small container, many of which can be filed in a larger container.

Rules for Using the Games

Encourage students to learn these three rules:

1. Before using a game, make sure all necessary materials are in the game's container. If not, report missing pieces to your teacher.
2. After using a game, put all the materials back in the container.
3. After using a game, return it to its proper storage place.

Recording Sheets

By recording problems solved while playing a mathematics game, children leave a mathematical trail that can be of great value to them and to their teachers and parents. Children can feel a sense of accomplishment as they look back and see all the mathematics they have done. Teachers can use the record for assessment. Parents will appreciate this "evidence" that their children are actually doing mathematics and not just playing games. Recording sheets that structure the recording process are very useful for many children, particularly when they are just learning to play a game. The next figure shows several ways of structuring recording sheets. Children should not always be required to keep a written record, but periodically requiring one is worthwhile.

Rectangles		
Length	Height	Score

Nines

1 2 3 4 5 6 7 8 9

Start Numbers	Sum	Equations of Used Numbers
___ + ___	= ___	=
___ + ___	= ___	=
___ + ___	= ___	=
___ + ___	= ___	=
___ + ___	= ___	=

Score [   ]

Three Hundred
+ + + + + + + + − −

More or Less		
Round	Problem	Score
1		
2		
3		
4		

Hit			
First Number	Second Number	Product	Cumulative Score

Bounded Playing Areas

You can use a piece of inexpensive felt as a playing surface so as to limit the area where a game's playing pieces are used. To confine the area within which cubes (or other materials) are rolled, make a rolling area by gluing felt to the bottom of a small box (about 4×6 inches). Felt also quiets the noise of playing pieces hitting the playing surface.

Introducing and Modeling Games

One of the most powerful ways of teaching children a new game is to model how it is played, while commenting on it. You can do this by playing for two opponents, playing against students while guiding their moves, or teaching a small group of children how to play the game and then having them demonstrate it to others while you and they make comments on the rules of the game. It is also possible to teach a small group how to play a game and then have them teach other children.

Ending a Game

If children are working in independent groups, they may need to be reminded of when they must finish playing their games and put the gaming equipment away. Telling children when the activity will end before they begin playing can help them finish on time. Or try setting a sand timer and announcing that there are three minutes until the end of an activity.

Groups

It is not necessary to make multiple copies of a game for use during instruction in a classroom. Groups of children can play the same game or different games. Depending on how children are grouped and how instruction is organized, you will need to construct different numbers of copies of a single game. For example, some groups can play one game while others play another, and the groups can then switch games. Or small groups of children can play different games at selected times of the day while other activities take place. To avoid making multiple copies of a game, use some type of contract, organizational, or rotation system for assigned groups that designates when which group plays what games. You can use an activity rotation chart (as shown) to designate who plays which games at a certain time of day. In this chart, games can be rotated while the children are kept in their groups. Cards with children's names and game names can be inserted into a pocket chart or affixed to a Velcro board, or you can write names on a chalkboard.

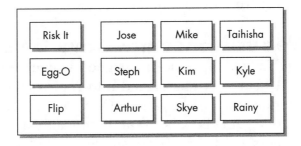

Children can be grouped in various ways. As mentioned earlier in the Who Goes First section, you can use a starting game to designate groups. You can also simply assign groups yourself or allow children to form their own groups, but in the latter case you must be sensitive to possible problems related to the popularity (or unpopularity) of particular children.

Cooperative Learning Groups

The games in this book are mostly for two or more people. Its puzzles are mostly for one person. Children learn most about them when they work in cooperative learning groups and discuss evolving strategies.

I suggest that you put children in cooperative groups of two to four people for much of their work. The goal of the groups should be to help every member learn and succeed while having fun. Groups should also share information with other groups, so that everyone in the class understands the mathematics. To encourage this, periodically hold whole-class discussions to share discoveries. Doing so raises two issues.

First, how can you encourage cooperative work on such things as magic tricks or strategy games, as once children learn a trick or strategy, they will want to use it on peers? Encourage children in a class to work together; their opponents should be friends in other classes and parents—these are the people to trick or beat while using newly discovered knowledge. Encourage children to view classmates as colleagues who help devise strategies to be used on others.

Second, how can you make sure that the child who first discovers a solution does not tell it to everyone else and spoil their ability to discover it themselves? Tell children they can give a hint to help someone discover something, but never to tell the answer outright and deprive someone of the fun of making a discovery. When giving instructions to groups, emphasize to children that small-group activity directed toward making discoveries should be distinguished from whole-group discussion directed toward sharing meaning.

Two practices are useful in facilitating groups. First, structure groups so that members see themselves as linked together in such a way that no one succeeds unless all members succeed and that if the group as a whole succeeds, then all members of the group have succeeded. Second, have children help each other learn by being each other's peer tutors, providing each other with constructive feedback, and teaching and learning from each other as necessary.

Competitive Versus Noncompetitive Games

Many of the games in this book have been designed as competitive games in which the high scorer wins. All can be transformed into games where the high scorer is not the winner or into noncompetitive games. One way of determining the winner of a game is to wait until a game is finished and then activate a randomizing device that designates the winners and losers. For example, after playing a game, determine the high scorers, low scorers, and middle scorers, then pick a card out of a deck. If it is 4 or less, then low scorers win; if it is between 4 and 8, then middle scorers win; if it is 8 or larger, then high scorers win. Doing this takes some of the emphasis off of always having to be the player with the most. In addition, most of the games in this collection can be played in such a way that players keep track of their individual score over a period of days and try to better their previous days' scores. Children often enjoy keeping graphs of this information about themselves.

No matter how the games are played, stress that the probabilities of randomizing devices play a role in determining winners and losers. Encourage children to ask serious mathematical questions about the role of chance and the role of choice during mathematical games. When children lose (or win) a game, encourage them to determine when to blame their fate on themselves (issues of choice) and when to blame it on whatever randomizing device might have been used in the game (issues of chance). Randomizing devices that determine the winner of a game are motivationally significant, for they can relieve children of the full responsibility of not winning.

Communication During Gaming

Many people think that learning can take place only in a quiet room. Many people think that a quiet room is one in which learning is taking place. When children are playing games or working puzzles, however, they need to talk to each other. The talk can be very constructive if children take the responsibility to make sure that all players understand the rules, algorithms, concepts, and facts required by an activity. Encourage children to communicate about mathematics in meaningful ways, with the stipulation that the talk is about the activity and its mathematics.

Communication helps children construct mathematical meanings. Math talk, math writing, math drawing, math gesturing, and math demonstrations with manipulatives can all help children make discoveries, construct meanings, and build understanding. If children write "memos" of "understanding, explanation, or proof" that explain their understanding of problems and solutions, these can help them construct mathematical meanings.

Calculators

Calculators should be available to children. They can play four important roles. First, when questions or disputes arise about answers, a calculator can be used as an arbitrator. There should be no need to run to a teacher immediately or have an argument about a disputed calculation. When calculations are in dispute, have children first describe to each other how they arrived at their answers before they turn to the calculator. They can then use the calculator to check both individual steps in the players' calculations as well as final answers.

Second, children can use calculators to develop mathematical reasoning and problem-solving abilities. During games where choices of number combinations are available, calculators help children focus on the mathematical ramifications of various choices. For example, if a player must use the digits 3 and 8 to make either the number 38 or 83, which will then be used during a calculation, a calculator can help the player think through the ramifications of using each number before making a final choice. I do suggest, however, that calculators should not always be available for games that emphasize mathematical thinking. For example, you might allow children to use calculators for every other game.

Third, children can use calculators to check their own recall of mathematical facts, check their execution of complex calculations, or use numbers during a game that are beyond their calculation ability. Doing so can help children learn self-reliance as well as avoid memorizing incorrect information.

Finally, calculators can be used as a device on which players keep track of their cumulative scores during a game. Using a calculator this way can help focus players' attention on the mathematics of the game. It can also allow players to use numbers that are beyond their calculation ability.

Assessment

Adults who observe and interact with children while they are playing mathematics games can diagnose a wide variety of their mathematical strengths and weaknesses, including arithmetic abilities (including use of algorithms, recall of facts, and conceptual understanding); mathematical reasoning and problem-solving skills (including the types of gaming strategies children develop and the reasons they give for their actions); and part-whole and figure-ground skills (which include seeing how the rules of a game work together, seeing how the parts of a problem relate to its solution, and being able to focus attention on relevant parts of a game). In addition, the recording sheets that children produce while playing games can be placed in assessment portfolios, where they will be of great value to children, teachers, and parents (as has already been discussed). Finally, games provide children a powerful way of assessing their own mathematical abilities. The immediate feedback children receive from their peers while playing games can help them evaluate their mathematical concepts and algorithms and revise inefficient, inadequate, or erroneous ones.

Gaming Etiquette and Cooperative Learning

Much has been written about how to help students learn together in groups. The following guidelines for gaming etiquette will help students successfully play mathematical games. You might want to post them in your classroom and discuss them with students.

- Play games to learn mathematics and have fun, not just to win.
- Teach each other and learn from each other. Every member of a group has the responsibility of helping other members understand the rules and mathematics of a game.
- Help your group be successful. Work together to make the game an enjoyable learning experience for all group members. Do your fair share of the work.
- Never insult another player. Disagree with answers and ideas, not people. Be sensitive to the feelings of others.

- Take turns. Listen to what others have to say and think about it before responding.
- Ask an adult for help only when the group cannot help itself.
- Speak and act in ways that will not disturb others. Never speak in a voice that is louder than a whisper, even if you have to whisper-yell (a yell done in a whisper that is no louder than a normal voice).

Varying Games to Meet Student and Curriculum Needs

I encourage you to vary the games and puzzles in this book to suit the needs of the children who will play them. You can do this by changing the operations used, the types of numbers used, or the rules. Be as creative as you like.

The randomizing devices in many of the games can also be changed. For example, you can use twelve cards instead of an egg carton, or replace a number cube with an egg carton by writing each of the numbers in the egg holes twice. Other randomizing devices that children enjoy using are paper cubes, pencils, teetotums, spinners, and tossing boards.

Making paper cubes is an enjoyable activity in itself. Copy the pattern provided here, write numbers on its faces, cut along the solid lines, and fold on the dashed lines. Glue or tape the flaps behind the faces to secure the paper into a cube shape. Now use the paper cube as a die.

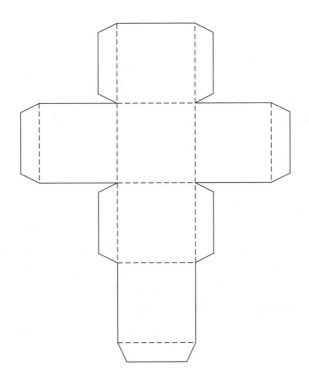

Students can also use pencils in place of a cube. Simply write on the six faces of a pencil, roll it, and see which side faces up when the pencil comes to rest.

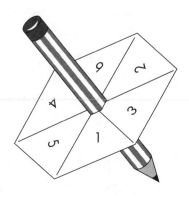

Teetotums are another randomizing device that children enjoy using. Cut a hexagon about 3 inches (7 cm) across from stiff cardboard and divide it into six equal triangles. Write the desired mathematical symbols in the triangles and stick a pencil point down through the center. Spin the teetotum. When it stops, the symbol in the triangle resting against the playing surface is your number (see the illustration).

Spinners are easy to make and use. Draw a circle on cardboard and divide it into as many wedge-shaped sections as you want to have on your randomizing device. Place a piece of tape over the center and attach a short pencil with a thumbtack pushed through the circle's center from the back. Try to impale the pencil approximately

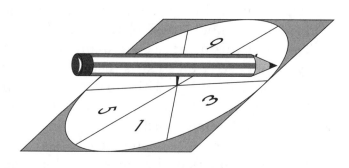

in the middle. Spin the pencil to get the number or symbol for play.

Tossing boards are fun for children to use. Divide a sheet of paper into however many sections you want to have on your randomizing device, and write a symbol or number in each. Children toss a button or pebble from a short distance away and use the symbol it lands on for play. Tossing boards can be placed in cardboard boxes so that the object tossed stays within a confined area.

| 4 |
| 6 |
| 2 |
| 5 |
| 1 |
| 3 |

Encouraging Children to Create Their Own Problems

Mathematicians love to create new problems to solve. Children should be encouraged to do likewise. They can vary the games and puzzles in many ways, just as you can (see the preceding section). They can also create new puzzles by varying the essential elements and relationships within a puzzle. Or they can change the stories that accompany the puzzles. Encourage children to build on the work of other mathematicians by finding, creating, and defining new games and puzzles and by varying the components of the activities in this book.

Enjoying the Games

Finally, I express here my hope that wherever and however the games and puzzles in this book are used, they will be truly enjoyed. They were devised as teaching tools and are practical and effective in that role. However, they need not always be used so purposefully. Parents and teachers can employ some as a substitute for a few hours of television; friends and siblings can add them to their rainy-day repertoire; and several may occupy the more tedious hours of an automobile trip or school field trip. The games will sharpen children's skills regardless of when or where they are played!

Part One

Math Skill Development Games

Chapter One

Paper-and-Pencil Games

Paper-and-pencil games are popular among children and require little preparation. The games in this book offer new ideas and variations on old ones. And they are not limited to paper and pencil. Students can play them on a chalkboard with chalk, a sidewalk with chalk, a laminated piece of paper or cardboard with crayons, or a whiteboard with dry erase markers. These alternatives help avoid the use of large amounts of paper.

Count

Object: Players take turns writing and saying the numbers from 1 to 45. Each player may claim one, two, or three numbers in sequence, starting where the other player left off. The player who claims 45 wins.

Skills: counting forward and counting back, place value, writing and saying numbers, problem solving, communication, representation, reasoning and proof

Number of players: 2

Grades: 1 to 5

Materials: paper and pencils

Preparation: none

Playing:

1. The players take turns writing and saying the numbers from 1 to 45. They write the numbers on a sheet of paper and say them aloud as they write them. The numbers are written and said in sequential order.

2. The first player starts by writing and saying one of the following: "one," "one, two," or "one, two, three." Thereafter, each player may write and say one, two, or three numbers in sequence, starting from where the other player left off counting.

Winning: The player who writes and says 45 is the winner.

Playing variations:

- Instead of using the numbers from 1 to 45, the players can use the numbers from *x* to *n*, where *x* and *n* are any counting numbers. For older children, 985 and 1005 work well.

- The player who says the last number can lose rather than win.

- Players can simply count aloud during the game, and forgo writing the numbers.

Skill variations:

Counting back: Instead of counting forward, players count backward from 45 to 0. The player who says 0 wins.

Fractions: Instead of using counting numbers, players can use a sequence of fractions (for example, the fractions from ¼ to 5 with a counting increment of ¼ can be used, as in ¼, ½, ¾, 1, and so on).

Note: This game has a winning strategy that children can discover if they search for it. Ask children to explain why their strategy works.

Capture the Fort

Object: Each player has 50 points to bet during a series of rounds. Whoever bets the most points wins a round and advances.

Skills: subtraction, inequalities, probability, problem solving, connections

Number of players: 2

Grades: 1 to 5

Materials: paper, pencils, and a counter (such as a coin or button)

Preparation: Have players draw a larger version of the playing board shown here on a sheet of paper, or make and duplicate copies for players.

Playing:

1. Place the playing board between the two players with a circle in front of each player. The circle nearest each player is that player's fort. The five lines between the circles are the positions on which the players can move the counter. The thick center line is the boundary between the players' territories.

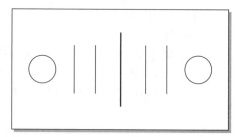

2. The game starts by placing the counter on the center boundary line. Subsequently the counter is moved in either direction, one line at a time, as determined by the betting. The object is to move the counter into the opponent's fort and thus capture it.

3. Moves are determined by making bets. Each player has 50 points to bet for the entire game.

4. The game is played as a series of rounds. During a round, each player first decides how many points to bet and secretly writes that number on a piece of paper. The players then simultaneously show each other their bets. The player with the larger bet wins the round and moves his or her counter one space toward the opponent's fort. If both players bet the same number, the counter is not moved. A new round then begins.

5. Players use up betting points as the game proceeds. Before play begins, they write 50 at the top of another small piece of paper. They subtract their first-round bet from 50, their second-round bet from the remainder of the first subtraction, and so on.

6. If a player runs out of points, he or she must bet zero points during each remaining round of the game, until the opponent either wins or runs out of points.

Winning: The first player to move the counter into the opposing fort wins. If neither player has sufficient points left to reach the opponent's fort, the game ends in a tie.

Playing variations:

- A player can be awarded a half-win if a tie results and the counter is in the opponent's territory.

- Players can avoid revealing their bets to each other by showing them instead to a third person, who announces only the winner of each round.

Foreheaded

Object: Each player writes a three-digit number on a slip of paper and attaches it to the forehead of the player on the left. Players then are given clues and try to guess their numbers.

Skills: reading, writing, and saying numbers using place value language; problem solving; reasoning and proof; communication

Number of players: 3 to 6

Grades: 1 to 5

Materials: paper, pencils, and tape (or sticky notes)

Preparation: Cut 1 × 2 inch (3 × 5 cm) slips of paper for each player. Sticky notes (about 1.5 × 2 inches) are ideal.

Playing:

1. The players sit in a circle.

2. Each player secretly writes a three-digit number on a slip of paper and then tapes it to the forehead of the player to the left. (If sticky notes are used, simply write on them and post them on a forehead.) The numbers are taped facing out so that every player sees all the opponents' numbers but not his or her own number.

3. Players take turns in clockwise rotation.

4. On each turn, a player must guess the number on his or her forehead. If a player guesses correctly, he or she wins. If a player guesses incorrectly, two things happen. First, opponents must tell him or her how many digits in the number he or she guessed are correct (the correct digit in the correct place). Second, the player must give every opponent a clue. This involves telling each opponent a three-digit number, using place value terminology, that contains at least one digit that is the same and in the same position as a digit in the opponent's number. For example, a player might give the clue 135 to an opponent with the number 237 taped to his or her head. Players should write down the clues they are given, for future reference.

5. If a player gives another player the exact same number as a clue that was already given on a previous turn by any player, that player must give another clue.

6. The game ends when a player guesses the number on his or her forehead.

Winning: The winner is the first player to guess his or her number.

Playing variations:

• Two-digit or four-digit numbers may be used instead of three-digit numbers.

• Foreheaded can be played so that a player is told both how many digits are completely correct (correct digit in the correct place) and how many digits are partially correct (correct digit in the wrong place). For example, if a player with 237 on his or her forehead guessed 532, he or she would be told, "One digit completely correct and one digit partially correct."

Googol

Object: One player secretly writes eight numbers on slips of paper. Another player tries to guess which slip has the largest number. Points are awarded for guessing and ordering numbers.

Skills: writing and reading numbers, inequalities, ordering numbers
Number of players: 2
Grades: 1 to 5
Materials: paper and pencils
Preparation: none
Playing:

1. There are ten rounds in the game. During each round, one player is the writer and the other is the picker. Players switch roles after each round. Thus, in ten rounds each player will be writer five times and picker five times.

2. To start a round, the writer tears a sheet of paper into eight small slips and secretly writes a different positive number on each one. The writer then turns them face down on the playing surface. The numbers written may range from small fractions to a googol (a 1 followed by a hundred 0s); they may be in fractional and decimal forms.

3. During the round, the picker turns the slips face up one at a time. The picker stops turning over slips when he or she believes that the one containing the largest of the eight numbers is turned face up. The picker cannot go back to a previously turned-up slip; the decision to turn over another slip is final, even though it is made without knowing what is written on all the slips. If the picker turns over all eight slips, the last one turned over is considered to be the chosen one.

4. To end a round, the picker turns all eight slips face up and arranges them in order from smallest to largest.

5. Score each round as follows: three points to a picker who chooses the largest number; one point to a picker who correctly arranges the slips in numerical order from smallest to largest.

Winning: The player with the highest total score after ten rounds is the winner.
Playing variation:

- The following scoring rule can be added: If the writer incorrectly marks slips of paper (with a negative number, the same number twice, and so on), the picker is awarded one point.

Number-Tac-Toe

Object: Players add (or multiply) numbers to get sums (or products) equal to numbers on a Tic-Tac-Toe grid. The first player to get three numbers in a row (as in Tic-Tac-Toe) wins.

Skills: addition (or multiplication), reasoning and proof, connections
Number of players: 2
Grades: 1 to 5
Materials: paper and pencils
Preparation: Create a Number-Tac-Toe grid by writing sums (or products) of the numbers from 1 to 9 in the nine cells of a regular Tic-Tac-Toe grid. (See the sample for addition or use the grids supplied. A blank playing sheet for reproduction is also provided.)

Playing:

1. Players decide who will mark X's and who will mark O's. If not provided a playing sheet, they draw a Number-Tac-Toe grid on a sheet of paper, and each list the numbers from 1 to 9 in a column on either side of the grid. (See the sample playing sheet.)

2. The first player crosses out any one number in his or her column of nine numbers. Beginning with the second player, the game continues as follows.

3. During a turn, a player crosses out any one number in his or her column of nine numbers that has not yet been crossed out. The player then adds (or multiplies) that number to (or by) the last number the opponent crossed out. If the sum (or product) is on the Number-Tac-Toe grid and if it is not yet marked, the player marks an X or O over it (depending on whether the player is marking X's or O's). Players should plan ahead.

4. The game ends when any of the following occurs:
   - Three of a player's marks are in a row (as in Tic-Tac-Toe).
   - All of the numbers on the grid are marked X or O.
   - All nine numbers in each player's column of numbers are crossed out.

Winning: The player who gets three marks in a row wins, as in Tic-Tac-Toe. If neither player gets three marks in a row, a tie is declared.

Playing variation:
- Players can construct their own Number-Tac-Toe grids by taking turns placing numbers in the nine cells of the grid at the start of a game. The Number-Tac-Toe grids shown here are samples that can be used to guide players in thinking about which numbers are appropriate to put in the cells of the grid.

Add-Tac-Toe Grids

5	7	12
16	9	15
2	6	8

14	3	12
8	16	6
2	18	10

7	9	15
16	11	5
3	13	4

6	4	10
12	14	8
16	9	5

13	8	9
15	5	11
17	10	7

15	12	9
16	7	5
2	8	6

Multiply-Tac-Toe Grids

25	15	56
12	36	16
49	20	8

24	6	56
8	35	14
63	8	15

8	10	5
48	24	3
36	6	30

12	24	4
35	27	18
15	21	5

3	36	63
15	30	9
18	24	8

15	12	36
16	25	49
20	8	56

Number-Tac-Toe

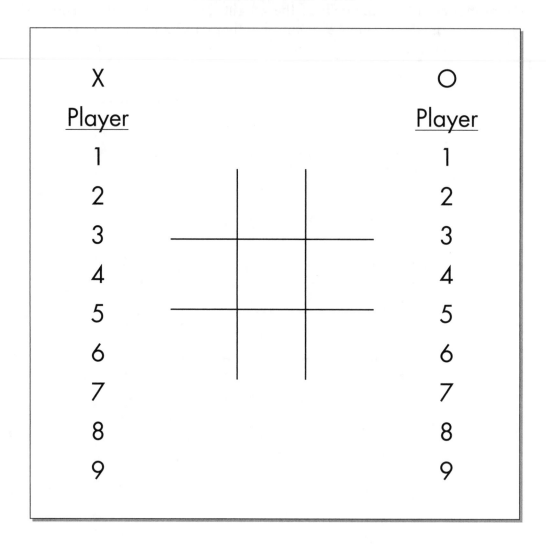

X		O
Player		Player
1		1
2		2
3		3
4		4
5		5
6		6
7		7
8		8
9		9

Ask and Give

Object: In this variation of Go Fish, players use place value skills to trade numbers.

Skills: place value, reading and writing large numbers, addition, subtraction, communication

Number of players: 2

Grades: 3 to 5

Materials: paper and pencils

Preparation: none

Playing:

1. At the top of separate sheets of paper, each player secretly writes a six-digit counting number, containing no 0s and no identical digits. Players keep their papers and numbers hidden from each other for the entire game.

2. As in Go Fish, players take turns being asker and giver. The game ends when each player has had five turns as asker. Their objective is to increase the size of their numbers by taking digits from each other.

3. A turn begins when the asker says, "Give me your ___'s," where ___ can be any digit from 1 to 9. (For example, "Give me your 6's.")

4. If that digit is in the giver's number, the giver announces its place value in the number. (For example, "You get 600.") If that digit is not in the giver's number, the giver announces this. (For example, "You get 0.") Note that the value of a digit that is asked for depends on its position in

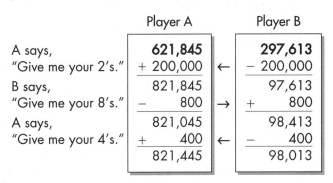

the giver's number. For example, if 6 is asked for and the giver's number is 512,639, then the giver responds, "You get 600." But if the giver's number is 561,243, then the giver responds, "You get 60,000."

5. As soon as the giver responds with a number, the asker adds that amount to his or her number (for example, + 600), and the giver subtracts that amount from his or her number (for example, − 600).

6. Each player's number changes with each new addition or subtraction. Players always use the most recent form of their numbers when adding, subtracting, or announcing the positional value of a digit. Players keep track of their changing number by adding to and subtracting from their original number and its successors directly under the original number. (See the sample game.)

7. If the same digit appears two or more times in the giver's number during the play, the giver may announce either of its values. For example, in 621,063 the giver may say, "You get 60" and say nothing about the 600,000.

8. The game ends after each player has five turns as asker. Players then check each other's additions, subtractions, and final numbers.

Winning: The player with the largest number at the end of the game wins. If either player's paper contains an error, that player automatically loses.

Hangmath

Object: This is a variation of Hangman. One player creates an arithmetic problem involving multidigit addition, subtraction, multiplication, or division. The other player tries to reconstruct the problem before being "hanged" (that is, within fourteen guesses).

Skills: place value, addition, subtraction, multiplication, division, problem solving, communication

Number of players: 2

Grades: 3 to 5

Materials: paper and pencils

Preparation: none

Playing:

1. Players take turns being hangman and guesser.

2. On one piece of paper, the hangman secretly writes a multidigit addition, subtraction, multiplication, or division problem (see sample).

3. On another piece of paper, the hangman makes a playing board that shows the type of problem and position of the digits in the problem (see sample). Problems up to the following sizes are suitable: four-digit addition and subtraction; three-digit by three-digit multiplication; and two-digit into four-digit division.

4. The hangman keeps the paper with the problem on it hidden, but gives the guesser the playing board.

5. The guesser tries to reconstruct the problem by guessing which digits belong where on the playing board. Guesses have the following format: "Is there a ___ in the ___ column?" (For example, "Is there a 5 in the ones column?")

Hangman's Problem

$$\begin{array}{r} 43 \\ \times\ 25 \\ \hline 215 \\ 860 \\ \hline 1075 \end{array}$$

Guesser's Playing Board

Math Skill Development Games

Is there a
five in the
ones column?

6. If the guesser guesses a correct digit in the correct column, the hangman must indicate every place the digit occurs in that column. (See the sample for the answer to the guess "Is there a 5 in the ones column?")

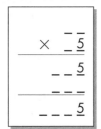

7. If the digit guessed does not appear in the specified column, the hangman begins or adds a line to the picture of a hanged man. The hanged man consists of fourteen lines drawn in this order: base of gallows, upright post, cross beam, rope, head, neck, body, leg, leg, arm, arm, eye, eye, mouth.

8. As the game progresses, the guesser tries to use information obtained from previous guesses to guide further guesses.

9. The game ends when either the hangman completes the picture or the guesser reconstructs the problem. Then guesser and hangman switch roles.

Winning: If the hangman picture is completed, the hangman wins. If the arithmetic problem is completed, the guesser wins.

Factors

Object: Players take turns giving and receiving numbers to factor. They score points equivalent to the numbers given and the factors identified.

Skills: factoring, multiples, division, multiplication, prime and composite numbers, addition, problem solving, communication

Number of players: 2 (or whole class in two teams)

Grades: 3 to 5

Materials: paper and pencils

Preparation: Have the players make a playing board or provide them with copies of the playing board on the next page. The playing board has a scoring column for each player on opposite sides of the paper, and the numbers from 1 to 30 in an array in the center.

Playing:

1. Players alternate roles as picker and factorer.

2. On a turn as picker, a player crosses out any legal number on the playing board. (A legal number is any number that is not crossed out and that has at least one factor that also has not been crossed out.) The picker writes that number in his or her scoring column.

3. On a turn as factorer, a player crosses out any remaining factors of the number the picker crossed out. The factorer writes all these numbers in his or her scoring column.

4. Neither player can reuse a number that is crossed out.

5. The factorer can cross out all possible factors of a number in one turn. For example, if the picker crosses out 30 as the first play of the game, the factorer can cross out 1, 2, 3, 5, 6, 10, and 15. The factorer may choose not to cross out a factor of a number.

Emilio	**Factors**					Sonya
30	~~1~~	~~2~~	~~3~~	4	~~5~~	1
	~~6~~	7	8	9	~~10~~	2
	11	12	13	14	~~15~~	3
	16	17	18	19	20	5
	21	22	23	24	25	6
	26	27	28	29	~~30~~	10
						15

6. Players switch roles after each round.
7. The game ends when there are no more legal numbers to cross out. Players then add the numbers in their columns to find their total score.

Winning: The player with the highest total score wins.

Playing variations:

- Have players keep cumulative sums of the numbers they acquire, rather than waiting until the end of the game to find the sum of the numbers.
- Use other numbers on the playing board—for example, 1 to 20, 1 to 35, or 1 to 40.
- Allow the picker to cross out illegal numbers (numbers that have no remaining factors on the playing board). Add the rule that if the picker crosses out an illegal number, then the factorer (who now has no numbers to cross out) gets two consecutive turns as picker, with the other player being factorer after each turn.

Factors

1	2	3	4	5
6	7	8	9	10
11	12	13	14	15
16	17	18	19	20
21	22	23	24	25
26	27	28	29	30

Get One

Object: Players choose a number and then take turns, first subtracting a factor of the number from itself, and then factors of the resultant differences from those differences, until one player leaves the other a difference of 1.

Skills: factoring, subtracting
Number of players: 2
Grades: 3 to 5
Materials: paper and pencils
Preparation: none
Playing:

1. Each player's objective is to leave the other player with the number 1.

2. To begin, the players jointly choose a positive whole number to start the game.

3. The first player subtracts any factor of this starting number (except the number itself) from the starting number to get a difference. The second player then subtracts any factor of this difference (except the number itself) from the difference to get a new difference. If a prime number comes up during the game (which has only factors of 1 and itself) the next player subtracts 1 (which is one of the factors of the number).

4. Players continue taking turns subtracting a factor of each new difference, always trying to leave the opponent a final difference of 1. (See the sample game.)

5. Both players do all subtracting on separate papers and check each other after each turn.

   Winning: The winner is the player who leaves the number 1 to the opponent.

Starting number	32
Player 1	− 8
	24
Player 2	− 12
	12
Player 1	− 6
	6
Player 2	− 3
	3
Player 1	− 1
	2
Player 2	− 1
Player 2 wins.	1

Write It

Object: Each player secretly writes a number. If the sum of the players' numbers is a multiple of some predetermined number, then one player wins a point. If not, the other player wins a point.

Skills: multiples, factors, probability, addition, multiplication, division
Number of players: 2
Grades: 3 to 5
Materials: paper and pencils
Preparation: none

Math Skill Development Games

Playing:

1. Before beginning, both players decide which whole number *x* the game will be about. (Excellent numbers to use are 2, 3, and 4.)

2. There are two sets of eight rounds in the game. During the first eight rounds, one player tries to get numbers to sum to a multiple of the chosen number *x*, and the other player tries to prevent this. The players switch roles for the second eight rounds.

3. To start a set of eight rounds, each player cuts a sheet of paper into eight smaller pieces.

4. During a round, each player takes a piece of paper and secretly writes a whole number on it. (The numbers may be limited, for example, to those between 0 and 100.) The players then show each other their numbers and add them together. If the sum is a multiple of *x*, the player trying for a multiple of *x* gets one point; if not, the other player gets one point. For example, John and Sue are playing a game about the number 2. John is trying to get numbers to sum to a multiple of 2, and Sue is trying to prevent this. John writes a 25 on his sheet of paper and Sue writes the number 5 on her sheet of paper. The sum of the numbers is 30, so John scores one point because he is trying to get sums to be a multiple of 2.

5. After the winner of a round is determined and the point awarded, a new round then begins. After eight rounds, the players switch roles (in terms of who is trying to get numbers to sum to a multiple of *x* and who is trying to prevent this). Each player then cuts another sheet of paper into eight pieces, and eight more rounds take place.

6. The game ends after two sets of eight rounds, when sixteen points have been awarded.

Winning: The winner is the player with the most points.

Skill variation:

Prime numbers: Limit the secret numbers to those between 1 and 40. The goal is to make the sum of the numbers be a prime number.

Coordinate Tic-Tac-Toe

Object: Two players try to get four marks in a row, as in Tic-Tac-Toe. Players cannot touch the game board and must tell their moves to a referee.

Skill: coordinate graphing

Number of players: 3

Grades: 2 to 5

Materials: copies of the Coordinate Tic-Tac-Toe game board, paper, and pencils

Preparation: If desired, decorate and then laminate the game board and have players write on it with grease pencils or crayons (which can be erased with a paper towel after each game); otherwise, players write on the game board with pencils.

Playing:

1. The game requires two players (or teams, if played in groups) and one referee. One player uses X and the other player uses O. The players cannot touch the game board; they must tell the referee where they want their mark to be placed on the game board by specifying a coordinate for their mark. The referee records a player's coordinates and marks on the game board a corresponding X or O for the player.

2. X's and O's are marked on line intersections of a 5 × 5 coordinate grid.

3. Players attempt to get four of their X's or O's in a uninterrupted horizontal or vertical straight line (a tic-tac-toe four in a row), while blocking their opponent from doing so.

4. Players take turns. Players cannot write on the game board or point at the coordinate grid on the game board. When it is their turn, players tell the referee the coordinates of the line intersection on the game board where they want their mark (either an X or an O) placed. The coordinates are given in the form (horizontal, vertical) or (across, up). The referee records a player's coordinates in that player's coordinate column on the game board, then verifies with the player that that is where he or she wants his or her mark placed, and then records an X or O in that location. Only the referee can place X's or O's on the game board.

5. If a player specifies an illegal move (off the game board or where another X or O already exists), the referee records it, but then the player loses his or her turn.

Winning: The first player to get four of their marks (X or O) next to each other in an uninterrupted straight horizontal or vertical line wins the game. Draw games in which neither player wins are possible.

Playing variations:

- Allow players to get a tic-tac-toe on a diagonal.

- Play on a larger grid (for example, a 12 × 12 grid), and players must get five in a row to have a tic-tac-toe. (This is similar to the Japanese game of GoMoku.)

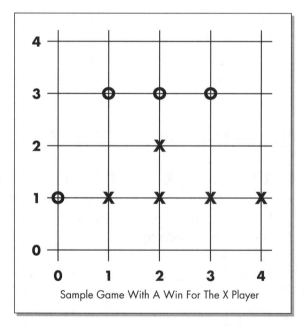

Sample Game With A Win For The X Player

Math Skill Development Games

Coordinate Tic-Tac-Toe

Name of X Player:_____

Name of O Player:_____

Name of Referee:_____

X's Moves	O's Moves

Coordinate format: (across, up) or (horizontal, vertical)

Chapter Two

Egg Carton Games

Give that empty egg carton a new life! Inside its lowly exterior lurks a randomizing device, a target, or a racetrack.

Use either plastic or cardboard egg cartons, but not those with large holes in their covers. Use either two-by-six cartons or three-by-four cartons. (The illustrations show two-by-six cartons; to use the three-by-four variety, simply rearrange the numbers.) Do not remove the tops from the cartons. You can also use the cartons to store game pieces. Game instructions can be pasted to the inside top of the cartons, and the cartons can be decorated.

When writing numbers in an egg carton, put them both on the bottom and the back side of the egg holes (so that the number in a hole can be read without removing objects from the egg hole). Buttons, centimeter cubes, pebbles, large beads, and other small objects are all appropriate to use as counters for egg carton games.

Egg-O

Object: Players take turns shaking a numbered egg carton containing two counters. The player's score after each turn is the sum, difference, or product of the numbers on which the counters land.

Skills: addition, subtraction or multiplication, communication
Number of players: 2 to 4
Grades: 1 to 5
Materials: one egg carton and two small counters (such as buttons, pebbles, or beads)

Preparation: Write the numbers from 0 to 10 in the holes of an egg carton, as shown. One number is written twice.

Playing:

1. Decide if Egg-O will be played as an addition, subtraction, or multiplication game.

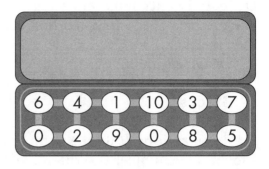

2. Egg-O is played in rounds, with play rotating clockwise. During each round, each player takes a turn putting the two counters in the egg carton, closing it, shaking it, and then opening the carton to see where the counters landed. The player then states aloud the numbers and their sum, difference, or product (depending on the game being played).

3. In the addition game, a player's score is the sum of the two numbers that the counters landed in. In a subtraction or multiplication game, players find either the difference or product of the numbers.

4. The player with the highest score wins one point for the round.

Winning: The first player to acquire five points wins.

Playing variations:

- Instead of acquiring points at the end of each round, players keep cumulative track of their scores from the rounds. The first player to get a cumulative score of 50 or more for the addition game wins (25 for the subtraction game, 200 for the multiplication game).

- Play ten rounds or for fifteen minutes. The winner is the player with the highest cumulative score.

- Use three, four, or five counters, instead of two.

- Require players to record their equations from each round on paper.

Skill variations:

Fractions or decimals: Use fractions or decimals instead of whole numbers.

Place value: Use two-, three-, or four-digit numbers in the egg cavities, such as 25 or 378.

Egg Race

Object: Twenty numbers are generated from an egg carton to form a racetrack. Players race to see who can first correctly add another number to each of those in the racetrack.

Skills: addition
Number of players: 2 to whole class
Grades: 1 to 3
Materials: one egg carton, one small counter (such as a button), paper, and pencils
Preparation: Write the numbers from 0 to 10 in the cavities of an egg carton, as shown. One number is written twice.

Playing:

1. To start, a player puts the counter in the egg carton, closes it, shakes it, opens it to see which number the counter landed on, and announces that number. This is done twenty times.

2. As the twenty numbers are announced, each player writes them down, one below another, in a straight column (using lined paper helps). The players then draw a line down their sheets of paper parallel to the column of numbers. (See the example.) These numbers now form a racetrack.

3. When all players are ready, a twenty-first number is generated by shaking the egg carton, and it is announced aloud. Players then race to see who can be first to add that last number to each of the other twenty numbers in their racetrack. The players record each sum next to the number they added to, but on the other side of the line. They must work from the top number down, without skipping.

4. As players finish, they raise their pencil up in the air and yell, "Done!" The order in which the players finish is recorded. The player who finished first reads his or her answers. If they are all correct, that player wins. If not, players read answers in the order in which they finished until a winner is found.

Winning: The first player to correctly complete the addition race wins.

Playing variations:

- Players can be provided with playing boards, such as those on the next page.

- Children can play alone by keeping track of how long it takes them to complete a race. They can keep track of their times and compare them over several days or weeks. Two children can take turns timing each other.

Skill variation:

Multiplication: Instead of adding, players can multiply the twenty-first number by each of the other numbers.

EGG RACE

Number + ☐ = Sum

EGG RACE

Number + ☐ = Sum

Egg Carton Games

More or Less

Object: Players bet on the size of the product of two numbers shaken in a numbered egg carton.

Skills: multiplication, probability, inequalities

Number of players: 2 or more

Grades: 3 to 5

Materials: one egg carton, two counters (such as buttons or pebbles), paper, and pencils

Preparation: Write the numbers from 0 to 10 in the egg carton, as shown. One number is written twice. Make copies of the playing sheet on the next page for each player.

Playing:

1. Give each player a More or Less playing sheet. Choose a person to be a caller.

2. The game lasts ten rounds, with every player playing simultaneously.

3. At the beginning of each round, every player bets whether the product of the two numbers to be shaken by the caller will be more than, equal to, or less than 20. Players bet by placing an X in the desired column of the playing board for that round in the game.

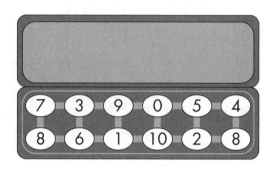

4. During each round, the caller places two counters in the egg carton, closes it, shakes it, opens it, and announces the numbers on which the counters landed.

5. At the end of each round, players write the numbers announced by the caller in the Numbers column of their playing sheet and write the corresponding multiplication problem and its answer in the Problem column of their playing sheet. For example, if the caller announced "4 and 5," the players would write a 4 and a 5 in the Numbers column and would write $4 \times 5 = 20$ in the Problem column.

6. When players have completed their multiplication problem for each round, the caller announces the answer to the multiplication problem. Players then calculate and record their scores. Players score one point if they solve the arithmetic problem correctly and two points if they win their bet about the size of the problem's answer.

7. After ten rounds, each player adds his or her ten scores to get a total score.

Winning: The player with the largest total score wins.

Skill variation:

Addition: Have children bet whether the sum of the numbers shaken is more than, less than, or equal to 10. Construct playing sheets accordingly.

More or Less

Round	Bets			Numbers		Problem	Score
	More than 20	Equal to 20	Less than 20				
1							
2							
3							
4							
5							
6							
7							
8							
9							
10							

Total Score =

Egg Bump

Object: Players shake two counters in a numbered egg carton, calculate the sum and difference of the resulting numbers, and record them by placing counters in another numbered carton.

Skills: addition, subtraction
Number of players: 2
Grades: 1 to 3
Materials: two egg cartons and 28 small counters (such as buttons or beads) that can be divided into two sets (by color or shape) of 14 counters each

Preparation: Label the inside top of one egg carton Shake Carton and write the numbers from 1 to 6 in its egg cavities, as shown. Label the inside top of the other egg carton Score Carton, write the numbers from 1 to 12 in its egg cavities, and write the number O inside its top, as shown.

Playing:

1. Put the Score Carton between the two players. Give each player a set of 13 similar counters. Put the two remaining counters in the Shake Carton.

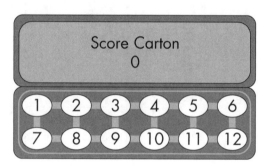

2. The game lasts ten rounds. Each player takes one turn during each round.

3. To begin a turn, a player takes the Shake Carton (with two counters inside it), closes it, shakes it, and opens it to see which numbers the two counters landed on.

4. The player then calculates the sum and the difference (as a positive number) of the two numbers.

5. At the end of a turn, a player puts his or her own counters into the Score Carton, either into its lid or its egg cavities. One counter is put on the number corresponding to the sum that was calculated. One counter is put on the number corresponding to the difference that was calculated. If one of the player's own counters is already on a number on which a counter is to be placed, the player does not place a counter on that number. If one of the opponent's counters is already on a number on which a counter is to be placed, the player removes the opponent's counter, gives it back to the opponent, and replaces it with his or her own counter. No more than one counter can ever reside on a single number.

Math Skill Development Games

6. After ten rounds (twenty turns), the game ends and the players count the number of their counters in the Score Carton.

Winning: The player with the most counters in the Score Carton wins.

Playing variation:

- At the end of the game, players find the sum of all the numbers on which their counters reside. The player with the largest sum wins.

Egg-a-Round

Object: Players move their counters clockwise around a numbered egg carton according to the shake of a number-generating carton. They acquire points according to the numbers on which their counters land.

    Skills: addition, counting

    Number of players: 2 to whole class

    Grades: 1 to 3

    Materials: one more egg carton than there are players, and as many counters (such as small beads, buttons, or pebbles) as there are egg cartons

    Preparation: In one egg carton (Leader's Carton), write the numbers from 1 to 6, as shown. In all the other egg cartons (Players' Cartons), write the numbers from 1 to 12, as shown.

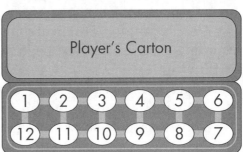

    Playing:

1. Choose a leader (either the teacher or a student). The leader takes the Leader's Carton and one counter.

2. Each player takes a Player's Carton and one counter. Each player puts his or her counter on any one of the twelve numbers.

3. The game is played as a series of six rounds.

4. To begin each round, the leader places a counter in the Leader's Carton, closes it, shakes it, opens it to see which number the counter landed on, and announces that number.

5. After the leader announces the number, all players move their counters that many egg cavities clockwise around their cartons, starting from where their counter rested at the end of the previous round. The number on which the player's counter lands after being moved is that player's score for that round.

6. Players add their scores cumulatively from round to round.

Winning: The player with the highest cumulative score after six rounds is the winner.

Playing variations:

- Use other numbers in the egg cartons. Try large numbers, such as 78 or 365, or fractions, such as ½ or ¾.

- Let the winner be the first player to get a score greater than 50.

Skill variation:

Multiplication: A player's score for a round is the leader's number times the number on which the player's counter lands.

Place-an-Egg Value

Object: Three counters designating hundreds, tens, and ones are shaken in a numbered egg carton. Players receive points for shaking large numbers and for reading and writing the numbers they shake.

Skills: place value, addition, inequalities, representation, communication

Number of players: 2 to 4

Grades: 1 to 4

Materials: one egg carton, three counters (such as wood cubes or cardboard squares), paper, and pencils

Preparation: Write the numbers from 0 to 9 in an egg carton, as shown. Mark the counters 100, 10, and 1. Duplicate copies of the recording sheet on the next page.

Playing:

1. The game is played in five rounds. During each round, each player takes one turn, in clockwise rotation.

2. During a player's turn, the player places the three counters in the egg carton, closes it, shakes it, and opens it to see which numbers the counters landed on. The player announces them aloud and records on the Place-an-Egg Value recording sheet the number of hundreds, tens, and ones acquired (for example, announcing 4 hundreds, 3 tens, and 5 ones and writing 4, 3, and 5 in the hundreds, tens, and ones columns). The player then writes and reads the number using place value notation and language.

3. After each round, players compare their numbers. The player with the largest number receives one point. In addition, players who correctly read and write their numbers using place value notation get one point.

4. After five rounds of play, each player adds his or her points from all five rounds.

Winning: The player with the most points wins.

Playing variations:

- Write both one- and two-digit numbers in the egg carton so that players must regroup numbers when writing and speaking using place value notation.

- If three or four people play, give one point to the player with the smallest number.

- Leave the counters blank and have players create the largest number possible by deciding, after shaking the carton, which object should be a hundred, ten, or one.

- Instead of having players shake the carton to obtain numbers, have them toss the counters into the carton from about three feet away to obtain numbers.

Skill variation:

Addition: Have players add together the numbers they receive starting with the second round. The player with the largest sum at the end of each round gets one point.

Bing-Egg-O

Object: This game is similar to Bingo. Egg cartons containing multiplication products serve as Bingo cards. Instead of picking Bingo balls, the caller shakes two numbered egg cartons containing counters to obtain factors.

Skills: multiplication

Number of players: 3 to whole class

Grades: 3 to 5

Materials: two more egg cartons than the number of players, and 11 small counters (such as buttons, beans, or pebbles) for each player

Preparation: In two egg cartons, write the numbers from 1 to 9, as shown. Three numbers are written twice. In the other egg cartons, write a random selection of the following numbers: 1, 2, 3, 4, 5, 6, 7, 8, 9, 10, 12, 14, 15, 16, 18, 20, 21, 24, 25, 27, 28, 30, 32, 35, 36, 40, 42, 45, 48, 49, 54, 56, 63, 64, 72, 81. These are the products of the numbers from 1 to 9.

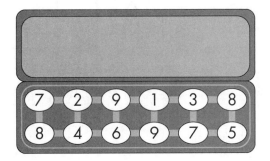

Playing:

1. Select a caller. Give the caller the two egg cartons numbered from 1 to 9 and two counters. Give each player one of the other egg cartons and 10 counters. Players open their cartons and place their counters in the lids.

Place-An-Egg Value

Round	Hundreds	Tens	Ones	Number	Score
1					
2					
3					
4					
5					

Final Score =

2. The caller places a counter in each egg carton, closes and shakes them, opens them to see which numbers the counters landed on, announces the two numbers out loud, and writes them down.

3. The players silently multiply the two numbers together and look to see if the product is written in their cartons. If it is, they place a counter on the number.

4. This continues until a player calls "Bing-Egg-O," meaning that the player has counters either in a straight line of six or in two adjacent rows of three (as shown).

5. The caller checks to see that this player has covered products that correctly match the pairs of numbers shaken.

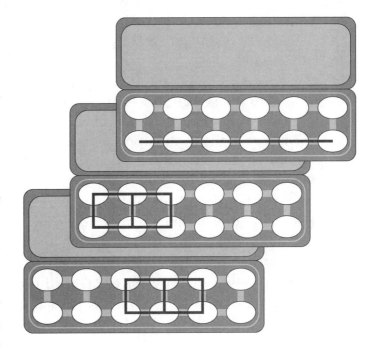

Winning: The first player to validly call "Bing-Egg-O" wins.

Skill variations:

Addition: Write any whole numbers in the caller's egg cartons, figure out all possible sums, and randomly write them in the player's egg cartons.

Fraction addition or multiplication: Follow the same setup procedure, but use fractions.

Three Hundred

Object: Players generate eight two-digit numbers, which they cumulatively add to or subtract from each other in an attempt to get a result that is as close as possible to 300.

Skills: two-digit addition and subtraction, place value, probability, problem solving

Number of players: 2 to whole class

Grades: 2 to 5

Materials: one egg carton, two small counters (such as pebbles or buttons), copies of the Three Hundred recording sheet or lined paper, and pencils

Preparation: Write the digits from 1 to 9 in the egg carton, as shown. Three numbers are written twice. Make copies of the Three Hundred recording sheet for players.

Playing:

1. Choose one person to be shaker for the entire game. Distribute copies of the Three Hundred recording sheet and a pencil to each player.

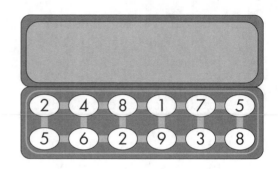

2. The game is played in up to eleven rounds. Players try to create a number as close as possible to 300 by the eleventh round.

3. To begin each round, the shaker puts the two counters in the egg carton, closes it, shakes it, opens it to see on which two digits the two counters landed, and announces those digits aloud. In the first round, each player then writes down those two digits in the uppermost two square spaces on the Three Hundred recording sheet, in either order, to make a two-digit number. (For example, if counters landed on 2 and 5, the players may create either 25 or 52.)

4. During the second round, the players record their second two-digit number directly under their first number and either add or subtract. The result is written under the two numbers. (See the sample game.)

5. In succeeding rounds, players record their two-digit number directly below the cumulative result of previous rounds, either add or subtract, and record the result directly below the problem.

6. During the game, players may add no more than eight times and subtract no more than two times. (Eleven rounds allow for the first number, eight additions, and two subtractions.) Each player decides when to add or subtract during the game. Players can black out plus and minus signs at the top of the recording sheet to help them keep track of how many additions and subtractions they have used.

7. At any time during the game, before the beginning of a new round, players can declare that they are satisfied with their cumulative result of the previous round and that they wish to stay with that result for the remainder of the game. Players do this if they feel that their cumulative result is as close to 300 as possible.

Winning: The player who creates the number closest to 300 (either above or below 300) wins.

Three Hundred
+++++++--

Three Hundred
+++++++--

Three Hundred
+++++++--

Egg Carton Games

55

Egg Throw

Object: Players take turns throwing numbered cardboard squares at an egg carton target. They score points by multiplying the numbers on the squares by the numbers on which they land in the egg carton.

Skills: multiplication, addition

Number of players: 2 to 4

Grades: 3 to 5

Materials: one egg carton, one piece of cardboard, lined paper or copies of the Egg Throw scoring sheet, and pencils

Preparation: From the piece of cardboard, cut four squares about ¾ inch (2 cm) on a side. Number them to correspond to the multiplication facts to be drilled. For example, to drill the 4, 5, 6, and 7 facts, number the squares 4, 5, 6, and 7. Write the numbers from 0 to 10 in the egg carton, as shown. If desired, make copies of the Egg Throw scoring sheet.

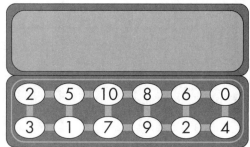

Playing:

1. Place the egg carton on the floor. Draw a tossing line behind which players must stand when tossing.

2. The game is played as a series of five rounds. Every player takes a turn during each round.

3. To begin a turn, a player stands behind the tossing line and tosses the four squares at the egg carton, one at a time.

4. To end a turn, players calculate their scores. First they multiply the number on each square by the number on which it fell. (Squares that do not fall into egg cavities do not score points.) Then they add their four products to get a score for the round. Finally, they add their score from the round to their scores from previous rounds.

Winning: The player with the largest total score after five rounds is the winner.

Skill variations:

Place value: Write the numbers 1000, 100, 10, and 1 on the squares. At the end of each turn, players record and read their scores using place value language.

Money: Use a penny, nickel, dime, and quarter instead of cardboard squares (or mark symbols for these coins on squares). The number in the egg cavity in which a coin lands indicates how many of that coin the player receives. Players calculate their scores using money language and notation.

Addition: The number on each square is added to the number on which it falls.

Egg Throw

Round	Calculations	Score	Cumulative Score
1			
2			
3			
4			
5			

Egg Throw

Round	Calculations	Score	Cumulative Score
1			
2			
3			
4			
5			

Egg Throw

Round	Calculations	Score	Cumulative Score
1			
2			
3			
4			
5			

Divide and Move

Object: Players move along a racetrack containing the numbers from 10 to 90. They move according to the remainders that result from dividing their playing position number by a number generated from an egg carton.

Skills: division with remainders

Number of players: 2 to 6

Grades: 3 to 5

Materials: one egg carton, one small counter (a button, pebble, or bead), lined paper, and pencils

Preparation: Write the numbers from 1 to 10 in the egg carton, as shown. Two numbers are written twice. Make copies of the Divide and Move playing board, or have each player write the numbers from 10 to 90 on lined paper, leaving about two inches between columns.

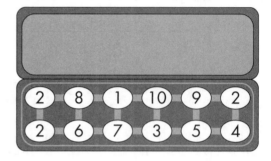

Playing:

1. The players circle the number 10 on their paper.

2. Players take turns, with play rotating clockwise. A turn involves three steps.

3. First, a player puts the counter in the egg carton, closes it, shakes it, and opens it to see which number the counter landed on.

4. Next, the player divides that number into the largest number circled on his or her paper and finds the remainder for this division problem.

5. The remainder determines how many more numbers will be circled on the player's paper. The player circles numbers successively, beginning with

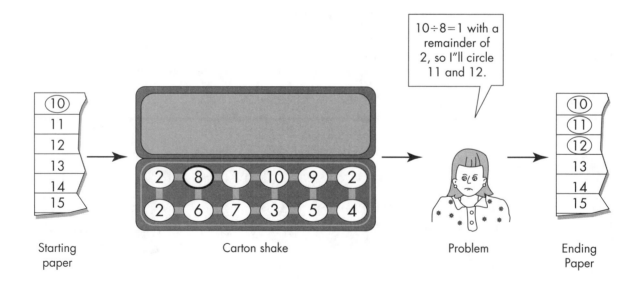

Starting paper   Carton shake   Problem   Ending Paper

10÷8=1 with a remainder of 2, so I"ll circle 11 and 12.

the one after the previously circled number. For example, if on the first turn the remainder is 2, then the player circles 11 and 12 (the first two numbers after 10). Note that a remainder of 0 means that no numbers get circled that turn.

6. Players check each other's papers for mistakes. A player who notices that another has made a mistake gets to take that player's next turn. In this way, a player who makes a mistake loses a turn, and a player who finds a mistake gets an extra turn.

Winning: The winner is the first player to circle all the numbers up to 90.

Playing variation:
- Use fewer numbers, either by having the largest number be smaller than 90 or by having players cross out any ten numbers they choose on their own paper.

Egg-Cala

Object: In this version of the old African game called mancala, players count as they "sow seeds" counterclockwise around a playing board.

    Skills: counting, problem solving

    Number of players: 2

    Grades: 1 to 5

    Materials: one egg carton with its lid removed, two small cardboard boxes (or cups or bowls) that can be placed at either end of the carton to form a game board, and 48 small objects (such as buttons, pennies, or pebbles)

    Preparation: Place the two small cardboard boxes or other small containers at either end of the egg carton.

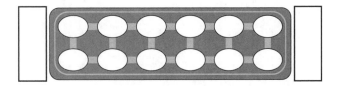

Playing:
1. The game board contains twelve small pits, six on each side of the egg carton, and two large home pits on either end (the cardboard boxes). Each player controls (or owns) the six pits on his or her side of the board and the home pit on his or her right-hand side of the board.

2. To set up the game, players sit facing each other with the game board between them and its long side perpendicular to them. The 48 small objects (called seeds) are distributed so that there are 4 in each of the small circles (called pits).

Divide and Move

10			
11	31	51	71
12	32	52	72
13	33	53	73
14	34	54	74
15	35	55	75
16	36	56	76
17	37	57	77
18	38	58	78
19	39	59	79
20	40	60	80
21	41	61	81
22	42	62	82
23	43	63	83
24	44	64	84
25	45	65	85
26	46	66	86
27	47	67	87
28	48	68	88
29	49	69	89
30	50	70	90

Math Skill Development Games

3. Players take turns. During a turn, a player takes all the seeds out of one of his or her pits and "sows" them around the board in a counterclockwise direction. Sowing seeds consists of placing one seed per pit in each successive pit going counterclockwise around the game board. Sowing begins in the first pit counterclockwise from the pit from which seeds are removed.

4. If the last seed a player sows lands in that player's home pit, the player takes another turn.

5. If the last seed a player sows lands in an empty pit on that player's side of the board, the player "captures" any seeds directly across from that pit on the opponent's side of the board. Capturing seeds involves removing them from the pit and placing them in the capturing player's home pit.

6. Seeds are never removed from a player's home pit.

7. When one side of the board is completely empty of seeds, the game ends, and players count the number of seeds in each home pit.

Winning: The player with the most seeds in his or her home pit at the end of the game is the winner.

Playing variations:

- At the beginning of the game, three seeds can be put in a pit instead of four.

- At the end of the game, any seeds remaining on the board are placed in the home pit of the player on whose side of the board they reside.

Chapter Three

Cube Games

One common way to generate random numbers from 2 to 12 is by rolling two dice. The games in this chapter, however, call for numbers anywhere from −25 to 100! You can create your own number cubes by covering the faces of regular dice with masking tape or small circular stickers available from stationery stores, and writing on the new symbols. The ideal materials to use for constructing cube games, however, are the blank wood cubes sold by many educational materials supply companies. The recommended size for blank cubes is between ¾ and 1 inch (or between 2 and 2.5 cm).

Other easily made devices will also randomize six items. As I described in the introduction to this book, you can also use the six sides of a pencil, a hexagonal tee-totum, a homemade spinner divided into six sections, and a tossing board with six sections as randomizing devices for all the cube games.

Nines

Object: Players cross out the digits from 1 to 9 according to the sum rolled on two numbered cubes. The player who crosses out the most numbers wins.

Skills: addition, subtraction, probability, connections, problem solving
Number of players: 1 to 4
Grades: 1 to 4
Materials: two cubes, paper, and pencil
Preparation: Write the numbers from 1 to 6 on the faces of each cube.

Playing:

1. Nines is played in turns, with each player completing a turn and scoring before the next player's turn begins.

2. A player begins a turn by preparing a playing board. This involves writing the numbers from 1 to 9 on a piece of paper, as in the sample game.

3. During a turn, a player rolls both cubes, adds the numbers rolled, then crosses out one or more numbers on the playing board equal to the sum of the numbers rolled. For example, if a player rolls a 4 and a 5, their sum is 9, and the player can cross out any of the following groups of numbers: 9; 8 + 1; 7 + 2; 6 + 3; 5 + 4; 6 + 2 + 1; 5 + 3 + 1; or 4 + 3 + 2. (See the sample game.) The player continues the process of rolling cubes and crossing out numbers until a sum is rolled that cannot be crossed out on the playing board. The player's score is then calculated.

4. A player's score may be either the number of digits not crossed out or the sum of the digits not crossed out. (Decide which before the game begins.) After a player's score is calculated, the next player's turn begins.

Winning: The player with the *lowest* score wins.

Roll It

Object: Players repeatedly roll numbered cubes (starting with five) and set aside one cube after each roll, in an attempt to cumulatively roll the largest sum possible.

Skills: addition, problem solving

Number of players: 2 to 6
Grades: 1 to 5
Materials: five cubes, and paper and pencils as needed
Preparation: Write the numbers 3, 4, 5, 6, 7, and 8 on the faces of each of the five cubes.

Playing:

Each player has only one turn during Roll It. When every player has taken one turn, the game ends. On a turn, a player follows these steps:

1. The player rolls all five cubes and sets aside the cube showing the largest number.

2. The player rerolls the remaining four cubes and again sets aside the cube with the largest number on it. The player adds the numbers on the two cubes set aside and announces the sum.

3. The remaining three cubes are rerolled, the cube with the largest number on it is set aside, and its number is added to the previous sum obtained.

4. The player rerolls the remaining two cubes, sets aside the cube with the largest number on it, and adds its number to the previous sum obtained from the first three cubes set aside.

5. Finally, the player rerolls the remaining cube, adds its number to the previous sum, and announces the result. This is the player's final score.

Winning: The player with the largest final score wins.

Playing variations:

• Use fewer or more than five cubes.

• Write different numbers on the cubes—for example, the numbers from 1 to 6 or those from 24 to 29.

Skill variations:

Multiplication: The numbers acquired in the game can be successively multiplied together to obtain a single product, which is a player's final score.

Multiple arithmetic operations: Play the game by first adding, then subtracting, then multiplying, and then dividing the numbers thrown and set aside, in that sequence. (Decimals can be used, or players can round off to the nearest whole number after dividing.) Or use just three cubes, with an addition and then a subtraction.

Cardinal-Ordinal

Object: Players cross out twelve cardinal numbers (in any order) and twelve ordinal numbers (in sequence from smallest to largest) according to the numbers thrown on three cubes. The first player to cross out all twenty-four numbers wins.

Skills: cardinal and ordinal, addition, connections
Number of players: 2 to 5
Grades: 1 to 2

Materials: three cubes, paper, and pencils

Preparation: Write the numbers from 1 to 6 on the faces of each cube. Have each player make a copy of the game sheet on the next page, or you can reproduce copies for all players.

Playing:

1. Each player attempts be the first to cross out all of the number names in both the cardinal and ordinal columns of their game sheets. Players may cross out cardinal numbers in any order. However, they must cross out ordinal numbers in sequence from first to twelfth.

2. Players take turns in clockwise rotation. Players write on their own game sheet.

3. To begin a turn, a player rolls the three cubes simultaneously.

4. Next the player crosses out number names according to the numbers rolled on the cubes. Number names may be crossed out if they match a number rolled on a single cube, the sum of the numbers rolled on two cubes, or the sum of the numbers rolled on all three cubes. A player may do any combination of these things on a single turn, so long as each number rolled is used no more than once. Number names in either column or both columns may be crossed out on a single turn. For example, if a player rolls a 1, 4, and 5, the player might cross out any one of the following:

   - one, four, and five
   - first, four, and five
   - ten (1 + 4 + 5)
   - first and nine (4 + 5)
   - one and nine
   - four and six (1 + 5)

   A player does not have to use all of the numbers rolled: in the previous example, the player might have just crossed out either *one* or *one* and *five*. If a player is not able to use any cubes, he or she passes, and the next player begins a turn.

5. A player's turn ends when he or she finishes crossing out number names and passes the cubes to the next player.

Winning: The winner is the first player to cross out all the cardinal and ordinal number names wins.

Playing variations:

- Allow players to steal a number another player rolls if the player who rolled the number can use it but does not do so. The stealer must claim the number as soon as the cubes are passed to the next player and must be able to use the stolen number immediately.

- Use a game sheet with two columns of cardinal numbers, with two columns of ordinal number names, or with two columns of numerals from 1 to 12.

Cardinal (any order)	Ordinal (in sequence)	Cardinal (any order)	Ordinal (in sequence)
one	first	one	first
two	second	two	second
three	third	three	third
four	fourth	four	fourth
five	fifth	five	fifth
six	sixth	six	sixth
seven	seventh	seven	seventh
eight	eighth	eight	eighth
nine	ninth	nine	ninth
ten	tenth	ten	tenth
eleven	eleventh	eleven	eleventh
twelve	twelfth	twelve	twelfth

Product Shot

Object: A numbered cube is rolled thirteen times. Players write the resulting numbers in the hexagons of a game sheet. Scores are calculated by multiplying together the numbers in adjacent hexagons.

Skills: multiplication, addition, probability, problem solving

Number of players: 2 to whole class

Grades: 3 to 5

Materials: one cube, and copies of the Product Shot game sheet

Preparation: Write the numbers 2, 3, 4, 5, 6, and 7 on the faces of a cube. Make a copy of the game sheet on the next page for each player.

Playing:

1. Give each player a game sheet and pencil.

2. Choose one person to roll the cube and announce the numbers rolled. This is done thirteen times during the game.

3. Immediately after each number is announced, every player writes that number in any empty hexagon on his or her game sheet. Once written, a number's position on the game sheet cannot be changed.

4. When all thirteen hexagons on the players' game sheets are filled, each player finds the products of the numbers in diagonally adjacent pairs of hexagons (indicated by the arrows on the game sheet). Each product is recorded in the appropriate circle.

5. Players cross out any product that appears in only one circle.

6. Players find the sum of the products that are not crossed out. These are their scores.

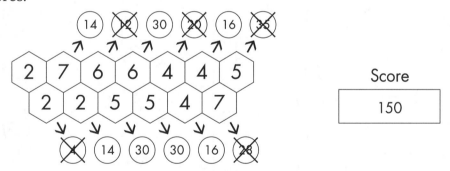

Winning: The player with the highest score wins.

Playing variations:

- Have a player's score be simply the number of circles not crossed out.
- Drill other multiplication facts by writing different numbers on the cubes.
- Play three games. The winner is the player with the highest cumulative score.

Skill variation:

Addition: Add the numbers and cross out sums that appear in only one circle. A player's score is the number of remaining circles.

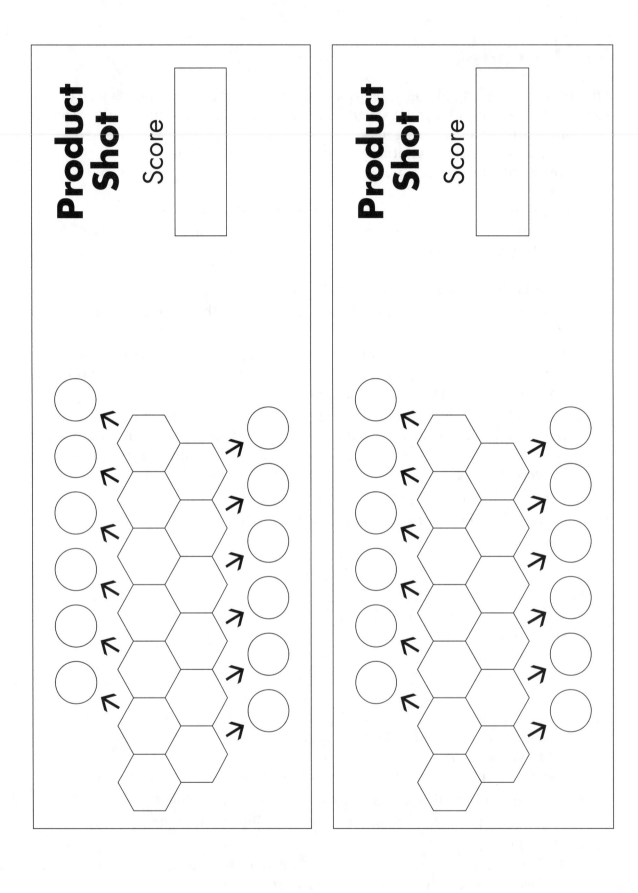

Product Shot

Score

Product Shot

Score

Rectangles

Object: During a series of rounds, players toss two numbered cubes that determine the length and width of rectangles that are constructed on 12 × 12 pieces of graph paper. Players score points by finding the areas of rectangles.

Skills: multiplication, geometry area calculations, problem solving, connections

Number of players: 2 to 5

Grades: 3 to 5

Materials: two dice or cubes, a pencil or crayon for each player, and copies of the Rectangles playing board on the next page (or graph paper)

Preparation: Number each cube from 1 to 6 and duplicate copies of the playing board (or have players mark off a 12 × 12 square on a piece of graph paper). To make playing boards reusable, laminate the boards.

Playing:

1. Players take turns. During a turn, a player tosses the cubes and constructs a rectangle by marking its length on the playing board (or graph paper) on a horizontal line according to the number thrown on one cube and marking its height according to the number thrown on the other cube on a vertical line starting at one of the ends of the length. The player then outlines the entire rectangle, colors it in, and calculates his or her score by determining the number of squares within the rectangle.

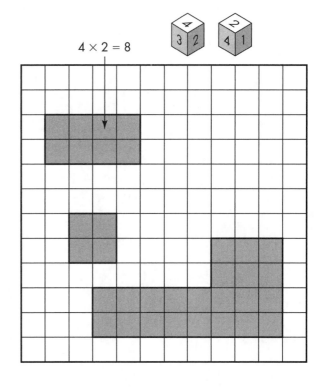

2. The rules for placing rectangles are as follows: all rectangles must be placed entirely within the major 12 × 12 square playing area; the edges of rectangles may touch (but do not have to); rectangles may not overlap each other; and no rectangle may be placed within another rectangle.

3. Players drop out of the game and calculate their cumulative score when their throw of the dice gives them a rectangle that will not fit on their playing board in the remaining empty space. The last player to place a rectangle on his or her graph paper gets a bonus of ten points. The game ends when all players have dropped out.

Winning: The player with the highest cumulative score wins.

Playing variations:

- Have players write down the method of calculation that they used to find the area of each rectangle under the rectangle. For example, for a 3 $\times$ 4 rectangle, they might write 3 $\times$ 4 = 12, 3 + 3 + 3 + 3 = 12, or 4 + 4 + 4 = 12.

- Have a game consist of five rounds, with the winner being the player who has the highest cumulative score after five turns.

Rectangles

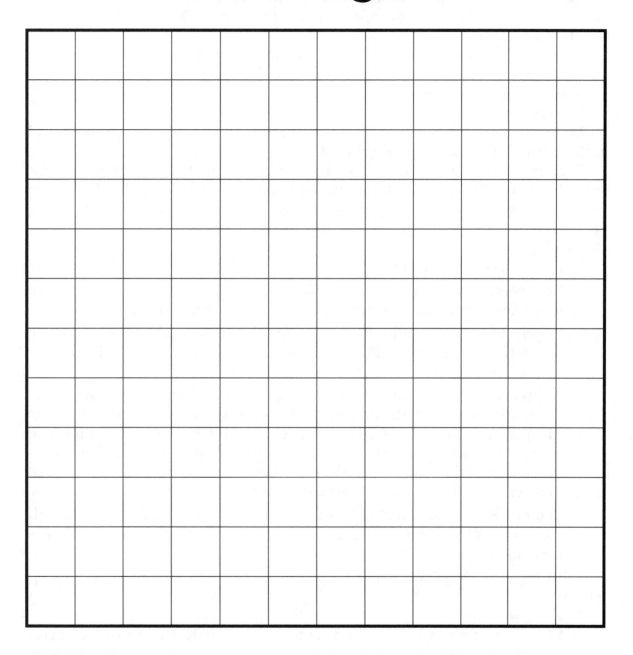

Off the Board

Object: Players move their counters in the positive or negative direction on a number line according to the throw of two numbered cubes. The first player to get a counter past either $+7$ or -7 wins.

Skills: positive and negative numbers, addition of signed numbers, connections, representation

Number of players: 2

Grades: 3 to 5

Materials: two cubes, two different counters (such as buttons or pebbles), and copies of the Off the Board playing board

Preparation: With a blue pen, write the numbers 0, 1, 1, 2, 2, and 3 on one cube. With a red pen, write the same numbers on the other cube. Make two larger-size copies of one of the playing boards on the next page. The first playing board is for beginners; the second is for advanced players.

Playing:

1. Give one copy of the appropriate board to each player.

2. Each player chooses a counter and places it on the "middle" (or 0) position on his or her playing board. Players move only their own counter.

3. Players decide which cube, the red one or the blue one, will move their counters in the "up" (positive) direction and which cube will move their counters in the "down" (negative) direction.

4. Players take turns. During a turn, a player rolls the two cubes and then moves his or her counter on the playing board, starting from where it last rested. The player moves the counter in the "up" (positive) direction a number of spaces equal to the number rolled on the "up" (positive) cube and then moves the counter in the "down" (negative) direction a number of spaces equal to the number rolled on the "down" (negative) cube.

5. The players continue taking turns until one player's counter is moved off either end of the playing board, past either "up 7" ($+7$) or "down 7" (-7). The game then ends.

Winning: The first player to move his or her counter off either end of the playing board wins.

Playing variations:

- For younger players, color one side of the playing board red and the other side blue to correspond to the colors on the cubes. This avoids the step of having children decide which side will be red or blue.

- Require older players to correctly say or write the equations that correspond to the numbers thrown during their moves.

Win		Win
up	7	+7
up	6	+6
up	5	+5
up	4	+4
up	3	+3
up	2	+2
up	1	+1
middle		0
down	1	−1
down	2	−2
down	3	−3
down	4	−4
down	5	−5
down	6	−6
down	7	−7
Win		Win

Number Grid

Object: Players create and write numbers in the cells of a 10 × 10 square grid, in an interlocking manner similar to Scrabble.

Skills: addition with trading, problem solving, communication

Number of players: 2 to 5

Grades: 3 to 5

Materials: three cubes, paper, and pencils

Preparation: On one cube, write the numbers 1, 2, 3, 5, 7, and 9. On the second, write the numbers 1, 2, 4, 6, 8, and 9. On the third, write the numbers 3, 4, 5, 6, 7, and 8. Have the players draw a 10 × 10 square grid. (If possible, have them outline the grid on a piece of graph paper or draw vertical lines on lined paper.) You can also reproduce the grid for the game Rectangles.

Playing:

1. Players take turns in clockwise rotation. All players write their numbers on the same 10 × 10 grid. Each player records points scored on a separate sheet of paper.

2. To begin a turn, a player rolls the three cubes. The player then tries to use the three digits rolled to form a three-digit number that will fit on the grid and read either from left to right or top to bottom.

3. The player writes the number on the grid, one digit per square. The first number created is written anywhere near the center of the grid. Thereafter, all numbers created must interlock with one or more previous numbers, as in Scrabble or crossword puzzles. Either one or two digits of the number created may overlap, but not all three. Each play must add at least one new digit to the grid. Players need not worry about digits adjacent to the three-digit number they place on the grid, only that their number has either one or two digits in common with the configuration of numbers already on the grid. In the example, the first number is 721. The second number, 374, interlocks with it in one place. The third number, 318, interlocks with the 3 in 374. Note that it is permissible for 318 to be adjacent to 721. The fourth number is 819 and the fifth is 439; both interlock with the previous configuration in two different places. The numbers 972 and 873 illustrate other ways that numbers can interlock. If a player cannot place a number on the grid, that player passes, and it becomes the next player's turn.

4. At the end of a turn, a player scores points equal to the number just created and placed on the grid. (For example, the player who created 374 gets 374 points.) Any points acquired are immediately added to points

acquired from previous turns, and the cumulative sum shown to the other players (to check the addition). Each successive score should be recorded in a straight column below the previous total. A player who cannot place a number on the grid scores 0.

5. The game ends either when the grid is filled or when each player has had to pass three times in succession.

Winning: The player with the most points at the end of the game wins.

Try It

Object: Players bet whether or not a 2 will be rolled as they keep a cumulative sum of the numbers rolled on two cubes.

Skills: addition, probability, communication

Number of players: 3 to whole class

Grades: 2 to 5

Materials: two cubes, copies of the Try It recording sheet (or lined paper), and pencils

Preparation: On each cube, write the numbers from 1 to 6. Reproduce copies of the recording sheet on the next page for players or have each player prepare a playing sheet on lined paper.

Playing:

1. Choose one person to be roller for the entire game.

2. Try It is played in rounds. A round ends when a 2 is rolled on one or both of the cubes. Players try to get a total score of 100 or more points before the game ends.

3. During a round, the roller rolls both cubes, announces the numbers rolled, the sum of the numbers rolled, and the cumulative sum of all the numbers rolled during the round. The cube roller repeats this until a 2 is rolled on a cube to end the round.

4. During a round, the players do two things. They keep track of the cumulative sum of all numbers rolled during the round, and they decide when to drop out. A player may drop out of a round at any time, and when he or she does, that player's round score is equal to the cumulative sum of all the numbers rolled during the round up to that point. Players announce when they drop out by recording their round score on their playing sheet, raising their pencil in the air, and saying, "I'm out!" Players must drop out between rolls of the cubes, not during a roll.

5. A round ends when the roller rolls a single 2 or a double 2. A player who has not dropped out before a single 2 is rolled receives a round score of 0. A player who has not dropped out when a double 2 is rolled loses all points thus far accumulated during the game and receives a 0 for both the round score and the total score.

Try It

Round	Round Score	Total Score
1		
2		
3		
4		
5		
6		
7		
8		
9		
10		

Try It

Round	Round Score	Total Score
1		
2		
3		
4		
5		
6		
7		
8		
9		
10		

6. When a round ends, the players calculate their total score for the game thus far. The total score is the round score from the just-completed round plus the total score from the previous round (unless a player lost all points on the roll of a double 2). The players announce their total scores after calculating them. (In a large group, only the players with the highest scores announce them.) If one or more players have a total score of 100 or more, the game ends. If not, a new round begins.

7. The roller should pause between each roll of the cubes so that players who wish to drop out of the round have a chance to do so. The roller should also call on players to help figure out cumulative sums. At any time, the roller may also ask all players who have not yet dropped out to raise a hand.

Winning: All players with a total score of 100 or more at the end of the game win. There can be more than one winner.

Numbers

Object: Players roll five cubes with numbers and operations written on their faces. They create as many different numbers as they can in three minutes using the numbers and operations rolled.

Skills: mental computation, addition, subtraction, multiplication, division, fractions, decimals, signed numbers, powers, roots, equations, problem solving, representation, connections

Number of players: 2 to whole class

Grades: 3 to 5

Materials: five cubes, paper, pencils, and a clock or egg timer

Preparation: Write the following numbers and operations on the cubes:

Cube one: 4, 5, 6, $-$, $\times$, $\div$

Cube two: 0, 1, 2, 3, $+$, $-$

Cube three: 0, 1, 2, 3, $\times$, $\div$

Cube four: 7, 8, 9 $+$, $-$, $\times$

Cube five: 4, 5, 6, $+$, $-$, $\times$

Playing:

1. Choose a person to act as roller. That person rolls all five cubes, announces the numbers and operations rolled, and starts the egg timer or checks the clock.

2. Players now record on their papers as many numbers as they can create using the numbers and operations rolled.

3. A player does not have to use all of the numbers and operations rolled to create a number: one, two, three, four, or all five of the cubes rolled can be used. Players may combine the numbers and operations rolled in any way, if doing so produces a legitimate number. For example, the following numbers are only a few of the many that can be made from a roll of a **5, 2,** $\times$ (multiply), $\div$ (divide), and $-$ (subtract): 5, 2, 25, 52, 10 (2×5), 32 (2^5), $\frac{2}{5}$; ($2 \div 5$), $2\frac{1}{2}$ ($5 \div 2$), 3 ($5 - 2$), -3 ($2 - 5$), 2.5 ($5 \div 2$), and 0.4 ($2 \div 5$).

4. After three minutes, the roller yells "Stop!" Every player must stop writing numbers, and the players count how many different numbers they wrote.

Winning: The player who creates the most numbers is the winner.

Playing variations:

- Play three games. The player who makes the most numbers in any one of the three games is the grand winner.

- Set a different time limit. Five minutes works well for experienced players.

- Change the operations on the cubes. For younger players, use only plus and minus signs.

- If two players work together, one of them can create numbers and announce how they were constructed while the other records them and the equations that produced them.

- Have each player write down both the numbers they create and the equations that produced them.

- One person can play Numbers as a solitaire game. The person plays three rounds a day for several weeks, records the high score for each day, and tries to keep beating the previous days' scores.

What's Up?

Object: Players cross out a number between 10 and 81 and then roll a numbered cube. The number rolled is divided into the number crossed out. The remainder is the player's score.

Skills: division with remainders, divisibility rules, probability

Number of players: 2 to 8

Grades: 4 to 5

Materials: two cubes, lined paper, and pencils

Preparation: On the faces of one cube, write the numbers 1, 3, 5, 7, 7, and 9. On the faces of the other cube, write the numbers 1, 2, 4, 6, 6, and 8. Write the numbers from 10 to 81 on a sheet of lined paper, leaving about two inches between columns of numbers, as shown. You can also reproduce the playing board on the next page.

10	28	46	64
11	29	47	65
12	30	48	66
13	31	49	67
14	32	50	68
15	33	51	69
16	34	52	70
17	35	53	71
18	36	54	72
19	37	55	73
20	38	56	74
21	39	57	75
22	40	58	76
23	41	59	77
24	42	60	78
25	43	61	79
26	44	62	80
27	45	63	81

What's Up?

10	11	12	13	14	15	16	17	18	19
20	21	22	23	24	25	26	27	28	29
30	31	32	33	34	35	36	37	38	39
40	41	42	43	44	45	46	47	48	49
50	51	52	53	54	55	56	57	58	59
60	61	62	63	64	65	66	67	68	69
70	71	72	73	74	75	76	77	78	79
80	81								

What's Up?

10	11	12	13	14	15	16	17	18	19
20	21	22	23	24	25	26	27	28	29
30	31	32	33	34	35	36	37	38	39
40	41	42	43	44	45	46	47	48	49
50	51	52	53	54	55	56	57	58	59
60	61	62	63	64	65	66	67	68	69
70	71	72	73	74	75	76	77	78	79
80	81								

Playing:

1. Players take turns, rotating clockwise.

2. First, a player crosses out any unused number on the number list. All players use the same number list. He or she then chooses one of the two cubes and rolls it.

3. Next, the player divides the number rolled into the number he or she crossed out and finds the remainder of this division problem.

4. The remainder for the division problem is the player's score for that round. Players keep a cumulative sum of their scores from round to round.

5. A player who notices another player make a mistake acquires that player's score for the turn.

6. The game ends when all the numbers on the number list have been crossed out.

Winning: The player with the largest cumulative score at the end of the game wins.

Playing variations:

- To shorten the game, use fewer numbers on the list. Try the numbers between 20 and 60.

- Put numbers larger than 100 on the list to provide practice in long division. For example, try those between 580 and 620. If two-digit numbers, such as 23, are written on the cubes, put still larger numbers, such as those between 7250 and 7275, on the list.

Roll 'n Add

Object: Players take turns rolling two numbered cubes, adding their numbers, and then marking the sum on a playing board. The first to reach a goal wins.

Skills: addition of one-digit numbers, probability

Number of players: 2

Grades: 1 to 2

Materials: two cubes, lined paper, and pencils

Preparation: On each cube, write the numbers from 1 to 6. (Conventional dice can be used.) Have each player prepare a playing sheet on lined paper or give players copies of the reproducible recording sheet.

Playing:

1. Players take turns. Each player has his or her own playing sheet.

2. During a turn, a player rolls the two cubes, announces the numbers rolled, adds the two numbers, announces the addition equation and the sum of the numbers, records the addition equation and sum on his or her playing sheet,

and then marks an X on the playing sheet in one of the boxes above the sum on the numbers rolled, as shown.

3. X's are marked in the squares above the numbers on the playing sheet. Only one X is to be placed in each square. The numbers on the playing sheet each represent one of the possible sums that can be rolled by the two cubes. X's are to be recorded from bottom to top above the sums, with no spaces between them.

						X				
					X	X		X		
		X			X	X		X		
X		X	X	X	X	X	X	X	X	
2	**3**	**4**	**5**	**6**	**7**	**8**	**9**	**10**	**11**	**12**

A Partially Completed Game Of Roll 'n Add

Winning: The winner is the first player either to have an X above each of the sums on the playing sheet or to fill up a complete column of six squares above one of the sums with X's on the playing sheet.

Playing variations:
- Place different numbers on the cubes. For example, to practice addition of numbers from 4 to 9, write the numbers 4, 5, 6, 7, 8, and 9 on the faces of each of the cubes and write the sums from 8 to 18 on the playing board. Or, for example, write the numbers from 1 to 6 on one cube, write the numbers from 4 to 9 on the other cube, and write the sums from 5 to 15 on the playing sheet.
- Reusable playing boards can be prepared by laminating the playing sheet. Have players write on it with crayons and then erase the crayon marks with a paper towel.
- The game can be played without requiring that players record their sums.

Roll 'n Add

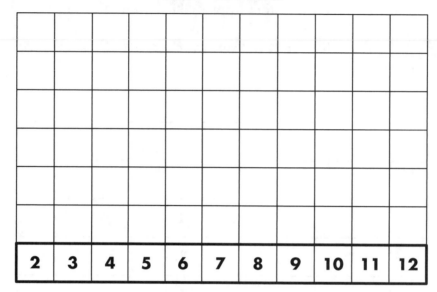

2	3	4	5	6	7	8	9	10	11	12

__ + __ = __   __ + __ = __   __ + __ = __   __ + __ = __

__ + __ = __   __ + __ = __   __ + __ = __   __ + __ = __

__ + __ = __   __ + __ = __   __ + __ = __   __ + __ = __

__ + __ = __   __ + __ = __   __ + __ = __   __ + __ = __

__ + __ = __   __ + __ = __   __ + __ = __   __ + __ = __

__ + __ = __   __ + __ = __   __ + __ = __   __ + __ = __

__ + __ = __   __ + __ = __   __ + __ = __   __ + __ = __

__ + __ = __   __ + __ = __   __ + __ = __   __ + __ = __

__ + __ = __   __ + __ = __   __ + __ = __   __ + __ = __

__ + __ = __   __ + __ = __   __ + __ = __   __ + __ = __

__ + __ = __   __ + __ = __   __ + __ = __   __ + __ = __

Math Skill Development Games

Roll Away

Object: This game is similar to Yahtzee. Players repeatedly roll ten numbered cubes, trying to turn up as many of a particular number as possible. Scoring involves multiplication and addition.

Skills: multiplication, addition, probability

Number of players: 2 to 6

Grades: 3 to 5

Materials: ten cubes, paper, and pencils

Preparation: On each cube, write the numbers 3, 4, 5, 6, 7, and 8. Prepare all ten cubes identically. Either make copies of the reproducible score sheet, or display a copy of it so that players can make their own.

Playing:

1. Each player gets or prepares a copy of the Roll Away score sheet.

2. There are six rounds in the game. During the first round, players roll for 3's (the smallest number on the cubes). During the second round, players roll for 4's (the next larger number on the cubes). During the subsequent rounds, players roll for each successively larger number, until during the last round, they roll for 8's (the largest number on the cubes).

3. During each round, each player takes one turn in clockwise rotation. On a turn, each player tries to roll as many as possible of the number being rolled for during that round.

4. At the beginning of a turn, a player rolls the cubes. First, the player rolls all ten cubes and chooses one cube (of the number being rolled for if one came up) to set aside in a reserve area. Second, he or she rerolls the remaining nine cubes and sets aside another cube in the reserve area with the first cube. Third, the player rerolls the remaining eight cubes and sets aside another cube in the reserve area. This process of rerolling the remaining cubes and setting one aside in the reserve area continues until only one cube remains. It is then rolled and set aside with the others. While setting aside cubes, the players must be careful not to change the numbers rolled (facing up).

5. At the end of a turn, the player calculates the score for that round. First, the player counts up the number of cubes set aside in the reserve area that show the number being rolled for during that round. He or she enters this number in the Quantity Thrown column of the score sheet, multiplies it by the cube number being rolled for during that round, and then enters the product in the Round Score column of the score sheet. The score sheet of a player who rolled seven 3's during the first round is shown in the sample.

6. After all six rounds, every player adds together the round scores and records the cumulative sum as the Total Score.

Number		Quantity Thrown		Round Score
3	×	7	=	21

7. Players check each others' score sheets during the game; any player who finds another's mistake receives an additional ten points, and the player who made the mistake loses ten points.

Winning: The player with the highest total score wins.

Playing variations:

- Write different numbers on the cubes. For an easier game, write the numbers from 1 to 6.

Number		Quantity Thrown		Round Score
3	×		=	
4	×		=	
5	×		=	
6	×		=	
7	×		=	
8	×		=	
Total Score =				

Chapter Four

Tongue Depressor Games

Tongue depressors, for the most part, are considered a tool for doctors. However, they are also useful to teachers, for they are one of the sturdiest, cheapest, and most easily stored materials for mathematics games. They can be written on, dealt like cards, moved around like dominoes, tossed into the air to land like pickup sticks, tied together in various quantities, or cast as randomizing devices like dice.

Tongue depressors can be bought in drug stores in either the adult size (6 × ¾ inches or 15.2 × 1.9 cm) or the child size (5½ × ⅝ inches or 14 × 1.6 cm). Craft sticks can also be used. They are sold in various sizes and colors in craft stores. In a pinch, ice cream sticks can be used.

Risk It

Object: This game is similar to Blackjack or Twenty-One. Players attempt to stop picking numbered tongue depressors from a face-down pile just before the cumulative sum of their numbers reaches 21.

> **Skills:** addition, probability
> **Number of players:** 2 or 3
> **Grades:** 1 to 3
> **Materials:** 25 tongue depressors
> **Preparation:** Mark each tongue depressor on one side, as shown, with one of the following numbers: 0, 0, 0, 1, 1, 1, 1, 1, 2, 2, 2, 2, 3, 3, 3, 3, 4, 4, 4, 5, 5, 6, 7, 8, and 9.

Playing:

1. Each player has only one turn. During a turn, the player places all the tongue depressors face down and mixes them up.

2. The player then turns over tongue depressors one by one and cumulatively adds his or her numbers. The object is to get a sum close or equal to, but not more than, 20.

3. A player may stop at any point and declare his or her score. The player then turns all the tongue depressors face down and mixes them up for the next player.

4. Players calculate their scores as follows. If the sum of the numbers on the tongue depressors is less than 20, the score is the cumulative sum. If the sum is equal to 20, the score is 30 (20 plus a bonus of 10). If the sum is more than 20, the score is 0.

Winning: The player with the highest score wins.

Playing variation:

- The game can end after each player has five turns. The player with the highest cumulative score wins.

Skill variations:

Multiplication 1: Choose any multiplier and have players multiply each tongue depressor they turn over by that multiplier. The number that players try to reach is the multiplier used times 20.

Multiplication 2: Use two sets of 20 tongue depressors each (40 altogether). On the backs of the tongue depressors in one set, draw a star; on the backs of the others, draw a circle. On the fronts of both sets, write the following numbers: 0, 0, 1, 1, 2, 2, 3, 3, 4, 4, 5, 5, 6, 6, 7, 7, 8, 8, 9, and 9. In this game, each player turns over two depressors at a time, one star depressor and one circle depressor, multiplies their numbers, and adds the product to his or her cumulative sum. Scoring: If a player's cumulative sum of products is less than 150, the score is that sum; if equal to 150, the score is 200; if more than 150, the score is 0.

Fractions: Write the following numbers on 25 tongue depressors: 0, ½, ½, ½, ½, 1, 1, 1, 1, 1½, 1½, 1½, 1½, 2, 2, 2, 2½, 2½, 2½, 3, 3, 3½, 3½, 3½, 4. Scoring: If the cumulative sum is less than 10, the score is that sum; if equal to 10, the score is 15; if more than 10, the score is 0. Other fractions, such as multiples of ¼, may also be used.

Pick

Object: Players receive five numbered tongue depressors. They take turns picking from one another's hands. After four rounds of picking, the player whose sum is the largest wins.

Skills: addition, column addition, communication

Number of players: 2 to 5

Grades: 1 to 2

Materials: 30 tongue depressors

Preparation: Mark three sets of 10 tongue depressors with each of the following numbers: 1, 2, 3, 4, 5, 6, 7, 8, 9, and 10. Write on only one side.

Playing:

1. Lay the tongue depressors face down and mix them up.

2. Each player draws five tongue depressors and holds them fan-style to conceal their numbers from other players.

3. The game is played as a series of four rounds.

4. During each round, every player picks one tongue depressor from the hand of the person on the right. The players lay their new tongue depressors face down in front of them until every player has picked. Then all players place their new tongue depressor in their hands, and a new round begins.

5. After four rounds, each player adds the numbers in his or her hand.

Winning: The player with the largest sum wins.

Skill variations:

Addition: Number the tongue depressors from 40 to 69.

Multiple arithmetic operations: End the game by having players combine the numbers in their hands as follows: First, each player adds the numbers on any two depressors, then subtracts the number on a third depressor from that sum. Next, the player multiplies the number on a fourth depressor by this difference and divides the resulting product by the last number. The player who creates the largest number wins.

Right On

Object: Players discard numbered tongue depressors, attempting to bring the sum of those in a discard pile to exactly 20. The player who does this most often wins the game.

Skills: addition, probability, problem solving, communication

Number of players: 2 or 3

Grades: 1 to 3

Materials: 40 tongue depressors

Preparation: Mark four tongue depressors with each of the numbers 1 through 10. Write on only one side of each tongue depressor.

Playing:

1. Place the tongue depressors face down between the players and mix them up. Each player picks seven tongue depressors and holds them so that opponents cannot see their numbers. The unpicked tongue depressors become a drawing pile.

2. The first player discards a tongue depressor, face up, to start a discard pile, and calls out its number. The next player discards a second tongue depressor face up onto the discard pile, adds their two numbers together, and calls out the sum of the numbers in the discard pile.

3. One after the other, each player discards one tongue depressor and calls out the cumulative sum of all the numbers thus far discarded. The player's object is to bring the discard pile's sum to exactly 20 and to get rid of all his or her tongue depressors.

4. The cumulative sum of the numbers in the discard pile cannot exceed 20. If a player cannot discard a tongue depressor without making the sum larger than 20, he or she must pick one tongue depressor at a time from the drawing pile until one is acquired that can be discarded.

5. The player whose discard brings the sum to exactly 20 gets one point. This player removes the completed discard pile and starts a new one by discarding another tongue depressor.

6. When a player gets rid of all his or her tongue depressors, the game ends and that player receives three points. Otherwise the game ends when no player can discard a tongue depressor and none are left in the drawing pile.

Winning: The player with the most points wins. Ties are possible.

Skill variation:

Fraction addition: To give practice in fraction addition, write fractions on the tongue depressors. To make a game based on multiples of ½, mark two tongue depressors with each of the numbers from ½ to 10, in increments of ½. To make a game based on multiples of ¼, mark one tongue depressor with each of the numbers from ¼ to 5, in increments of ¼. You can make games based on other fractions in a similar way.

Flip

Object: Players flip nine numbered tongue depressors into the air. The numbers that land face up are all multiplied together. The player with the largest product wins.

Skills: multiplication, addition, probability

Number of players: 2 to 6

Grades: 3 to 5

Materials: nine tongue depressors, paper, and pencils

Preparation: Mark one side of each tongue depressor with a number from 1 to 9.

Playing:

1. There are ten rounds. Each player takes one turn during each round.

2. To begin a turn, a player flips the nine tongue depressors into the air one by one. (They can be flipped the same way a coin is flipped.)

3. During a turn, a player multiplies together all the tongue depressor numbers that land face up. For example, if a 3, 4, 5, 6, and 9 landed facing up, the player would multiply $3 \times 4 \times 5 \times 6 \times 9$ and get a product of 3240. This is the player's score for the turn.

4. A player completes a turn by adding the score just made to the sum of scores he or she has made in previous turns. The next player then takes a turn. (Players should carefully check each other's multiplication and addition calculations. Make calculators available to settle disputes.)

5. The game ends after ten rounds.

Winning: The player with the largest total score wins.

Playing variations:

- Have players use the recording sheet on the following page to record their work.

- At the end of each round, award one point to the player with the largest product. The player with the most points wins.

- Any player who gets a product larger than 2500 gets one point. The player with the most points after ten rounds wins.

- Reduce the number of rounds.

Skill variation:

Addition: Have players add the numbers on the face-up tongue depressors.

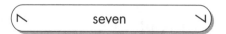

Flip Record Sheet

Round	Numbers Flipped	Product	Cumulative Score
1			
2			
3			
4			
5			
6			
7			
8			
9			
10			

Total Score =

Slide

Object: This game is similar to the game Pea Under Thimble. Three tongue depressors whose numbers a player has just viewed are placed face down and mixed up. The player then points to two and guesses their product.

Skills: multiplication

Number of players: 2 to 6

Grades: 3 to 5

Materials: nine tongue depressors

Preparation: Mark the tongue depressors on one side with the numbers from 1 to 9.

Playing:

1. Choose a dealer.

2. The game is played in rounds.

3. To begin a round, the dealer turns all nine tongue depressors face down and mixes them up. The dealer then randomly chooses three tongue depressors and turns them face up so that all players can see their numbers. The other six tongue depressors are pushed aside.

4. Next, the dealer turns the three chosen tongue depressors face down in front of the players and quickly mixes them up by sliding them around using both hands. The dealer then lines up the three chosen tongue depressors in a row and asks the players for bets. Each player bets by pointing to two tongue depressors and guessing the product of their numbers. Players can be required to write their bets down by recording which depressors they are betting on and what the product is. For example, they might write: (left TD) × (middle TD) = 36.

5. To end a round, the dealer turns the three chosen tongue depressors face up, examines players' bets, and each player who bet correctly scores one point. A new round then begins.

6. Players keep track of their cumulative scores.

7. The game ends either after a designated period of time or when a player makes a total score of ten points.

Winning: The player with the highest score at the end of the game wins.

Skill variation:

Addition: Players guess the sum of the numbers on the tongue depressors, rather than the product.

Togol

Object: Players take turns guessing which of eight numbered tongue depressors lying face down is the largest. Points are awarded for accurately guessing and ordering numbers.

Skills: reading numbers, inequalities, ordering numbers, probability, communication

Number of players: 2

Grades: 1 to 3

Materials: 20 tongue depressors and a small box that will hold them

Preparation: Number the tongue depressors from 1 to 20. Use both written and numeric forms. Write on one side only.

Playing:

1. There are ten rounds in the game. During each round, one player is a picker and the other a guesser. Players switch roles after each round.

2. To start a round, the picker places all the tongue depressors in the box, then secretly picks eight of them from the box and places them face down on the table. This is done without letting the guesser see what the numbers are.

3. During the round, the guesser turns the tongue depressors face up one at a time. The guesser attempts to stop turning over tongue depressors when the one with the largest of the eight numbers is turned face up. The guesser cannot go back to a previously turned-up depressor; the decision to turn over another depressor is final, even though it is made without knowing the number on it. If the guesser turns over all eight depressors, the last one is considered to be the chosen one.

4. To end a round, the guesser turns all eight tongue depressors face up and orders them from smallest to largest.

5. Score each round as follows: three points to the guesser if the guesser chooses the largest number; one point to the guesser if the guesser correctly arranges the tongue depressors in order from smallest to largest; and one point to the picker if the guesser does not choose the largest number.

Winning: The player with the highest cumulative score after ten rounds is the winner.

Playing variations:

- A simpler scoring system awards only one point to the guesser if the guesser chooses the largest number and correctly arranges the tongue depressors from smallest to largest.

- Other numbers can be used. For example, the numbers from 1 to 100 can be written on a set of 100 tongue depressors.

Guess It

Object: Two players take turns picking numbered tongue depressors and letting each other guess if they are marked with an odd or even number. Players acquire tongue depressors if they guess correctly. The player who acquires the most wins.

Skills: odd and even, probability, communication, and associating spoken, written, and numeric forms of numbers

Number of players: 2

Grades: 1 to 5

Materials: 100 tongue depressors

Preparation: Number the tongue depressors from 1 to 100. Use both written and numeric forms. Write on only one side.

Playing:

1. Turn the tongue depressors face down.

2. The first player picks up a tongue depressor, keeping its blank side toward the second player. The second player guesses whether it has an odd or even number on it.

3. If the second player guesses correctly, he or she takes the tongue depressor. Otherwise, the first player gets to keep it.

4. The players then switch roles—the second player picks up a tongue depressor, and the first player guesses whether the number on it is odd or even.

5. Players continue alternating until there are no more tongue depressors left face down. Each then counts the tongue depressors acquired.

Winning: The player with the most tongue depressors wins.

Playing variation:

- Use 30 tongue depressors numbered 1 to 10; 38 numbered 1 to 19; or 50 numbered 1 to 50.

Skill variations:

Inequalities 1: Players guess whether the number is greater than 50, equal to 50, or less than 50.

Inequalities 2: The player who picks up a tongue depressor also chooses any whole number, ____ , between 1 and 100 and asks, "Is the number smaller than ____ , larger than ____ , or equal to ____ ?"

Multiples and factors: Have the player who picks up the tongue depressor ask any of these questions: "Is the number a multiple of ____ ?" "Does this number have a factor of ____ ?" or "Is this number prime or composite?" (____ would be a whole number between 2 and 10.)

Metric: Write 100 different metric lengths on the tongue depressors, half of them greater than one meter and half of them less than one meter. Players ask, "Is the length greater than or less than one meter?" You can make similar games emphasizing other metric units.

Get Seven

Object: Each player receives seven tongue depressors with division problems marked on them. Players pass one tongue depressor to the player on their left and receive one from the player on their right. The first player to get seven tongue depressors with the same quotient wins.

Skills: division, problem solving
Number of players: 4 to 6
Grades: 3 to 5
Materials: 48 tongue depressors
Preparation: Write the following problems on one side of each tongue depressor.

$1\overline{)4}$	$2\overline{)8}$	$3\overline{)12}$	$4\overline{)16}$	$5\overline{)20}$	$6\overline{)24}$	$7\overline{)28}$	$8\overline{)32}$	$9\overline{)36}$	$10\overline{)40}$	$11\overline{)44}$	$12\overline{)48}$
$1\overline{)5}$	$2\overline{)10}$	$3\overline{)15}$	$4\overline{)20}$	$5\overline{)25}$	$6\overline{)30}$	$7\overline{)35}$	$8\overline{)40}$	$9\overline{)45}$	$10\overline{)50}$	$11\overline{)55}$	$12\overline{)60}$
$1\overline{)6}$	$2\overline{)12}$	$3\overline{)18}$	$4\overline{)24}$	$5\overline{)30}$	$6\overline{)36}$	$7\overline{)42}$	$8\overline{)48}$	$9\overline{)54}$	$10\overline{)60}$	$11\overline{)66}$	$12\overline{)72}$
$1\overline{)7}$	$2\overline{)14}$	$3\overline{)21}$	$4\overline{)28}$	$5\overline{)35}$	$6\overline{)42}$	$7\overline{)49}$	$8\overline{)56}$	$9\overline{)63}$	$10\overline{)70}$	$11\overline{)77}$	$12\overline{)84}$

$6\overline{)30}$

Playing:

1. Lay the tongue depressors face down.

2. Every player draws seven tongue depressors, hiding the problems on them from other players. The remaining tongue depressors are removed, except for one, which remains face down.

3. The first player chooses one tongue depressor he or she does not want. He or she places it face down in front of the player to the left, and then picks up the extra tongue depressor left on the table.

4. Play now rotates clockwise. Each player in turn passes an unwanted tongue depressor face down to the player on his or her left and then picks up the one given by the player on the right. The objective is to get seven tongue depressors with the same quotient.

5. The game continues in this manner, with players always placing one tongue depressor on the table before picking up the next one.

Winning: The first player to get seven tongue depressors with the same quotient wins.

Playing variation:

- Players sit in a circle. Simultaneously, everyone gives a tongue depressor to the person on their left and immediately picks up the tongue depressor received.

Skill variations:

Division, fractions, decimals, percents, multiple arithmetic operations: Mark sets of 48 tongue depressors to drill other arithmetic facts: other division quotients; division remainders (38 ÷ 6 will then have a value of 2); equivalent forms of fractions, decimals, and percents (½, .5, and 50% will be equivalent); or different ways of writing the same number (5 + 4, 3 × 3, 12 − 3, and 27 ÷ 3 will be equivalent). For each game, construct four sets of twelve equivalent numbers or problems.

Equato

Object: Players race to be the first to use five numbers, along with any arithmetic operations they choose, to form a specified number.

Skills: constructing equations using addition, subtraction, multiplication, and division; problem solving; reasoning and proof; communication

Number of players: 2 to 6

Grades: 2 to 5

Materials: 50 tongue depressors

Preparation: Write one of each of the following numbers on one side of a tongue depressor: 1, 1, 1, 2, 2, 2, 3, 3, 3, 4, 4, 4, 5, 5, 5, 6, 6, 6, 7, 7, 7, 8, 8, 8, 9, 9, 9, 10, 10, 10, 11, 11, 12, 12, 13, 13, 14, 14, 15, 15, 16, 17, 18, 19, 20, 21, 22, 23, 24, and 25.

Playing:

1. Equato is played in rounds, during which everyone plays simultaneously.

2. To begin a round, place the tongue depressors face down and mix them up. Each player then picks five tongue depressors and places them face up in front of him or her. A final tongue depressor is then turned face up—its number is the "goal" for the round, and it is called the goal depressor.

3. The players race to be the first to use the numbers on their five tongue depressors along with any arithmetic operations—addition, subtraction, multiplication, or division—to form a number equal to the goal for the round. Each tongue depressor number must be used exactly once, they may be used in any sequence, and the player may move the tongue depressors around. Any arithmetic operation may be used any number of times in any sequence. (See sample game.)

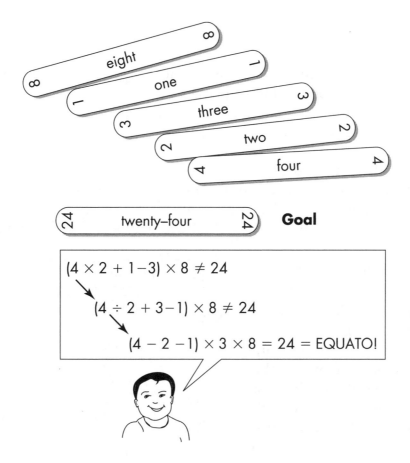

4. The first player to create an equation calls out "Equato!" and slaps the goal depressor. Within thirty seconds, that player must state the equation created. If it is valid, that player gets one point. If not, the round continues with that player disqualified for the remainder of it. If no player can create an equation in a reasonable amount of time (say, three minutes) the round is ended with no score.

5. All the tongue depressors are laid face down and a new round begins.

6. The game ends when one player earns three points.

Winning: The first player to get three points is the winner.

Playing variations:

• Have players record the equations they create, as well as state them.

• Create simpler games by marking the tongue depressors with only the numbers from 1 to 20 (or 1 to 10) and by allowing players to use four (or three) of their five tongue depressors to make the equation.

Ladders

Object: Players pick six numbered tongue depressors and try to be the first to arrange them in order from smallest to largest.

Skills: ordering numbers, comparing numbers, fractions, problem solving

Number of players: 2 to 4

Grades: 3 to 5

Materials: 50 tongue depressors

Preparation: Write one of each of the following fractions on one side of two tongue depressors: $^0/_2$, $^1/_2$, $^2/_2$, $^0/_4$, $^1/_4$, $^2/_4$, $^3/_4$, $^4/_4$, $^0/_3$, $^1/_3$, $^2/_3$, $^3/_3$, $^0/_{12}$, $^1/_{12}$, $^2/_{12}$, $^3/_{12}$, $^4/_{12}$, $^5/_{12}$, $^6/_{12}$, $^7/_{12}$, $^8/_{12}$, $^9/_{12}$, $^{10}/_{12}$, $^{11}/_{12}$, $^{12}/_{12}$. Use both written and numeric forms.

Playing:

1. Place the tongue depressors face down and mix them up.

2. Each player picks six tongue depressors. Each tongue depressor is turned face up and placed in front of the player, just above the last tongue depressor picked. Thus the first tongue depressor picked will lie closest to the player, and the last one picked will lie farthest from the player, forming a ladder, as illustrated. Players may not alter this initial sequencing, except when taking a turn.

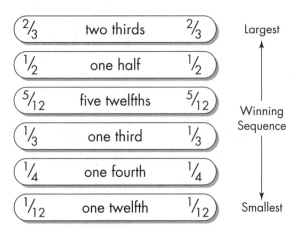

$^3/_{12}$	three twelfths	$^3/_{12}$	← sixth pick
$^1/_4$	one fourth	$^1/_4$	← fifth pick
$^5/_{12}$	five twelfths	$^5/_{12}$	← fourth pick
$^1/_3$	one third	$^1/_3$	← third pick
$^3/_4$	three fourths	$^3/_4$	← second pick
$^1/_{12}$	one twelfth	$^1/_{12}$	← first pick

3. Players take turns in clockwise rotation. The players try to replace tongue depressors in their ladders so that the numbers become ordered from smallest to largest, with the smallest number closest to a player. Two equivalent numbers cannot be in a player's ladder.

$^2/_3$	two thirds	$^2/_3$	Largest
$^1/_2$	one half	$^1/_2$	
$^5/_{12}$	five twelfths	$^5/_{12}$	Winning
$^1/_3$	one third	$^1/_3$	Sequence
$^1/_4$	one fourth	$^1/_4$	
$^1/_{12}$	one twelfth	$^1/_{12}$	Smallest

4. In turn, players pick one tongue depressor from those lying face down on the table or face up in the discard pile, and decide whether to discard it or use it. Discarded tongue depressors are placed face up on a discard pile. (The first player who discards starts the pile.)

If the player uses the tongue depressor, he or she exchanges it with one of the tongue depressors in his or her ladder—without disturbing the order of the tongue depressors—and the exchanged tongue depressor is discarded. For example, at some time during the illustrated game, the player picked a $2/3$, exchanged it with the $3/12$, and discarded the $3/12$.

Winning: The winner is the first player to get all six tongue depressors sequenced from smallest to largest, with the smallest one closest to the player.

Playing variation:

- Players can start with eight tongue depressors or can have the option of arranging them either from smallest to largest or largest to smallest.

Skill variations:

Signed numbers: Write the integers from -25 to $+25$ on the tongue depressors.

Counting numbers: Write the counting numbers from 1 to 50 on the tongue depressors.

Decimals, mixed numbers, or equations: Make up other games using decimals, mixed numbers, or unsolved equations (which must be sequenced according to their answers).

Chapter Five

Card Games

Playing cards have long been a means of entertainment for both children and adults. The following games do not use regular playing cards, but many are otherwise similar to established card games.

You can use index cards to make playing cards, or purchase blank playing cards from an educational materials supply company. Number 68 round-corner tickets, sold by most printers, are also ideal. Another alternative is to cut cards from any stiff paper stock, such as oak tag or tag board, to the size of approximately 2.5 × 4 inches (5 × 8 cm). If you are cutting cards from stiff paper stock, a good way to make sturdy cards is first to draw the cards on the paper stock, then laminate the entire piece of paper, and then cut out the cards. You can use clear contact paper instead of lamination film. Regular playing cards, without the face cards, can be used for some games.

Operations War

Object: This game is similar to the card game War. Two numbered cards are dealt to each player. Players multiply the numbers on their two cards, and the player with the larger product wins and takes all four cards.

Skills: multiplication, inequalities, communication, connections

Number of players: 2

Grades: 3 to 5

Materials: 40 cards

Preparation: On four sets of 10 cards, write one of each of the numbers from 1 to 10. Write on only one side of each card.

Playing:

1. Each player receives 20 cards.

2. Both players place their cards face down in front of themselves, in a neat stack.

3. From the top of their stack of cards, both players simultaneously deal themselves one card face down—without looking at it—and then deal their opponent one card face up.

4. Both players then simultaneously turn over their face-down cards, multiply the numbers on their cards together, and announce their products. The player with the larger product acquires all four cards and places them face down on the bottom of his or her stack of cards. (Players should check each other's multiplication.)

5. Play continues repeatedly as described above.

6. If a tie occurs, both players repeat the process of dealing a face-down card and a face-up card. The winner of this second round takes all eight cards. If additional ties occur, repeat this process.

Winning: If a player acquires all 40 cards, that player wins. Otherwise, the player with the most cards after some predetermined time is the winner.

Skill variations:

Addition or subtraction: Players either add or subtract the numbers on the cards.

Three-person addition and multiplication war: Each player gets 13 cards. Every player deals himself or herself one card face down and then deals each opponent one card face up. Players then add together their face-up cards and multiply the sum by their face-down card. The player with the largest result acquires all nine cards.

Bongo

Object: This game is a variation of Bingo using two sets of cards, one with problems and the other with answers. Five problem cards are dealt to each player. Players match their problems to the answers called.

Skills: multiplication, communication

Number of players: 3 to 11, or whole class if several sets are used

Grades: 3 to 5

Materials: 55 red cards and 55 blue cards (or any other two colors)

Preparation: Write one these 55 multiplication problems on one side of each red card.

1×1	1×2	1×3	1×4	1×5	1×6	1×7	1×8	1×9	1×10
	2×2	2×3	2×4	2×5	2×6	2×7	2×8	2×9	2×10
		3×3	3×4	3×5	3×6	3×7	3×8	3×9	3×10
			4×4	4×5	4×6	4×7	4×8	4×9	4×10
				5×5	5×6	5×7	5×8	5×9	5×10
					6×6	6×7	6×8	6×9	6×10
						7×7	7×8	7×9	7×10
							8×8	8×9	8×10
								9×9	9×10
									10×10

Write the following 55 products on one side of each blue card.

1	2	3	4	5	6	7	8	9	10
	4	6	8	10	12	14	16	18	20
		9	12	15	18	21	24	27	30
			16	20	24	28	32	36	40
				25	30	35	40	45	50
					36	42	48	54	60
						49	56	63	70
							64	72	80
								81	90
									100

Playing:
1. Decide whether to deal problem cards or answer cards to players. Either can be dealt, but not a mix of both. (These directions assume that problem cards are dealt.)
2. Choose a dealer. The dealer deals five problem cards to each player and sets aside any that are left over.
3. The players place their five problem cards face up in front of themselves.
4. The deck of answer cards is placed face down in front of the dealer, who picks them up one by one, holds each facing the players, and announces its number.

5. All players with a problem card that matches the dealer's answer card turn that card face down. A player may turn over *only one problem* card for each answer card held up, even if several cards match.

6. The dealer continues turning up answer cards until a player calls "Bongo!" A player calls "Bongo!" as soon as all of his or her cards are turned face down.

7. The player who called "Bongo!" announces the problems on his or her cards while the dealer checks that they match the answer cards turned up. If not, play continues.

Winning: The first player to correctly call "Bongo" wins.

Skill variations:

Addition, subtraction, division, fractions: Different types of Bongo can be constructed by creating 55 pairs of matching mathematical expressions and writing them on two sets of different colored cards.

Little Shot

Object: As numbered cards are drawn from a deck nine times, players write the resulting numbers in the nine cells of a 3 × 3 grid. Players calculate scores by adding the numbers in the grid's rows, columns, and one diagonal.

Skills: addition, probability

Number of players: 2 to whole class

Grades: 1 to 3

Materials: Six cards, paper, and pencils

Preparation: Write one of each of the numbers from 1 to 6 on one side of each card. Have each player make his or her own copy of the Little Shot game sheet or duplicate copies for players.

Playing:

1. Each player gets a game sheet and a pencil.

2. Choose one person to hold, shuffle, and draw the cards and to announce each number drawn. Cards are drawn nine times during the game. After each card is drawn and its number announced, the card is returned to the deck, and the deck is shuffled.

3. After each number is announced and before the next card is drawn, players write the announced number in any empty square on their game sheet. Once written, a number cannot be moved.

4. After the nine numbers are written, the players find the sums of the numbers across the three rows, down the three columns, and through the diagonal. They record the sums in the corresponding circles.

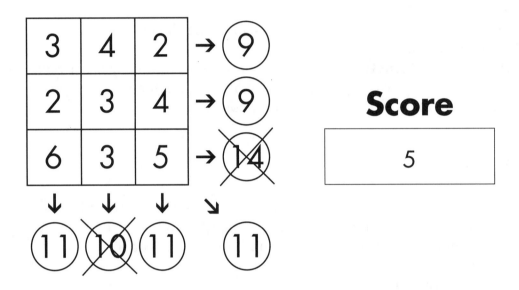

5. Players cross out any sum that appears in only one circle.

6. The number of sums that are **not crossed out** is a player's score.

Winning: The player with the largest score wins.

Playing variations:

- Drill other addition facts by writing different numbers on the cards—for example: 4, 5, 6, 7, 8, and 9.
- Play three successive games of Little Shot. The winner is the player with the largest cumulative score.

Math Skill Development Games

Little Shot

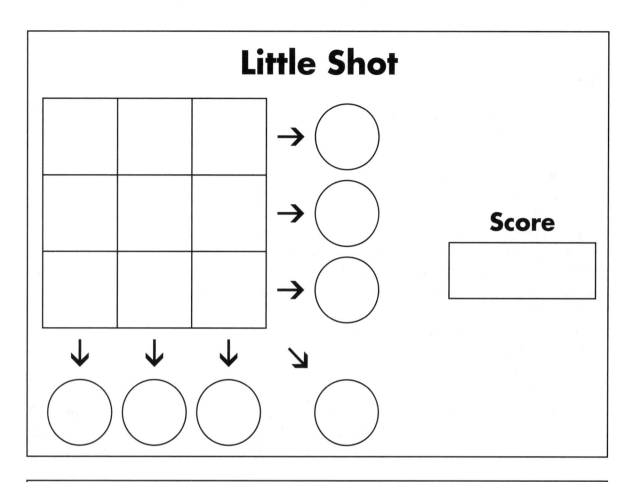

Score

Little Shot

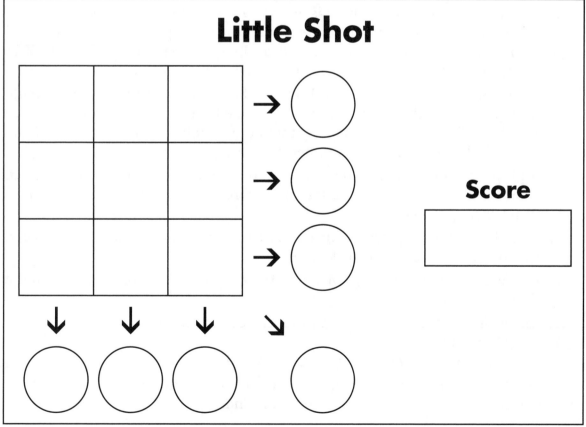

Score

Place-a-Bet

Object: Players secretly construct a three-digit number from three numbered cards dealt to them. Then they each bet whether their number is the highest, in the middle, or lowest.

Skills: place value, inequalities, communication, representation

Number of players: 3

Grades: 2 to 5

Materials: 40 cards, and copies of the Place-a-Bet playing sheet

Preparation: Mark four sets of 10 cards with each of the numbers from 0 to 9. Write only one number on one side of each card. Reproduce copies of the playing sheet for each player or have each player make a copy of it.

Playing:

1. Give each player a playing sheet, choose a dealer, and have the dealer shuffle the cards.

2. There are ten rounds in a game. To begin each round, deal three cards to each player and proceed as follows.

3. Players look at their cards, without letting their opponents see them, and secretly put them together in any way they wish to form a three-digit number. They secretly record that number in the Number column of their playing sheets.

4. Each player now bets whether his or her number is the highest, in the middle, or lowest of the three numbers created by the three players. They all record their bets on their playing sheet next to their numbers by marking an X in either the High, Middle, or Low column. They mark in **only one** column.

5. When all three players have marked their bets, they turn their cards face up. Each player tells the others, using place value terminology, the number he or she made. Each player shows the others this number written on the playing sheet. Each player reveals his or her bet.

6. A player who makes a correct bet gets one point. A player who makes an incorrect bet gets zero points. Players record 0 or 1 in the Points column of their playing sheets.

7. To end each round, players return their cards to the dealer, who shuffles and redeals them to begin the next round.

8. At the end of ten rounds, players add their points and record the sum in the Total Score box.

Winning: The player with the largest total score wins.

Playing variations:

- Play the game with two-, four-, five-, or six-digit numbers.

- Penalize players who incorrectly read their number during a round by ruling that they may not score a point on that round.

Place-a-Bet

Round	Number	Bets			Points
		High	Middle	Low	
1					
2					
3					
4					
5					
6					
7					
8					
9					
10					

Total Score

Running Sum

Object: Players place numbered cards end to end to form a connected network of cards, in a manner similar to Scrabble. To place cards, card numbers must add up to a predetermined sum.

Skills: column addition
Number of players: 2 to 4
Grades: 1 to 3
Materials: 63 cards
Preparation: Mark seven sets of nine cards with each of the numbers from 1 to 9. Write one number on one side of each card.

Playing:

1. To begin, remove two 5's, two 6's, two 7's, two 8's, and two 9's from the deck. Place these 10 cards face down, mix them up, and then pick two of them. The sum of the numbers on these two cards is the running sum for the game.

2. Return the 10 cards to the deck, shuffle the deck, and deal each player 15 cards face down. Players keep the numbers on their cards hidden from opponents until they play them.

3. Players take turns in clockwise rotation. Their objective is to get rid of as many cards as possible.

4. On the first turn of the game, the first player places two or more cards face up on the table. The numbers on the cards must add up to the running sum. The player lays the cards down end to end in a straight line (called a run). For example, if the running sum is 16, the first player could play 3, 5, and 8. (See the sample game.)

5. During each succeeding turn of the game, a player adds a new run of cards to those already on the table. Each new run must be connected to a card in a previous run, as in Scrabble. Also, the sum of the new cards plus the interconnecting old card must equal the running sum. For example, note in the sample game that the cards in each line (or run) add up to 16 (the running sum in this game).

6. If a player cannot play any cards on a turn, that player must pass and lose the chance to get rid of cards.

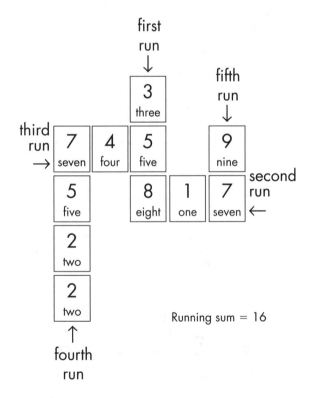

Running sum = 16

Math Skill Development Games

7. The game ends either when one player has no more cards left or when all players have passed and none can play any of their remaining cards.

Winning: The player who first uses up all 15 cards wins. If the game ends with all players still holding some cards, then the player with the fewest cards wins.

Slap It

Object: Players take turns flipping over face-down cards. When two match, the first player to slap one of them gets both. The player who gets the most wins.

Skills: multiplication, reasoning and proof, communication

Number of players: 2 to 4

Grades: 3 to 5

Materials: 36 cards

Preparation: On one side of each card, write one of the following numbers or problems:

8	12	16	20	24	28	32	36	40
2×4	3×4	4×4	5×4	6×4	7×4	8×4	9×4	10×4
4×2	2×6	2×8	2×10	2×12	2×14	2×16	2×18	2×20
1×8	1×12	1×16	1×20	3×8	1×28	1×32	1×36	5×8

Playing:

1. Place all the cards face down on the playing surface and mix them up.

2. Play rotates clockwise. In turn, each player chooses one card and immediately places it face up on the playing surface. Cards that are turned face up remain that way throughout the game, until they are won by a player and removed from the playing surface.

3. Each time a player turns up a card that has a value that is equal to a card that is already face up, all players try to be the first to slap a hand over the matching card that was previously face up. The player to first slap the card with the equivalent value to the card that was just turned over wins both cards and removes them from the table. That player must also explain why the two cards are equal.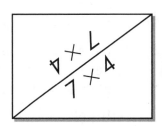

4. The game ends when all the cards are face up. Players then count the number of cards they have won.

Winning: The player with the most cards wins.

Playing variation:

- Have players turn over two cards at the same time. If they match, the player keeps them; otherwise the player turns them face down before play passes to the next person. This is similar to Concentration.

Skill variations:

Money equivalents: Put the following monetary amounts on the cards: penny, nickel, dime, quarter, half-dollar, dollar, 1 dollar, 5 dollars, ¢, 1¢, 5¢, 10¢, 25¢, 50¢, 100¢, 4 quarters, $5.00, cents, $.01, $.05, $.10, $.25, $.50, $1.00, 10 dimes, 10 dollars, 2 quarters, one cent, 5 pennies, ten cents, 2 bits, fifty cents, $, 20 nickels, $10.00, and 5 dimes.

Fractions and decimals: Put equivalent fractions and decimals on the cards.

Call It

Object: Players attempt to discard numbered cards by taking turns placing a card onto a discard pile and then multiplying its number by the number on the previously discarded card.

Skills: multiplication, communication

Number of players: 2 to 5

Grades: 3 to 5

Materials: 40 cards

Preparation: On four sets of 10 cards, write one of each of the numbers from 1 to 10. Write on only one side of each card.

Playing:

1. Deal six cards to each player. Deal another card face up to start a discard pile. Place the rest of the cards aside.

2. Players take turns clockwise. Players attempt to get rid of all their cards.

3. On a turn, a player places one card onto the discard pile, multiplies its number by the number of the card on the top of the discard pile (the previously played card), and calls out the product.

4. If the product is correct, the player leaves the card on the discard pile and the next player takes a turn. If the product is incorrect, the player must take back the discarded card. The next player then takes a turn.

Winning: The winner is the first player, after each player has had six turns, to discard all of his or her cards. If several players discard all six of their cards within their first six turns, they are all declared winners.

Playing variations:
- Play several games, have players take turns going first, and see who wins the most games after each player has had a turn going first.
- Players can be required to state aloud the multiplication problem as well as its product.

Skill variations:

Addition or subtraction: Have players either add or subtract the card numbers.

Fractions: This game can be used for practice with addition or subtraction of fractions by writing one of each of the following numbers on one side of each card.

0	1	2	3	4	5	6	7	8	9
¼	1¼	2¼	3¼	4¼	5¼	6¼	7¼	8¼	9¼
½	1½	2½	3½	4½	5½	6½	7½	8½	9½
¾	1¾	2¾	3¾	4¾	5¾	6¾	7¾	8¾	9¾

What's Next?

Object: Each player draws an arrangement of placeholders that represent an arithmetic problem. As numbered cards are drawn one by one, players fill in the placeholders with numbers and then solve their problems.

Skills: addition, subtraction, multiplication, division, place value, probability, problem solving

Number of players: 3 to whole class

Grades: 2 to 5

Materials: 10 cards, paper, and pencils

Preparation: On one side of each card, write a number from 0 to 9. Decide which type of arithmetic problem the game will deal with. (See samples.) Draw a picture depicting the form of the problem on a chalkboard or chart paper, and display it for players to copy.

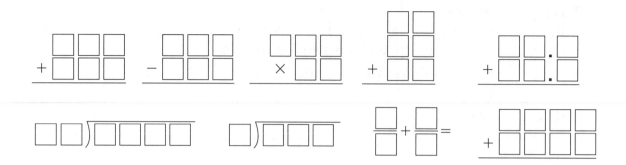

Playing:

1. Choose a person to be a caller. Have each player copy the picture of the arithmetic problem on a sheet of paper.

2. The game is played in rounds with all players playing simultaneously. There are as many rounds as there are empty placeholders in the problem.

3. To begin a round, the caller shuffles the cards, holds them so that the numbers on the cards cannot be seen, randomly picks one card, holds it up so that all players can see the number, and announces the number aloud.

4. During a round, each player writes the number announced by the caller in any empty placeholder. Once a number is written, it may not be moved.

5. At the end of a round, the caller replaces the card in the deck and begins another round.

6. When all the placeholders in the players' problem have been filled, the players solve their own problem. They then check each other's problems and solutions.

Winning: The player whose problem produces the largest answer wins. Ties are possible.

Playing variations:

- Once the caller picks a card, it is not returned to the deck for the rest of the game. This variation works only when there are fewer than seven placeholders in the problem.

- With fewer than six players (or an entire class divided into fewer than six teams), play ten games and see who wins the most.

- The winner can be the player whose problem produces the smallest answer.

- Allow players to discard one of the numbers the caller announces. Have a special place next to the problem where players write the number they discard. In this variation, the caller picks one more card than there are placeholders in the problem.

- Construct recording sheets for students to use while playing the game. Including two to eight problems on a recording sheet, either of the same or of different types, allows students to play a number of games during a single sitting.

Two Numbers

Object: Cards with two numbers on them are dealt face up. Players calculate a card's value by adding, subtracting, multiplying, or dividing its numbers. If two cards have the same value, players can capture them.

Skills: addition, subtraction, multiplication, division, problem solving, reasoning and proof, communication

Number of players: 3 to 6

Grades: 3 to 5

Materials: 75 cards

Preparation: Mark one side of each card with one of the pairs of numbers listed below, as illustrated in the diagram.

1, 1	2, 2	3, 3	4, 4	5, 5	6, 6	7, 7	8, 8	9, 9	10, 10
1, 2	2, 3	3, 4	4, 5	5, 6	6, 7	7, 8	8, 9	9, 10	
1, 3	2, 4	3, 5	4, 6	5, 7	6, 8	7, 9	8, 10		
1, 4	2, 5	3, 6	4, 7	5, 8	6, 9	7, 10			
1, 5	2, 6	3, 7	4, 8	5, 9	6, 10				
1, 6	2, 7	3, 8	4, 9	5, 10	6, 12				
1, 7	2, 8	3, 9	4, 10	5, 15	6, 18				
1, 8	2, 9	3, 10	4, 12	5, 20	6, 24				
1, 9	2, 10	3, 12	4, 16	5, 25	6, 30				
1, 10	2, 12	3, 15	4, 20	5, 30					
	2, 14	3, 18	4, 24						
	2, 16	3, 21							
	2, 18								

Playing:

1. A card's values are calculated by adding, subtracting, multiplying, or dividing its two numbers. For example, the card with 2 and 4 on it has the following values: 6 (2 + 4); 2 (4 − 2) or (4 ÷ 2); 8 (4 − 2); 8 (4 × 2); ½ (2 ÷ 4); −2 (2 − 4). (Note: Values can be limited to positive whole numbers.)

2. The dealer shuffles the cards and places the deck face down. The dealer then deals the top card face up. This card is called the object card. Players calculate all its values.

3. The dealer now takes cards from the top of the deck and places them face up in a heap called a playing pile. The interval of time between dealing each card can vary from five to forty seconds, depending on the players' skills.

4. As each card lands face up on the playing pile, the players calculate its values. If any of these values equal a value of the object card, the players slap the object card.

5. The first player to slap the object card captures both it and all the cards that have accumulated in the playing pile. The player must explain the equivalence. A player who erroneously slaps the object card is eliminated from the game until another player slaps it.

6. As soon as a player captures the object card and playing pile, that player takes them. The dealer deals a new object card and begins dealing cards onto a new playing pile.

7. When the dealer has dealt all the cards in the deck, players count up the number of cards they captured, and record this number. Then a new player becomes dealer.

8. The dealer does not capture cards while dealing. During the game, the dealer role rotates clockwise. After all players have had a turn dealing, the game ends. Players then calculate the number of cards they captured during the entire game.

Winning: The player who captures the most cards wins.

Playing variation:

- For an easier game, have the dealer choose only one of the values of the first card turned over to be the objective. For an even easier game, its value can also be limited to a whole number between 1 and 10.

Mathino

Object: This game is similar to the card game Casino. Players acquire numbered cards by constructing arithmetic equations with them.

   Skills: addition, constructing equations, problem solving, reasoning and proof, communication

   Number of players: 2 to 4

   Grades: 1 to 5

   Materials: 60 cards

   Preparation: Mark five sets of 12 cards with each set having the numbers from 1 to 12. Mark cards on only one side.

   Playing:

1. Players try to acquire as many cards as possible, which they place in a pile in front of them.

2. Mathino is played in rounds. To start the first round, the dealer deals four cards face down to each player and four cards face up on the table. In successive rounds, four cards are dealt face down to each player. A round ends when each set of four cards is played.

3. During each round, players pick up the cards dealt to them, concealing their values from others. Players take turns, with play rotating clockwise. On a turn, a player plays only one card and can do one of the following:

   - *Match:* If one of a player's cards is the same as a card on the table, the player can match them on the table and acquire both.

   - *Combine:* If one of a player's cards equals the sum of two or more cards on the table, the player may combine them in an equation on the table and acquire them all. For example, a 7 may acquire a combination of a 4 and 3. The player can simultaneously acquire several combinations.

   - *Hold:* If several of a player's cards contain the same number as a single card or sum of cards on the table, the player may play one of the cards onto its match on the table (or onto a sum that equals it), say "Holding ___'s" (naming the cards), and then leave them on the table. A player doing this must plan to acquire all the "held" cards on a later turn in the same round. For example, if a player holds two 3's that match a 3 on the table, he or she can place one of the 3's on the 3 on the table with the words "Holding 3's," and acquire both with the other 3 later in the round.

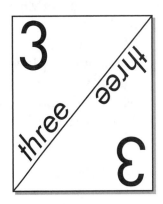

- *Build:* One or more cards on the table may be combined with one card from a player's hand to build an equation that equals another card in the player's hand. To do this, a player puts the cards in a single pile on the table and says "Building ___" (naming the sum). The player must posses a card that equals the "built sum" and must plan to use it during a later turn to acquire the build. For example, a 3 from a player's hand can be put into a pile with a 5 and 2 from the table with the declaration "Building 10 = 3 + 5 + 2."
- *Steal:* A player may match and acquire any pile of cards that an opponent is holding or building, if that player has the necessary card to do so.
- *Rebuild:* A player may build on an opponent's build or on his or her own build. For example, if a player is building 6 with 2 and 4, another player may add a 3 and say "Building 9 = 3 + 2 + 4."
- *Discard:* If a player cannot match, combine, hold, build, steal, or rebuild, the player must discard a card face up on the table.

4. Players cannot build on a hold. They can rebuild on a build. A player does not have to acquire a hold or build immediately.
5. In the final round of the game, deal any remaining cards face up on the table play. The last player who acquires cards also acquires all cards remaining on the table.

Winning: The player who acquires the most cards wins.
Skill variation:
  Multiple operations: In making combinations, permit players to use subtraction, multiplication, or division.

Mathominoes

Object: This is a variation on Dominoes for learning to recognize equivalent mathematical expressions.
  Skills: addition
  Number of players: 2 to 4
  Grades: 1 to 3
  Materials: 28 cards
  Preparation: Draw a line down the middle of each card and mark them as shown.

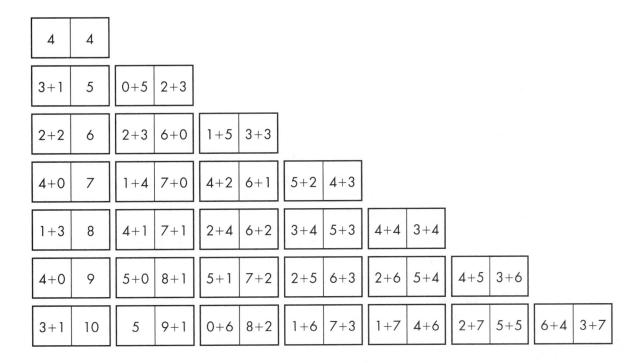

Playing:

1. Place the mathominoes face down on a table, spread them out, and mix them up.

2. Each player picks seven mathominoes. Remove the remaining mathominoes from the center of the table. Players may either lay their mathominoes face up in front of themselves (beginners and young players) or hold them in their hands to conceal their markings from opponents.

3. The object of the game is to match mathominoes end to end in a line so that their equivalent ends are adjacent to each other. In the example, the mathomino with 3 + 1 on it was the first one played. The second player then added the mathomino with 2 + 3 on it because 2 + 3 equals (or is equivalent to) 5. Note how the other two mathominoes match the 3 + 1 and the 6 + 0. Mathominoes can be played at either end of the line of mathominoes, either right side up or upside down, or at right angles to each other (but only at the end of the line).

4. To begin the game, the first player places a mathomino on the table to start a line. Thereafter players take turns with play rotating clockwise.

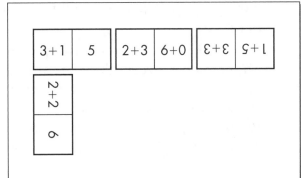

5. On a turn, a player may either place one matching mathomino next to one of the two ends of the line of mathominoes (if

the player can) or pass and lose the chance to get rid of a mathomino (if a mathomino cannot be played).

6. The game ends either when all of one player's mathominoes have been played or when no one can place a matching mathomino on the end of the line of mathominoes.

Winning: The player with the fewest mathominoes at the end of the game wins.

Playing variations:

- **Draw mathominoes:** Form a draw pile with the mathominoes not distributed at the beginning of the game. Any player who cannot play a match onto the line of mathominoes must then pick from the draw pile. Play then passes to the next player.

- **Branching mathominoes:** Mathominoes with equivalent numbers on both sides ("doubles") can be played across a line of mathominoes at right angles to it (if a player chooses to do so). In the next illustration, for example, the mathomino with 1 + 5 and 3 + 3 on it was played at right angles to the mathomino with 6 + 0. Playing a double at right angles to a mathomino line opens up another end to the line because players may now play mathominoes on either end of the double. In the example, players can now play mathominoes adjacent to 1 + 5 and 3 + 3, as well as 6.

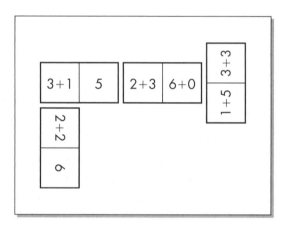

Skill variations:

Division: The game is played like regular Mathominoes, but mark the cards as shown in the next figure.

Fractions: The game is played like regular Mathominoes, except that the cards are marked with equivalent fractions and illustrations of fractions. Construct seven sets of equivalent fractions, with each set containing eight items (for example, one set might contain $^{1}/_{2}$, $^{2}/_{4}$, and $^{3}/_{6}$ drawings of these fractions, such as half of a circle, $^{2}/_{4}$ of a square, and $^{3}/_{6}$ of a hexagon; and the words "one half"). Then combine elements from each set so that there are two per card.

Fractions, decimals, and percents: The game is played like regular Mathominoes, except that the cards are marked with equivalent fractions, decimals, and percents. Construct seven sets of equivalent mathematical expressions with each set containing eight items (for example, one set might contain $^{1}/_{2}$, .5, 50%, and a drawing of half of a square). Then combine elements from each set so that there are two per card.

Math Skill Development Games

3)9	2)6												
4)12	3)12	2)8	6)24										
5)15	6)30	7)28	4)20	2)10	7)35								
6)18	3)18	5)20	8)48	8)40	9)54	2)12	4)24						
7)21	5)35	8)32	6)42	3)15	7)49	6)36	9)63	2)14	8)56				
8)24	4)32	4)16	5)40	5)25	3)24	5)30	8)64	3)21	6)84	2)16	9)72		
9)27	9)81	9)36	8)72	9)45	7)63	7)42	6)54	4)28	5)45	7)56	4)36	2)18	3)27

Varied skills: The game is played like regular Mathominoes, except that the cards are marked with a wide variety of mathematical skills, including subtraction, multiplication, money, time, and measurement equivalents. Construct seven sets of equivalent mathematical expressions with each set containing eight items. Then combine elements from each set so that there are two per card.

Pass It

Object: Players receive seven cards. They pass one card to the player on their left, while simultaneously receiving one card from the player on their right. The first player to acquire seven matching cards wins.

    Skills: place value, reading numbers

    Number of players: 4 to 6

    Grades: 2 to 4

    Materials: 48 cards

    Preparation: Mark one side of each card with one of the following numbers.

411	421	431	412	422	432	413	423	433	414	424	434
311	321	341	312	322	342	313	323	343	314	324	344
211	231	241	212	232	242	213	233	243	214	234	244
121	131	141	122	132	142	123	133	143	124	134	144

Playing:

1. There are three rounds. During the first round, players try to get seven cards with the same digit in the units place; during the second round, players try to get seven cards with the same digit in the tens place; and during the third round, players try to get seven cards with the same digit in the hundreds place.

2. To start each round, players are dealt seven cards. They conceal their numbers from opponents. Any undealt cards are set aside.

3. Each player then chooses one card to get rid of, and lays it face down in front of the player to his or her left. When all players' unwanted cards are on the table, everyone simultaneously picks up the card given to them by the player on their right, and places it with their other cards. This process is repeated until a round ends.

4. A round ends when a player gets seven cards with the same digit in the proper place (units, tens, or hundreds, depending on the round), announces this, and demonstrates it to the other players by showing the seven cards and reading the seven numbers aloud correctly.

Winning: The winner of each round is the first player to acquire seven cards with the same digit in the proper place. The winner of the game is the player who wins the most rounds. Ties can occur.

Playing variation:

- To remind players what they are playing for during a given round, mark three cards with the words "units," "tens," and "hundreds," and place the appropriate one in the center of the table during each round.

Measure

Object: A card is picked that has an object to measure and the units to measure it in. Players estimate the length and then measure. The player with the best estimate wins a point.

Skills: measurement, estimation, fractions, problem solving, communication, connections

Number of players: 2 to 4

Grades: 1 to 5

Materials: index cards; copies of the Measure recording sheet; a measuring tape, ruler, and yard (or meter) stick with either U.S. customary or metric units (depending on the units you want players to use); and paper and pencils

Preparation: Prepare at least 20 cards for the game. On one side of each card, clearly specify an object that is to be measured and the units in which it is to be measured. The following are examples of things that could be in a game: in inches, to the nearest half inch, what is the height of the teacher's desk; in inches, to the nearest inch, what is the length of the fish tank; in feet, to the nearest foot, what is the length of the classroom.

> In inches,
> to the closest half inch
>
> What is the height
> of the teacher's desk
> from the floor
> to the top of the desk?

Playing:

1. Shuffle the cards and place them in a face-down stack between the players.

2. The game is played in rounds. A complete game consists of five rounds.

3. During a round, the top card from the deck is turned face up. Players then estimate the length of the object to be measured and record their estimate on their recording sheet. Next, players measure the object and record the measurement on their recording sheet. Players then calculate and record how far their estimate was from the actual measurement of the object. Finally, points are awarded. The next round then begins.

4. Points are awarded as follows: If a player's estimate is accurate, the player gets two points. If no player's estimate matches the actual length of the object, then the player with the smallest difference between the estimate and the actual length gets one point. If several players have the same estimate, they can all be awarded either one or two points.

Winning: The player with the highest score wins.

Playing variations:

- Have students write suggestions about things to be measured. Select only those things to put on cards that can easily be measured and that do not offend anyone (such as a person's girth).

- Do not award points. After five rounds, a player's score is the sum of the differences between the estimates and the actual measurements.

Skill variations:

Nonstandard measurement: Measure with such things as paper clips, unifix cubes, or new crayons.

Weight measurement: Have students estimate and then weigh objects.

Angle measurement: Use pictures from magazines, as well as classroom objects.

Name: _____

MEASURE

Round	Item to be Measured	Estimate	Actual Measurement	Difference	Points
1					
2					
3					
4					
5					

Total Number of Points =

Bluff

Object: This game is similar to the card games I Doubt It or Cheat. Players discard two numbered cards and state a multiplication product. The discarded cards may or may not equal the stated product, and the player's statement may or may not be challenged.

Skills: multiplication, factors, division

Number of players: 3 to 6

Grades: 3 to 5

Materials: 72 cards

Preparation: Mark eight cards with one of each of the numbers from 1 to 9. Write on only one side of each card.

Playing:

1. If there are three or four players, deal each player 18 cards. If there are five or six players, deal each player 12 cards. Put any extra cards aside. Players conceal the numbers on their cards from opponents.

2. Players take turns clockwise. They attempt to discard all their cards.

3. On a turn, a player must discard two cards into the center of the table and announce a multiplication product that may or may not be the product of the numbers on the two cards. The cards are discarded sandwiched together back-to-back, with one card face up and the other card face down. **The product announced must be larger than the product announced by the previous player** (unless the discarder is the first player to discard; in this situation, any product may be announced).

4. If a player suspects another player of not telling the truth, that player may challenge the other by saying "Bluffer!" (or, more politely, "I doubt it!"). This must be done before the next player takes a turn. Bluffing consists of announcing a product that does not equal the product of the numbers on the two discarded cards. If a player is challenged, that player must turn the two cards just discarded face up. If the player bluffed, that player must pick up all the cards in the central pile and add them to his or her hand. If the player did not bluff, the challenger must pick up all the cards in the central pile and add them to his or her hand. The player who was correct (who played what was announced or who correctly detected bluffing) then takes the next turn and begins that turn by announcing any product desired, no matter how small or large. (Note: sooner or later a player must bluff, for once the product 81 is announced, only a bluff can follow.)

5. The game ends when a player successfully discards all his or her cards.

Winning: The first player to successfully discard all his or her cards wins.

Skill variation:

Addition: Players announce a sum rather than a product.

Geo 20 Questions

Object: Players lay out 36 cards face up on the playing surface. The leader secretly chooses one to be It. Guessers ask yes-or-no questions to try to determine which card is It.

Skills: geometry shapes, area, attributes of geometric figures, problem solving, reasoning and proof, communication

Number of players: 2 to 4

Grades: 3 to 5

Materials: 36 Geo 20 Questions cards

Preparation: Copy the Geo 20 Questions cards on the following pages onto card stock. (Card stock that can be used in duplicating machines is available from stationery stores.) The card stock can be laminated, if desired. Then cut the cards from the card stock.

Playing:

1. The game is played in rounds. During each round, one player is the leader and the rest are guessers. The role of leader rotates clockwise until each player has a turn being the leader.

2. At the beginning of a round, the leader mixes up the cards and then places the 36 cards face up on the playing surface. The leader then secretly chooses one card to be It.

3. Guessers take turns asking the leader one question about It that can be answered by either yes or no. Turns rotate clockwise, starting from where the leader is located.

4. On his or her turn, a guesser can either ask a question about It or guess which card is It.

5. Questions asked can be about such things as the area of It (for example, is it equal to, larger than, or smaller than a given number of units), the shape of It (for example, is It a hexagon), the number of sides on It, or the number of vertices that It has.

6. During a round, the leader keeps track of the number of questions asked about It. If a player correctly guesses which card is It, that player's score for the round is equal to the number of guesses made thus far during the round, and the other players receive 36 points each. If no player guesses which card is It after twenty guesses, then the round ends and all players get 36 points for the round. The role of leader then passes clockwise, and a new round begins. Players record their score for a round at the end of each round.

7. The game ends when each person has had a chance to choose It. Players then add up their scores for each round of the game.

Winning: The player with the smallest cumulative score wins.

Playing variations:

- The leader can be required to secretly record the location of It on a piece of paper, keep the paper hidden during a round, and reveal it to guessers at the end of the round.

- The leader can be required to place the cards in a rectangular arrangement, such as a six-by-six array.

- A blank template is included in case children or adults desire to construct additional shapes.

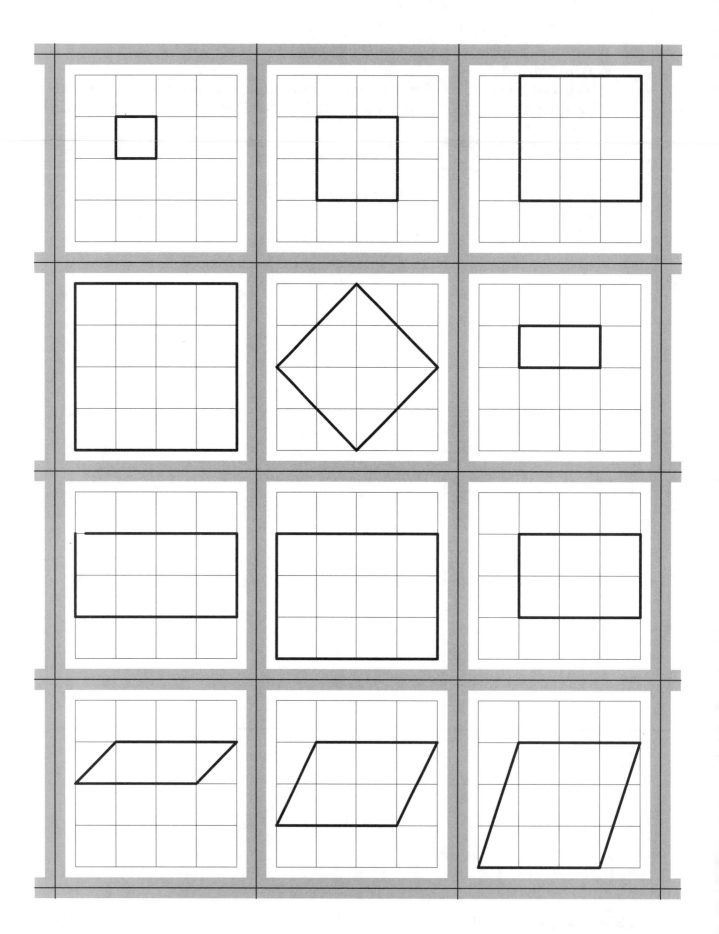

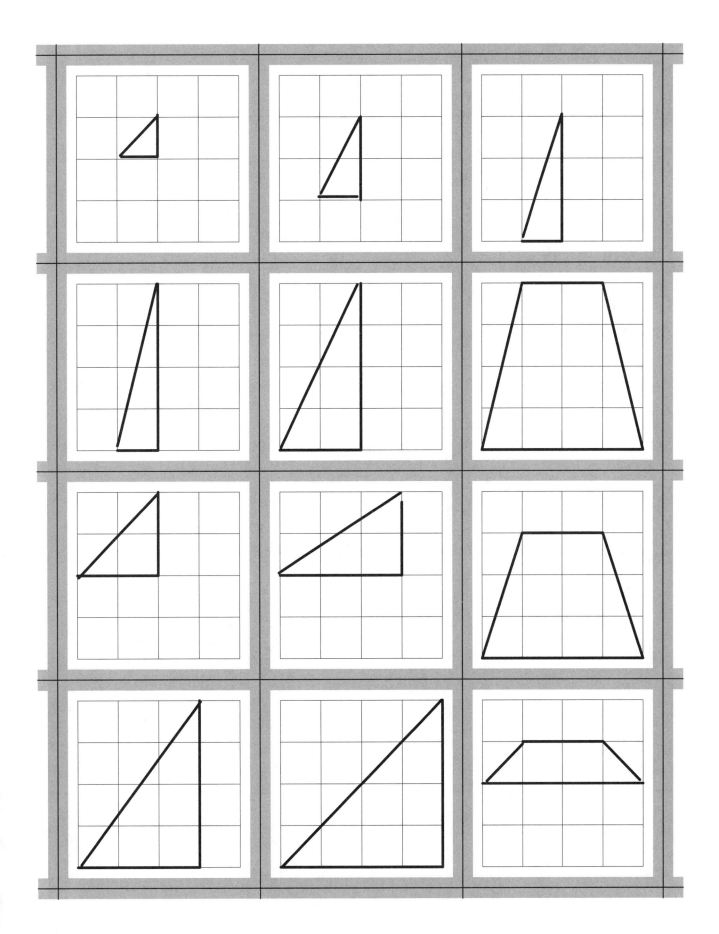

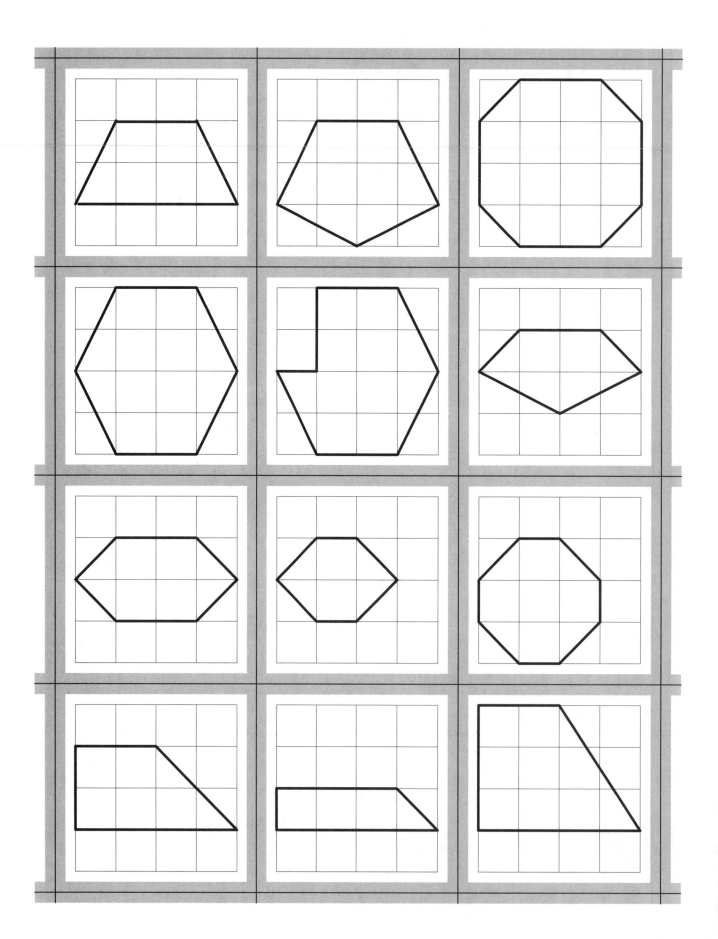

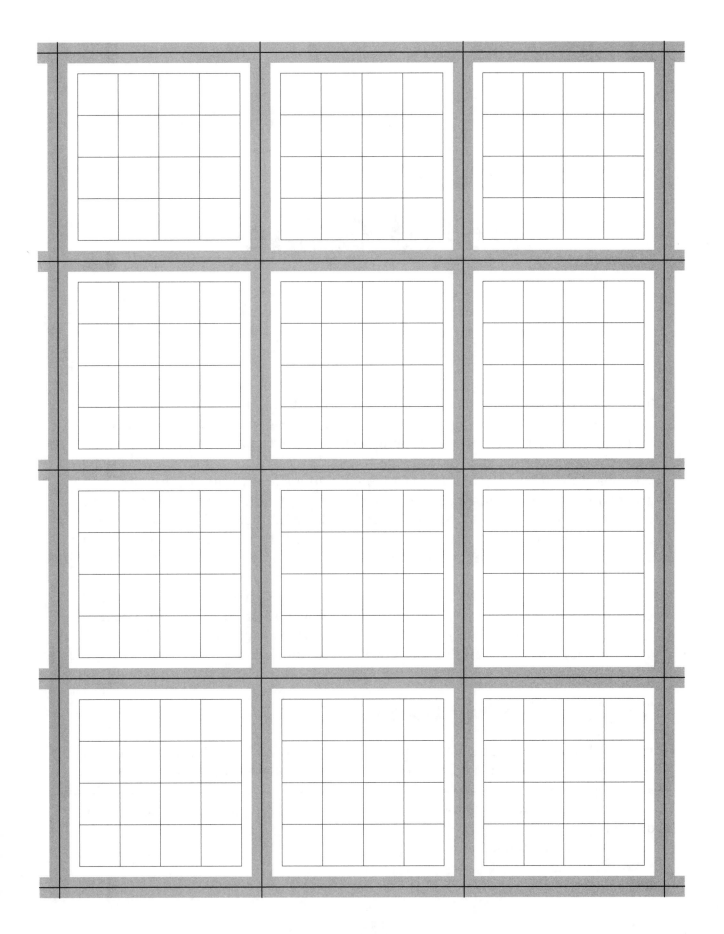

Chapter Six

Board Games

Board games have been popular since the time of the ancient Egyptians. Some involve several players playing together around a single game board. Others involve several players each using a similar game board seated around a "bank."

Thick paperboard is an ideal material to use. You can draw a game board on the paperboard or photocopy one from this book and paste it to the paperboard. You can enlarge a board to almost any size desired using a photocopier. Decorate the game boards with colored crayons, pencils, or felt tip markers to highlight a theme. Instructions can be pasted to the back of a game board. To protect game boards, you can laminate them or cover them with clear contact paper. Doing so also allows a game board to be written on and erased, if players use appropriate writing implements. Dry erase markers and wax crayons work well. Constructing a game board on the inside of a large flat cardboard box (such as a shirt box) is useful because playing pieces can be stored in the box. Game boards can also simply be photocopied and used without lavishing any further attention on them.

The Great Trading Game

Object: Players roll dice to determine how many pennies they receive in a race to be the first to get one dollar. Trades for dimes and dollars must take place as the game progresses.

Skills: place value, addition facts, addition with trading, money, connections, communication

Number of players: 2 to 4

Grades: 1 to 5

Materials: paper or paperboard (about 8.5 × 11 inches), two dice, three sets of 50 counters of three different colors (such as colored cubes, poker chips, or slips of colored paper; play money is also fine), and a box to hold all the counters

Preparation: Draw a playing board for each player or make enlarged copies of the reproducible provided.

Playing:

1. Players sit in a circle around the box of counters. Players agree on which counters will represent pennies, dimes, and dollars.

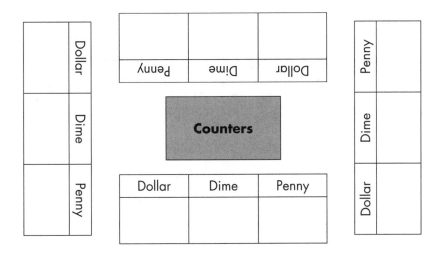

2. Players take turns, rotating play in a clockwise direction.

3. During a turn, a player rolls the dice, adds the numbers thrown, and takes the number of pennies equal to the sum thrown on the dice. They are placed on his or her playing board in the penny column.

4. As soon as a player collects 10 pennies, he or she must trade them for a dime. If dimes can be traded for dollars, this must also take place. This is called *legalizing.* If a player does not legalize when it is possible, either by trading pennies for dimes or dimes for dollars, an opponent who notices wins one penny from the player who did not legalize.

Winning: The first player to earn a dollar wins the game.

Playing variations:

- One player can be a banker. The banker checks all sums, gives out chips, and exchanges coins during trading transactions.

- Wood cubes can be used instead of dice. A cube might be numbered with 3, 4, 5, 6, 7, and 8 to give children practice adding these numbers.

- The game board can be set up to contain an area for Ten Dollars.

- Base 10 blocks can be used instead of counters.

- Players can be asked to record on a sheet of paper equations that represent their progress during the game (previous score + new pennies acquired = new score).

Skill variations:

Subtraction: Players start with two dollars on their board and remove a number of pennies equal to the sum of the numbers rolled on the dice. The first player with no money wins.

Decimals: Players record equations corresponding to their moves using decimal notation.

The Great Trading Game		
Dollar	Dime	Penny

The Great Trading Game		
Dollar	Dime	Penny

0 to 99 Guess

Object: A leader secretly circles one number on the game board. Players try to guess the number by asking questions that the leader can answer with either yes or no.

Skills: inequalities, number patterns, counting, problem solving, reasoning and logic, communication

Number of players: 3 to 5

Grades: 1 to 5

Materials: paper and crayons (or erasable markers)

Preparation: Make five enlarged photocopies of the 0 to 99 game board. For sturdier game boards, glue them on paperboard and laminate.

Playing:

1. The game has a leader, who hides a number on the game board; the other players try to guess the hidden number. The game is played in rounds. Players take turns being the leader in successive rounds.

2. To begin a round, the leader secretly circles one number on his or her game board and then hides it, by either turning the game board over or placing something on top of it.

3. During a round, after the secret number is hidden, players take turns, rotating clockwise. On a turn, they ask the leader one question about the number that can be answered with either a yes or no. Examples of valid questions are "Is the number 25?" and "Is the number larger than 25?" Such questions as "What number is one larger than the number?" are not allowed because they cannot be answered with a yes or no. After a question is asked and answered, all players can cross out or circle numbers on their game board. For example, if the hidden number is less than 25, players might cross out all numbers larger than 24.

4. A round ends when a player guesses the hidden number. A player can only guess the hidden number on his or her turn, when asking the leader a question. Even if a player determines what the hidden number is before his or her turn, the player cannot simply interrupt another player's turn to guess the number. If a player determines what the hidden number is as a result of asking a question, the player must still wait until his or her next turn to guess the number.

5. The player who guesses the hidden number ends the round and gets one point. Players keep cumulative track of their points. At the end of a round, players clean their game boards.

Winning: The player with the largest number of points after a specified number of rounds or playing time is the winner.

Playing variations:

- To play with a large group of children, divide them into two teams.

- For experienced players, do not use a game board. Have players visualize the game board and write the results of their guesses on paper.
- In a two-person game, players take turns being leader; at the end of a round, a player receives a score equal to the number of guesses it took to determine the hidden number; the player with the smallest cumulative score wins.

Skill variations:

Decimals: Use the numbers from 0 to 9.9 on the game board, in increments of .1, with all decimals between two consecutive whole numbers on a single line.

Fractions: Place fractions on the game board.

0 to 99 Guess

0	1	2	3	4	5	6	7	8	9
10	11	12	13	14	15	16	17	18	19
20	21	22	23	24	25	26	27	28	29
30	31	32	33	34	35	36	37	38	39
40	41	42	43	44	45	46	47	48	49
50	51	52	53	54	55	56	57	58	59
60	61	62	63	64	65	66	67	68	69
70	71	72	73	74	75	76	77	78	79
80	81	82	83	84	85	86	87	88	89
90	91	92	93	94	95	96	97	98	99

In the Basket

Object: Players roll two dice and occupy positions according to the sum of the numbers rolled. Rolling a 7 results in a penalty. Rolling a sum occupied by another player results in a reward.

Skills: addition

Number of players: 2 to 5

Grades: 1 to 3

Materials: large sheet of paperboard, 50 counters (such as poker chips, buttons, or dried beans), and two dice

Preparation: Copy the In the Basket game board onto paperboard. The game board can also be enlarged and photocopied and used as is.

Playing:

1. To begin, give each player 10 counters and determine the order in which players will take their turns.

2. In turn, the players roll the two dice and calculate the sum of the numbers rolled (face up on the dice). If the circle on the game board with that sum is not occupied by a counter, the player places one counter on that circle, and the player's turn ends. If the circle is occupied by a counter, the player takes the counter off of the game board, adds it to his or her collection of counters, and takes another turn. A player continues rolling the dice and taking his or her turn until he or she can place a counter on an empty space on the game board. This brings the player's turn to an end. If a player rolls a sum of 7 on the dice, the player deposits one counter in the basket, and his or her turn ends.

3. When a player runs out of counters, the player loses and is out of the game.

4. Players continue taking turns until only one player remains in the game.

Winning: The winner is the last player remaining in the game.

Playing variations:

- For a game that takes less time to play, give players only six counters at the start of the game.

- If several games will be played, the winner gets a score equal to the number of counters possessed at the end of the game. The "grand winner" of several games is the player with the largest cumulative score.

- Players can be asked to record the equations that correspond to the numbers rolled on the dice. If an equation is incorrect, the player gives the basket one counter, and his or her turn ends.

Skill variation:

Addition of three numbers: The game can be extended to larger numbers by using three dice. In this case, the game board should contain circles with the numbers 3 to 8, 10 and 11, and 13 to 18. Both 9 and 12 are penalty numbers that require players to deposit one counter in the basket.

In the Basket

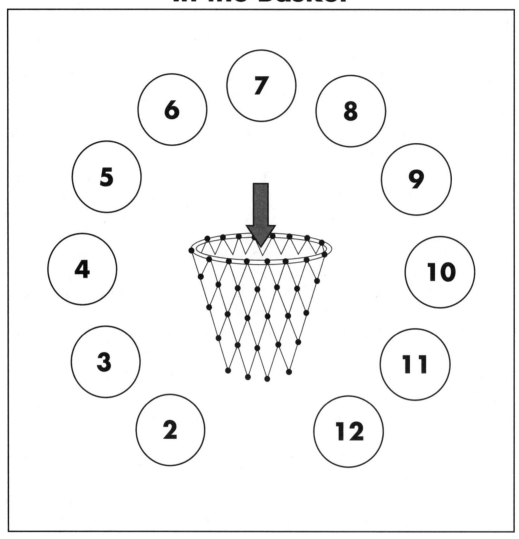

Math Skill Development Games

Race to the Nineties

Object: Players pick cards that contain vectors that designate moves as they race from 0 to any number between 90 and 99.

Skills: addition with trading, connections, communication

Number of players: 2 to 4

Grades: 1 to 5

Materials: paperboard, four different small objects for playing pieces, and 44 blank index cards

Preparation: Make and decorate the game board. It can be enlarged and photocopied using the Race to the Nineties reproducible. Color the top row (Start) on the board light green and the bottom row (90 to 99) light blue (numbers and words must show through the coloring). On one side of each of four sets of 11 cards, draw vectors (arrows) as shown in the diagram. On the top of each card draw a green line, and on the bottom draw a blue line. (Use the same colors as on the game board, for they give orientation to the cards.)

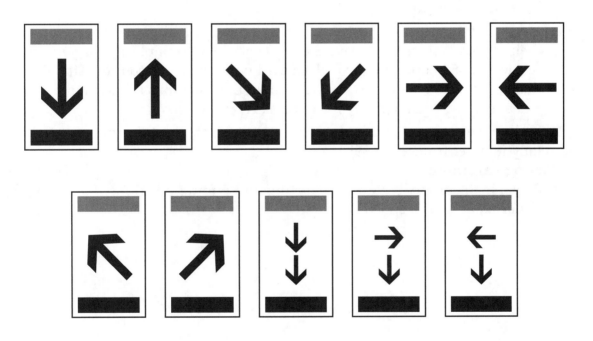

Playing:

1. Each player chooses a playing piece and places it on the green row at the top of the game board. Shuffle the cards and place them in a neat deck face down next to the game board.

2. To start, players move their pieces to 0 and follow directions from 0.

Board Games

3. Players take turns. During a turn, a player picks a card from the deck, turns it arrow side up, and follows the instruction given by the arrow(s) on the card. The arrow pointing straight down means move the playing piece down one row (which is the same as adding 10 to the number that the playing piece is on). The arrow pointing diagonally down and to the right means move the playing piece down one row and to the right one space (which is the same as adding 11 to the number that the playing piece is on). To determine the orientation of the arrows, match up the colored lines on the cards with the top and bottom rows of the game board (which should be similarly colored). After a player has moved, the player's card is placed face down on the bottom of the deck.

4. If a playing piece is moved onto a space already occupied by another playing piece, the playing piece that was first on the space is removed and placed in the green row at the top of the board. It starts over from 0.

5. When a card is picked that designates a move that will take a player's piece off the game board, he or she picks a second card and follows its instructions. If the second card also takes the player off the board, the player stays put and loses his or her turn.

6. During a turn, players must state (or write) the equation that corresponds to their moves. (You can also have them do both.) For example, if a player's piece resides on 25 and the player picks a card with an arrow pointing straight up, the player would say "25 − 10 = 15." If all the equations are written down in a neat row, a player's progress can be easily reviewed.

Winning: The winner is the first player to reach the bottom row of the game board (any number from 90 to 99).

Playing variation:

- Players can simply state their starting and ending positions. For example, "I started at 25 and ended at 15."

Race to the Nineties

Start									
0	1	2	3	4	5	6	7	8	9
10	11	12	13	14	15	16	17	18	19
20	21	22	23	24	25	26	27	28	29
30	31	32	33	34	35	36	37	38	39
40	41	42	43	44	45	46	47	48	49
50	51	52	53	54	55	56	57	58	59
60	61	62	63	64	65	66	67	68	69
70	71	72	73	74	75	76	77	78	79
80	81	82	83	84	85	86	87	88	89
90	91	92	93	94	95	96	97	98	99

Checker Math

Object: This is a game similar to Checkers in which the goal is to get the highest cumulative score.

    Skills: addition, problem solving

    Number of players: 2

    Grades: 1 to 4

    Materials: checkerboard, set of checkers, and markers to write on the checkerboard

    Preparation: On the lighter-colored squares of the checkerboard, write numbers with the marker as shown.

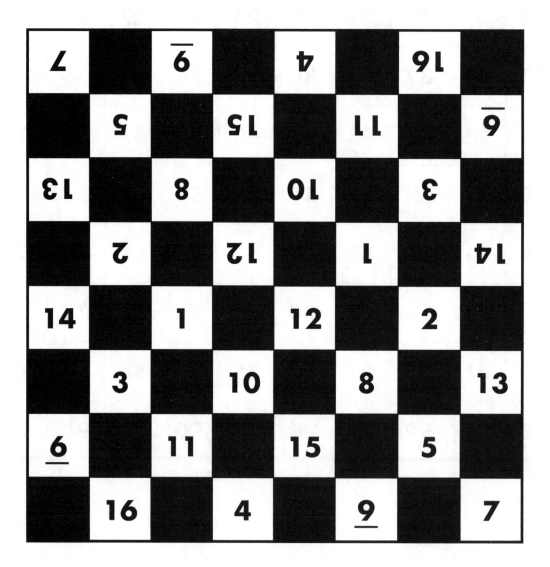

Playing:

1. Players sit opposite each other with the board positioned between them and with a dark corner square to their left. One player has 12 dark checkers; the other has 12 light checkers. Each player puts his or her checkers on the numbered squares in the three rows of squares closest to himself or herself, as in regular checkers.

2. Players take turns. On a turn, a player moves or jumps with one of his or her checkers. Checkers are moved or jumped only on numbered squares. A move consists of displacing a checker one space forward in a diagonal direction toward the opponent's side of the board onto an empty space, as in regular Checkers. A jump consists of jumping a checker over an opponent's checker that is in a square one space diagonally in front of the checker to an empty space directly on the opposite side of the jumped checker, as in regular Checkers. When an opponent's checker is jumped, it is removed from the board. On a single turn, one checker can jump several of an opponent's checkers in sequence if each jumped checker has a vacant space directly beyond it.

3. A checker is turned into a king when it reaches the furthest row of the game board. Two checkers are placed on top of each other to make a king. A king can move and jump forward or backward.

4. If on a turn a player can jump an opponent's checker, the jump must be taken.

5. Scoring: When a player moves a checker from one square to another, he or she is awarded the number of points equal to the number on the square onto which the checker is moved. If a player jumps an opponent's checker, the player is awarded points equal to the number on the square onto which the checker lands after jumping. If a player makes repeated jumps, the player is awarded points equal to the sum of the numbers on the squares on which the jumping checker landed after each jump. Players keep track of their cumulative scores by adding any new points obtained during a turn to points obtained during previous turns.

6. The game ends either after all of one player's checkers have been jumped and removed from the board or after some preset time period.

Winning: The player with the highest cumulative score at the end of the game wins.

Playing variation:

- Have players write down all their scores and cumulative scores in sequence, so that their addition can be checked.

Skill variations:

Addition, subtraction, multiplication, division: Any type of problem can be put in the squares. The value of each square is the answer to the problem on it. One- or two-digit whole number addition, subtraction, multiplication, or division problems can be used, as well as problems with fractions and decimals.

Down the Tubes

Object: Players move their playing pieces along the squares of a game board based on a hundreds number chart, according to the throw of a die.

Skills: place value, addition, subtraction

Number of players: 2 to 4

Grades: 1 to 3

Materials: one die, four different colored playing pieces that fit in the game board's squares, 16 index cards, and a large piece of white paperboard

Preparation: Copy the Down the Tubes game board onto the large piece of paperboard. (The game board can be enlarged on a photocopying machine and pasted onto the paperboard.) Circle in red all numbers with a 5 in the ones place. Decorate the board if desired. To prepare the index cards, write each of the following numbers on one side of two cards: $+5$, -5, $+10$, -10, $+9$, -9, $+11$, -11.

Playing:

1. To start, each player chooses a playing piece and places it on the game board at 0. All the cards are shuffled and placed face down in a pile.

2. Players take turns throwing the die and moving their playing piece along the game board the number of spaces designated by the die, starting from where they were located at the end of the previous turn.

3. When players move their pieces onto the dotted space at the end of each row, they slide them into the funnel and down the tube to the leftmost rectangle in the row of numbers below the row the player was on. For example, if a player is on space 8 and throws a 4 on the die, the player moves to 9, moves one more space, slides down the tubes to 10, then moves on to 11, and finally places the playing piece on space 12, where it comes to rest.

4. If a player's playing piece comes to rest at the end of a move on a number with a 5 in the ones place (the numbers circled in red), the player must pick the topmost card off of the card pile and follow its instruction. "$+5$" means move ahead five spaces; "-5" means move back five spaces. If as a result of picking a card a player moves back beyond 0, the player just restarts the game from 0 on the next move. If as a result of picking a card a player lands on another circled number, the player stays there and does not pick again. After moving, the player puts the card picked on the bottom of the card pile.

Winning: The first player to reach the Finish box wins.

Playing variation:

- Use two dice instead of one.

Skill variation:

Factors: On the playing cards, write statements such as "go forward to the next prime," "go back to the last composite number," "go back to the last number that was a multiple of 3," or "go forward to the next number with both 2 and 3 as factors."

Math Skill Development Games

Down the Tubes

| 0 | 1 | 2 | 3 | 4 | 5 | 6 | 7 | 8 | 9 | 10 |

| 10 | 11 | 12 | 13 | 14 | 15 | 16 | 17 | 18 | 19 | 20 |

| 20 | 21 | 22 | 23 | 24 | 25 | 26 | 27 | 28 | 29 | 30 |

| 30 | 31 | 32 | 33 | 34 | 35 | 36 | 37 | 38 | 39 | 40 |

| 40 | 41 | 42 | 43 | 44 | 45 | 46 | 47 | 48 | 49 | 50 |

| 50 | 51 | 52 | 53 | 54 | 55 | 56 | 57 | 58 | 59 | 60 |

| 60 | 61 | 62 | 63 | 64 | 65 | 66 | 67 | 68 | 69 | 70 |

| 70 | 71 | 72 | 73 | 74 | 75 | 76 | 77 | 78 | 79 | 80 |

| 80 | 81 | 82 | 83 | 84 | 85 | 86 | 87 | 88 | 89 | 90 |

| 90 | 91 | 92 | 93 | 94 | 95 | 96 | 97 | 98 | 99 | 100 |

Finish

Hit

Object: Players slap two coins so that they slide across a table onto a target. The two numbers on which the coins land are multiplied for a score.

Skills: multiplication, addition

Number of players: 2 to 4

Grades: 3 to 5

Materials: two coins (or similar objects, such as poker chips), tape, and paper

Preparation: Enlarge and photocopy the target provided or draw the target on a sheet of paper (8.5 × 11 inches). Each rectangle should be at least 4 × 1.2 inches. Tape the target onto a table about 12 inches from an edge. That edge will be the hitting edge. (Tape the paper smoothly so that coins do not get stuck on it.) Mark or tape arrows on the coins.

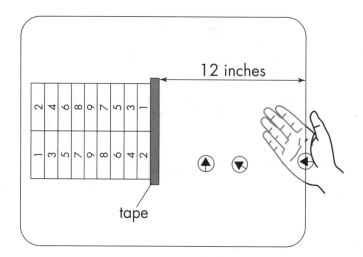

Playing:

1. There are ten innings in the game. Each player takes one turn during each inning.

2. On a turn, a player places a coin on the hitting edge of the table, as shown. The player then gives the coin a sharp, light slap with the palm of the hand so that the coin slides onto the target. The player repeats this with the other coin.

3. The player multiplies the two numbers on which the arrows on the coins land. For example, if the arrows land on 5 and 9, the player multiplies 5 × 9 and gets the product 45. This is the player's score for the turn. If an arrow lands off the target, the player's score is zero for the turn.

4. A player completes a turn by adding the new score to the sum of previous scores. (Players should check each other's calculations.)

5. After ten innings, the game ends.

Math Skill Development Games

Hit

1	2
3	4
5	6
7	8
9	9
8	7
6	5
4	3
2	1

Winning: The player with the largest cumulative score wins.

Playing variations:

- Put the target in a shirt box lid or on the floor and have players toss the coin onto it.

- At the end of each inning, compare players' products and award one point to the player with the largest product. The player with the most points at the end of the game wins.

- Reduce the number of rounds.

Skill variations:

> **Addition:** Have players add instead of multiply.

> **Fractions, decimals, place value:** Put other numbers on the target, such as fractions, decimals, or three-digit numbers.

Drop the Die on the Donkey

Object: Blindfolded players toss a die on a game board, which is a drawing of a donkey, and score points equal to the product of the die number and the value of the part of the board on which the die lands.

> **Skills:** multiplication
>
> **Number of players:** 2 to 5
>
> **Grades:** 3 to 5
>
> **Materials:** a square piece of paperboard, one die, a blindfold, and colored markers for decorating the game board
>
> **Preparation:** Enlarge and copy the game board onto the paperboard and color or decorate it if desired. To practice facts other than those from 1 to 6, use a wood cube numbered as desired instead of a traditional die.

> **Playing:**

1. The game is played as a series of rounds, during which each player takes a turn and scores points. Players obtain cumulative scores by adding together points from successive rounds.

2. During a turn, a player first puts on the blindfold. The die is placed in the player's right hand. Other players in the game rotate the game board in front of the player. The first finger on the player's left hand is then placed on one corner of the game board, so that the player can locate where it is. The player raises the hand holding the die about five inches above the game board and drops the die. The blindfold is then removed.

3. A player's score for a turn is the product of the number on the die and the number in the playing board area on which the die landed. If the die touches two different areas on the playing board, the player can take the higher value of the two areas, even if only a small corner of the die is touching the area.

Drop the Die on the Donkey

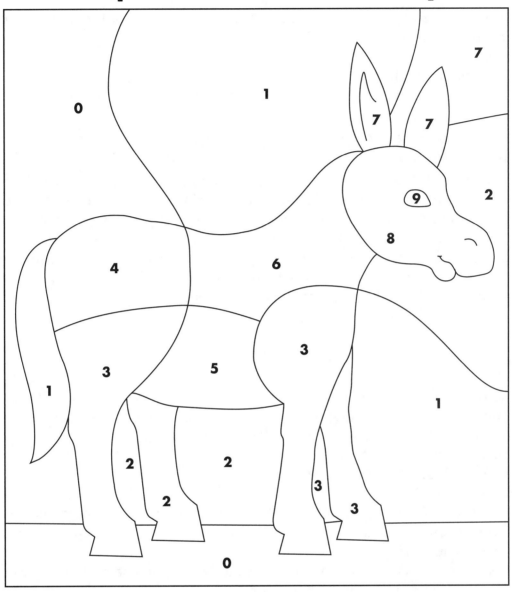

The player adds the score from the current turn to his or her cumulative score.

Winning: The player with the highest cumulative score after some agreed-on time or number of rounds is the winner.

Playing variation:

• Play as the traditional Pin the Tail on the Donkey, only have a player select a numbered tail from a grab bag to start a turn. Score as described.

Skill variations:

Addition 1: Have players add the number on the die to the number on the playing board. Play each round as a separate game.

Addition 2: Use different numbers on the playing board. Numbers less than 20 are good for a game in which the first player with a cumulative sum of more than 80 wins. Numbers less than 200 are good for a game in which the first player with a cumulative sum of more than 800 wins. Use a button instead of a die, and a player's score for a round is equal to the number in the area of the game board on which the button lands. Cumulative scores are determined by adding together scores from successive rounds.

Divi

Object: A dealer takes a handful of counters (n) and throws a die (d). Players bet on the integer result of dividing the number of counters by the die number ($n \div d$) and the number of counters remaining after the division.

Skills: division, estimation

Number of players: 3 or more

Grades: 1 to 5

Materials: 60 small counters (such as buttons, pebbles, or dried beans), a container to put them in, one die, paperboard on which a game board can be constructed, paper, and pencils

Preparation: Make an enlarged copy of the Divi game board (at least 12 inches per side). Laminate and decorate it as desired.

Playing:

1. Divi is played in rounds. To begin each round, the dealer takes a handful of counters and places them in a pile in the center of the game board, rolls the die, announces the number thrown on the die, and asks players to place their bets. Two bets are placed. One bet is for the number of groups that will be created when the counters are divided into groups, each of which has as many counters in it as the number thrown on the die. The other bet is for the number of counters that will remain at the end of the division process, if there are not enough counters to make a whole group. Players record their bets on a sheet of paper.

Bets		Points
#Groups	Remainder	
6	3	0
5	2	1
4	0	

2. After all bets are placed and recorded, the dealer separates the counters into groups, each of which has an amount equal to the number thrown on the die. Each group of counters is placed in one of the small squares on the game board. When no more groups equal in size to the die number can be created, the dealer announces the number of groups created and the number of counters remaining.

3. Players score one point if they guessed the number of groups correctly and one point if they guessed the remainder correctly.

Winning: The winner is the player who has the largest number of points after a specified number of rounds or a specified time period.

Playing variations:

- Bet just on the remainder or bet just on the number of groups.
- Do not use the die and have a predetermined size of the groups for the entire game. The number 4 works best; the numbers 3 and 5 work well too.
- If playing with a large group, use an overhead projector as the playing surface and project the division process.
- Have older players record the division problem once they know the number of groups, die number, and remainder.

Skill variation:

Place value: Guess the number of counters put on the table. A correct guess gets two points; if either the ones or tens digit is correct, the player gets one point.

Divi

Race

Object: Players select slips of paper from a bag. Each slip contains an arithmetic problem and a distance to move on the game board. Players move accordingly.

Skills: addition, subtraction, multiplication, division

Number of players: 2 to 4

Grades: 1 to 5

Materials: paperboard, four small objects for playing pieces, a paper or cloth bag about 8 inches wide and 12 inches high, and 50 to 100 small index cards

Preparation: Enlarge and copy the Race game board on the next page onto the paperboard. Decorate as desired. Laminate or cover the board with clear contact paper. On each of the cards, write an equation and directions to move 1 to 5 spaces, as shown. Match moves of 1 or 2 spaces to easy problems and moves of 3, 4, or 5 spaces to more difficult problems. The problems put on the cards can correspond to any skill or operation. Prepare between 50 and 100 cards for the game.

$$4 \times 5 =$$

move 2 spaces

$$\begin{array}{r} 25 \\ +38 \\ \hline \end{array}$$

move 4 spaces

Playing:

1. Each player chooses a playing piece and places it on the Start space. The cards with arithmetic problems are placed in the bag, the bag is closed, and the cards are mixed up by shaking the bag. Players determine the order of play.

2. Players take turns. During a turn, a player reaches into the bag and randomly picks a card from it. The player attempts to solve the problem on the card. If successful, the player moves his or her playing piece toward the finish line the number of spaces designated on the card. If the player does not answer the problem correctly, the playing piece is not moved. At the end of each turn, the player returns the card to the bag and shakes it to mix up the cards.

Winning: The first player to reach Finish wins.

Playing variations:

- Place penalty cards in the bag, which require the player to move backward a certain number of spaces.

- Ask players to record on paper the arithmetic problems they draw from the bag and to record their answers.

Skill variations:

Money: Use coin stamps to place pictures of several coins on each card. Players calculate how much money is represented on a card.

Fractions: Draw fractional amounts on the cards, and have players state the amount represented.

Factors: Place one number or several numbers on a card. Have players state the factors of the number (or the common factors of the several numbers).

Race

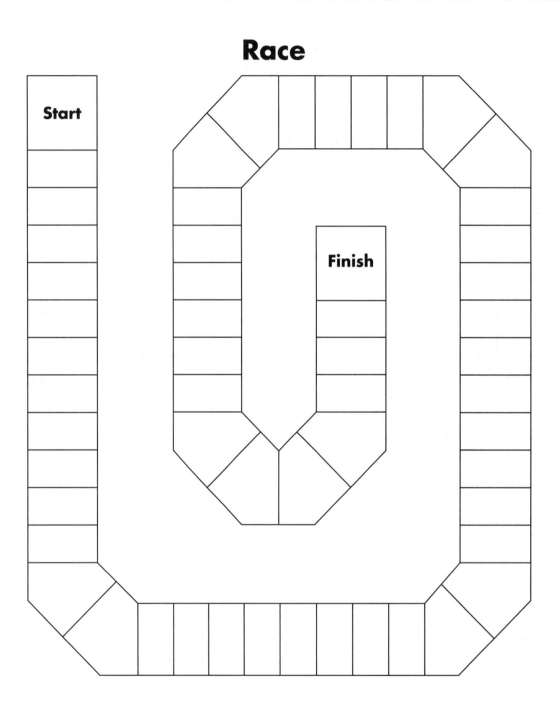

Math Skill Development Games

Coordinate Submarine

Object: This game is somewhat similar to Battleship. Two players try to sink the other's submarine, which is hidden on a coordinate grid, by calling out coordinates that designate where depth charges are dropped.

   Skills: graphing
   Number of players: 2
   Grades: 2 to 5
   Materials: six pieces of paperboard (four about 8 × 8 inches in size and two about 8 × 16 inches), colored markers to write on the paperboard, about 120 small counters (such as buttons, poker chips, or cubes) of one color and 25 of another color, a small box in which to store the counters, paper, and pencils

   Preparation: On the four smaller pieces of paperboard, draw and number an 8 × 8 grid, as shown, to make game boards. Decorate them or laminate them, if desired. Fold the two larger pieces of paperboard in half to make blinds that will hide the game boards, as shown.

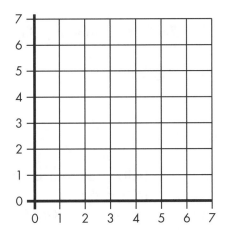 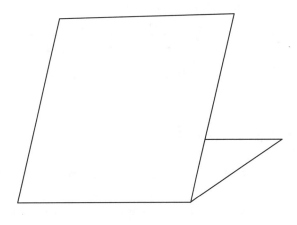

   Playing:
   1. Players sit opposite each other. Each player takes two game boards and one blind, and hides one game board in a blind. Each player places the other game board next to the hidden one. It is called a recording board. Put the box of counters between the players. The counters in greater number are called miss counters; the others are called hit counters.

   2. Each player takes three counters from the box and places them on three adjacent horizontal or vertical line intersections on their hidden game boards. These three counters are called a submarine. Once the game begins, players can not move their submarines.

   3. Players take turns. During a turn, each player tries to guess where the other's submarine is hidden and to sink it by dropping depth charges on the line

intersections where its counters are hidden. A player drops depth charges in the following manner. A player writes down an ordered pair on a sheet of paper. It has the format of (horizontal axis number, vertical axis number). Each ordered pair represents a position on the opponent's grid where a depth charge is dropped. The ordered pair is shown to the opponent, who must state whether or not the depth charge hit a coordinate that is part of the submarine. If the depth charge hit part of the submarine, the player who dropped the depth charge records this on his or her recording board by taking a hit counter out of the box and placing it on the coordinates on his or her recording board. If the depth charge misses a submarine, the player records this by placing a miss counter on his or her recording board.

4. Play continues with players taking turns dropping depth charges until one player has dropped depth charges on all three coordinates that define the opponent's submarine, thus sinking it.

Winning: The first player to sink the opponent's submarine wins.

Playing variations:

- The blinds can be replaced by a book or shoe box, behind which playing boards are hidden.

- Players can drop three depth charges during a turn. The opponent tells which depth charges landed on a submarine.

- Diagonal submarines can be placed on the game board.

Off the Grid

Object: Players place 36 counters of two colors, one color belonging to each player, on a 6 × 6 grid. They then roll two dice to obtain an ordered pair, and remove the counter on the grid corresponding to the ordered pair. The player with the most counters left on the grid after twenty-five dice rolls wins.

Skills: graphing, probability
Number of players: 2
Grades: 2 to 5
Materials: paperboard (at least 8 × 8 inches), colored pens to construct a game board, two dice of different colors or sizes, and 36 counters that can be separated into two distinct groups of 18 each (for example, 18 red and 18 blue buttons, poker chips, or cubes)

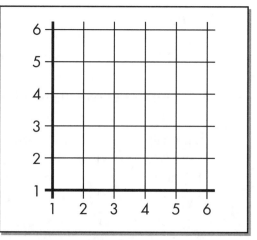

Math Skill Development Games

Preparation: On the paperboard, draw a 6 × 6 grid as shown. If desired, decorate and laminate the game board or cover it with clear contact paper.

Playing:

1. Separate the 36 counters into two distinct sets of 18. Each player takes one set. Place the game board between the two players. Decide which die will generate numbers that correspond to the horizontal axis and which die will generate numbers that correspond to the vertical axis, so that when the two dice are rolled, they generate an ordered pair that corresponds to one and only one point on the game board.

2. The game begins with players taking turns placing their counters, one at a time, on the game board at points where lines intersect. No more than one counter can be placed at any line intersection. When all 36 counters are placed on the game board, covering all 36 line intersections, play proceeds to the next stage.

3. Players next take counters off the board in the following manner. Each player takes one die, and the two players simultaneously roll the dice (on the count of "One, two, three" if necessary). The numbers rolled are written on a sheet of paper as an ordered pair. The counter residing on the game board at the intersection corresponding to the ordered pair is removed and given to the player to whom it belongs.

4. The process of rolling the dice, writing the corresponding ordered pair, and removing a counter from the grid takes place twenty-five times. If a counter does not reside on an intersection because it has already been removed, no counter is removed, but the turn counts as one of the twenty-five rolls of the dice.

5. The game ends after twenty-five rolls of the dice. Players then count the number of their counters that still remain on the game board.

Winning: The player with the most counters left on the grid after twenty-five dice rolls is the winner.

Playing variation:

- The game can be played with three or four players. Simply use 36 counters that can be divided into three distinct sets of 12 or four sets of 9.

Chapter Seven

Physical Education Games

Physical education games have long been a favorite of children. Kids love any chance to run, jump, and move about. For those children who learn best through large motor activity, physical education games are an ideal way to help them learn mathematics.

Most physical education games need a large empty space, such as a playground or gym. Many can be played in a hall. Some of the best can even be played in a classroom, as long as there is sufficient room. Always make sure that the playing areas in which physical education games take place are safe for children and that an accidental fall will not result in a child colliding with a desk, door, or wall.

Jump the Answer

Object: Players race to be the first to jump answers to problems on a number grid.
 Skills: addition, subtraction, multiplication, division
 Number of players: two teams of any size
 Grades: 1 to 5
 Materials: chalk or crayons, a chalkboard or sheet of paper on which problems can be written, paper, and pencils
 Preparation: Draw two number grids and a starting line, as shown in the figure, on a floor, sidewalk, or playground. Squares in the number grid should be about one foot long. The distance between the starting line and the number grid should be between 8 and 20 feet.

Playing:

1. Choose a problem giver and two teams. The players of each team line up behind the starting line.

2. The problem giver writes a problem on a chalkboard or sheet of paper and shows it to the first players on the starting line. The problem can involve any operation with any size numbers, so long as it has a solution that is a whole number (for example, addition problems can vary from $7 + 5 = ?$ to $3567 + 8456 = ?$).

3. The two players on the starting line calculate the answer (using either mental math or paper and pencil) and then run to their number grid and jump the answer on the grid, with digits being jumped according to their position in the number from highest place value position to lowest place value position. (For example, if the answer is 36, the 3 would be jumped into first and the 6 would be jumped into second.) A digit is jumped by jumping with either both feet or one foot into the square on the number grid that contains the digit. Once the answer to the problem is jumped, the players race back to the starting line.

7	8	9
4	5	6
1	2	3
	0	

7	8	9
4	5	6
1	2	3
	0	

Starting line

4. The player who returns to the starting line first, after having jumped the correct answer to the problem, wins one point for his or her team. Players waiting in line for their turn to jump must calculate answers to the problem and watch to make sure that the other team's player jumps the correct answer.

5. The players who just jumped go to the back of the line after the point is awarded, and the next players in line move up to the starting line to get ready for the next problem. The process then repeats until each player has a turn to jump.

Winning: The team with the largest number of points when the game ends is the winner. The game can end after a specified number of points has been acquired or after a set time period.

Playing variations:

- Simple problems can be spoken aloud rather than written.
- Players can be given numbers instead of equations to jump.

Math Ball

Object: Players stand in a circle and toss a ball to each other in a random order. As a player catches the ball, that player must say the number one higher than that said by the previous person who caught the ball.

Skills: counting up or counting down

Number of players: 3 or more

Grades: 1 to 2

Materials: a ball about 4 to 12 inches in diameter

Preparation: none

Playing:

1. Players stand in a circle. The size of the circle depends on the skill level and number of the players.

2. The first player, who is the one holding the ball at the start of the game, yells "Zero!"

3. Then the player holding the ball (the tosser) throws it to any other player in the circle (the catcher). Before catching the ball, the catcher must yell the number one higher than that yelled by the tosser.

4. If the catcher does not yell the appropriate number, does not yell the number before catching the ball, or does not catch the ball, that player must drop out of the game and stand outside the circle. The ball is then passed back to the tosser, who throws it to another player.

5. If the tosser does not throw the ball to the catcher in a way that the catcher can catch it, the tosser must drop out of the game, and the designated catcher restarts the game's count where the tosser left off.

Winning: The last player left in the game wins.

Playing variations:

- Play as a counting down game with the first number being 100 (or 1000).
- Start the count at a number larger than 0 (perhaps 347).
- Slow the game down by ruling that the ball must bounce on the ground once between the tosser and the catcher.

Skill variations:

Multiples: Count by a multiple other than one.

Fractions: Count by adding a fraction to the previous number said.

Buzz: Play like Buzz, with the ball being passed clockwise and with players having to say "Buzz" (instead of the number) whenever the multiple of some designated number is to be said. The word "buzz" can also be used as a substitute for any digit in a number equal to the multiple (thus for multiples of 5, the number 55 would be said as "buzz-buzz").

Simon Says Math

Object: This game is similar to Simon Says, except that the leader asks players to do things involving mathematics, such as jump the answer to $42 \div 6$.

Skills: addition, subtraction, multiplication, division, communication

Number of players: 3 or more

Grades: 1 to 5

Materials: none

Preparation: none

Playing:

1. Choose a leader. Have all players stand in an area where they can move about freely.

2. The game is played as a series of rounds. The leader begins each round by making a statement that has three parts: a Simon Says part, an action part, and an equation part. The Simon Says part either contains the words "Simon says" or does not. The action part describes some action that players are to engage in. The equation part of the statement gives an addition, subtraction, multiplication, or division equation. Different operations can be used in a game. Two examples of statements are "Simon says jump the sum of 3 plus 2" and "Clap your hands to show the number of tens in the product of 7 times 6."

3. Once the leader has made the three-part statement, players carry out the action described in the statement if the statement begins with the words "Simon says." If the statement does not begin with these words, the players stand still.

4. A player drops out of the game and sits down if any of the following occurs: the player stands still when a statement beginning with "Simon says" is made; the player acts out all or part of the answer to the equation in the statement when the statement lacks the phrase "Simon says"; the player performs the described action incorrectly (for example, hops on the right foot when directed to use the left foot); or the player incorrectly acts out the equation. Such errors are monitored by the leader and other players.

5. A player stays standing and remains in the game if the action was correctly performed.

6. A round ends when it is determined which players will stay in the game and which must drop out. A new round then begins.

Winning: The last player or players to remain standing after some specified period of time win.

Playing variations:

- Write actions on one set of 3×5 index cards and equations on another set. Have the leader pick one card from each set to determine what is to be said. Here the leader simply decides whether or not to add "Simon says."

- Entire statements can be written on index cards. The leader then has the job of shuffling the cards to begin the game, picking a card, reading it, and helping determine who remains in the game and who drops out.

Skill variation:

Place value: In place of an equation, the leader says a number with two to six digits. In the action part of the statement, the leader specifies if the players are to act out the digit in the ones, tens, hundreds, thousands, ten thousands, or hundred thousands place in the number. For example, the leader might say "Simon says clap your hands the number of tens in 475."

Number Calisthenics

Object: Two teams take turns doing a series of exercises to instructions related to place value. The place value of the digits of a number determines how many of which exercises will be done.

Skills: place value, communication

Number of players: two teams of any size

Grades: 1 to 4

Materials: none

Preparation: none

Playing:

1. Choose two teams and a leader to announce numbers. The two teams alternate turns as exercisers and watchers.

2. A turn begins with the leader announcing a four-digit number. The exercisers must then act out the four-digit number in unison by doing the following exercises in sequence: as many jumping jacks as specified by the value of the digit in the thousands column of the number; as many toe touches as specified by the value of the digit in the hundreds column; as many hand claps as specified by the tens digit; and as many finger snaps as specified by the value of the digit in the ones column. For example, for the number 5432, the exercisers would do 5 jumping jacks, 4 toe touches, 3 hand claps, and 2 finger snaps.

3. While the exercisers are acting out their number, the watchers watch them to see if anyone makes a mistake. Anyone who makes a mistake exercising must drop out of the game. Players who are out of the game become permanent watchers for their team.

4. Once one team has completed exercising to a number, the teams switch roles and a new number is announced by the leader.

5. Play continues either until all the members of one team are out, until the amount of time allocated for playing the game elapses, or until a specified number of rounds have been played.

Winning: The team that has the most players still in the game when it ends is the winner.

Playing variations:

- Have the leader write the number rather than saying it aloud.

- Replace any of the exercises with others. For example, the hand claps might be replaced by push-ups.

- Any size number can be used: two-, three-, four-, or five-digit numbers all work well.

- This can be played as a whole-group activity where there are no winners and losers.

Fingers

Object: Two players face each other with one of their fists closed. Simultaneously, they extend from one to five fingers while also calling out a number between 2 and 10. If a player's called number equals the sum of the extended fingers, that player wins a point.

Skills: addition, counting, probability, communication

Number of players: 2

Grades: 1 to 2

Materials: none

Preparation: none

Playing:

1. Fingers is played as a series of rounds.

2. During each round, two players face each other with one of their fists closed. On the count of three, they both simultaneously extend from one to five fingers while at the same time calling out a number between 2 and 10. Fingers are to be extended with a shake of the fist in a manner similar to that used in the game Rock-Paper-Scissors.

3. If the number called out by a player equals the sum of the fingers extended by both players, that player scores one point. Both players can score a point during the same round.

4. A player's score is the sum of the points acquired during the game.

Winning: The player with the highest score wins.

Playing variations:

- Allow a maximum of fewer than five fingers to be extended. This allows the probability of guessing to be higher.

- Allow players to use two hands when extending fingers, so that numbers up to 20 can be used.

Skill variations:

    Subtraction: Have players bet on the difference between the numbers of fingers extended, by calling a number between 0 and 4.

    Multiplication: Have players bet on the product of the number of fingers extended. Bets that are within four numbers above or below the product win a point (thus a bet of 15 would win a point if the product was either 12, 15, 16, or 18).

Hands In

Object: Each player hides from one to three small counters in his or her left hand and guesses the sum of the counters hidden in all players' hands.

    Skills: counting, addition, probability

Number of players: 2 to 10

Grades: 1 to 3

Materials: three small counters (such as pennies, paper clips, dried beans, buttons, or pebbles) for each player

Preparation: none

Playing:

1. Each player is given three small counters at the start of the game. The game is played as a series of rounds.

2. Players start each round by hiding from other players both of their hands and their counters (in their lap, under a table, behind their back); placing one, two, or three counters in their left hands; and concealing the remaining counters from the other players in their right hands. On the count of three, all players extend their left hand in front of them.

3. Players look at each others' hands that conceal the counters and then guess, one at a time in clockwise rotation, the total number of counters contained in all the outstretched left hands. Once all players have guessed, they open their outstretched hands and calculate the total number of counters (by either adding or counting them).

4. At the end of each round, players receive points. All players who guess correctly score two points. If no player guesses correctly, the player (or players) with the closest guess score one point.

5. A player's cumulative score is the sum of the points received during the game.

Winning: The player with the highest cumulative score wins.

Playing variations:

- Change the number of counters given to each player. Two to five counters can be used.

- Have the players record their guesses on a sheet of paper during each round so that there is no doubt about what they guessed.

Twist-'em

Object: Players give each other four-digit numbers that they must represent by placing their hands and feet on a numbered grid. The player who falls over first while attempting to represent the number loses.

Skills: place value, communication, connections
Number of players: 2 to 4 (or two larger teams)
Grades: 1 to 5
Materials: chalk or crayons for drawing on the floor or ground, paper, and pencils

Preparation: Draw the numbered grid, as shown, on a floor, sidewalk, or playground. The side of each cell should be from 8 to 15 inches long, depending on the size and skill of the players.

7	8	9
4	5	6
1	2	3
	0	

Playing:

1. Players take turns as number giver and twister.

2. The number giver writes a four-digit number on a sheet of paper and reads it aloud to the twister using correct place value language. The twister checks the paper to make sure the number giver read it correctly.

3. The twister then puts his or her hands and feet in the appropriate cells of the grid in the following order:
   - Right foot on the digit representing the thousands
   - Left foot on the digit representing the hundreds
   - Right hand on the digit representing the tens
   - Left hand on the digit representing the ones

4. After getting into position, the twister tries to count from 1 to 10 without falling.

5. If the twister falls while attempting to get into position or while counting from 1 to 10, or if he or she succeeds in the endeavor, players switch roles.

6. Score as follows: The number giver gets one point for reading the number correctly. The twister gets five points for not falling and for counting to 10. Players must have an equal number of turns in the roles of number giver and twister.

Winning: The player with the highest score wins. Equal scores produce a tie.

Playing variation:
- If playing with two teams, the game moves faster and is more exciting if two number grids are used and each team simultaneously gives the other team a number and receives a number to act out on their own grid.

Skill variation:

Addition or subtraction: Addition or subtraction problems involving four-digit numbers can be used, with the twister solving the problem before acting out the answer. A correct solution to the problem earns the twister two points.

Math Rover

Object: This game is a version of Red Rover (which is a form of Tag). Players, with numbers attached to them, run across a rectangular playing field while a person who is "It" tries to tag them. Players run when It calls out a problem whose answer is equal to the player's number.

Skills: addition and subtraction

Number of players: 7 to about 30

Grades: 1 to 3

Materials: a placard for each player (piece of paper or cardboard) about 8 × 11 inches, string, and a large playing field

Preparation: On each of the placards, write a different number from 1 to *x*, where *x* is the number of placards being created. Make holes in each placard and attach string in such a way that placards can be hung around players' necks or tied around their middle. Mark out a rectangular playing field that is about 20 × 40 feet. A blacktop is ideal.

Playing:

1. To begin, each player puts on a numbered placard. One player is chosen to be It. It stands inside the playing field. The rest of the players are divided into roughly equal groups and stand along the outside of the longest sides of the field.

2. It decides which player is going to run from one side of the playing field to the other, and constructs an addition or subtraction problem that is equal to the number on that player's placard. It then sings out the chant "Math Rover, Math Rover, let [state the problem] come over!" (For example, "Math Rover, Math Rover, let 9 − 4 come over!" forces 5 to run.) After the chant, the player with the answer to the problem attempts to run from

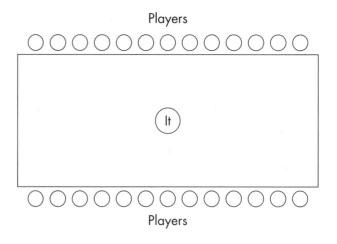

one side of the rectangle to the opposite side without being tagged. It attempts to tag the player while he or she is on the inside of the playing field.

Math Skill Development Games

3. If the runner reaches the other side without being tagged, that player is safe and waits for his or her number to be called again. If the runner is tagged or does not run because he or she did not calculate correctly, that player goes to the center of the rectangle and becomes Its assistant, and helps tag other players. A player who runs across the field when it is not his or her turn must enter the rectangle and become an assistant to It.

4. The game continues with It calling and players running until only one person is left who has not yet been tagged.

Winning: The winner is either the last untagged player or It and all Its assistants.

Playing variations:

- An adult can construct and call problems out so that It and his or her aides need only tag players.

- Problems can be put on index cards, with two or three problems for each placard. It picks them one by one and uses their problems in the Math Rover chant. If a tagged player's number is called, another card is picked.

- Use only the numbers from 1 to 10 on the placards, so that several players have the same number. When It calls a problem, all players with the answer must run. One or more might be tagged. Only those tagged become assistants to It.

Skill variations:

Inequalities: It can call out inequalities that force more than one player to run. (Examples: "All players greater than $5 - 3$ and less than $8 - 2$"; or simply "All players less than $8 - 2$.")

Division: It calls out division problems. Placards contain only the numbers from 1 to 10, and more than one player might have to run when a problem is called. Players run if either the quotient or remainder equals the number on their placard.

Equivalent fractions: Put fractions on the placards. It calls out fractions that are equivalent to, but different from, those on the placards.

Operation Hopscotch

Object: This game is similar to Hopscotch, but before each hop, players call out the product of the number onto which they are going to jump and the number on which their stone presently resides.

Skills: multiplication
Number of players: 2 to 4
Grades: 3 to 5

Materials: chalk or crayons for drawing, and a small stone for each player

Preparation: Draw the numbered grid, as shown, on the floor, sidewalk, or playground.

Playing:

1. Players take turns. To start the first turn, a player stands in 0 and throws his or her stone into square 1. He or she jumps over 1 into 2 and 3 (with one foot in 2 and the other in 3), hops onto 4 (with one foot), jumps into 5 and 6, hops onto 7, jumps into 8 and 9, hops into 10, turns around in square 10, and then goes back the same way, jumping over square 1 and back into square 0.

2. Each time a player puts a foot on a number or numbers, and before hopping or jumping to succeeding numbers, the player must call out the product of that number (or numbers) and the number on which his or her stone presently resides. (For example, a player whose stone resides on 2 would call out the following while jumping, "2, 6, 8, 10, 12, 14, 16, 18, 20, 20, 18, 16, 14, 12, 10, 8, 6, 2, 0.") If the product is incorrect, the player loses that turn and must start over and toss the stone into the numbered square it was in when the incorrect product was called out.

3. After each player gets to back to 0 or loses a turn, the next player takes a turn.

4. If during a turn a player touches any of the lines with a foot, puts a foot down when hopping, loses balance and falls, or throws his or her stone out of the desired square, that player loses that turn and must start over on the next turn from where he or she was on the previous turn.

5. Players must always jump or hop over any square containing their stone or an opponent's stone.

6. Once a player succeeds in completing a turn with his or her stone in square 1, on the next turn the player picks up his or her stone from square 1, throws it into square 2, and repeats the hop and jump sequence described above. On future turns, the player repeats this process, throwing the stone into the next square in the sequence whenever he or she successfully completes a turn.

Winning: The first player to complete a turn with his or her stone in square 10 is the winner.

Playing variation:

- Have players pick up their stone just before they jump over it on their return from 10 to 0. This way there is only one stone on the playing board at a time.

Skill variation:

Addition: Players add the numbers on which they are going to jump to the number on which their stone presently resides.

Bean Bag Toss

Object: Players take turns tossing a bean bag at a target containing a blank multiplication table. Players score points equal to the answer to the multiplication problem they toss, if they can solve the problem.

    Skills: multiplication, use of a multiplication table, addition

    Number of players: 2 to 5

    Grades: 3 to 5

    Materials: one bean bag, large piece of cardboard, drawing marker, and piece of tape

    Preparation: Use the marker to draw a multiplication table on the cardboard, without the answers. This will be the target for the game. A target for the numbers from 1 to 5 is shown. You can construct targets for the numbers 1 to 10, or any numbers desired. Place the target on the floor and put a two-foot strip of tape on the floor about five feet from the target to indicate a throw line.

X	1	2	3	4	5
1					
2					
3					
4					
5					

    Playing:

1. Players take turns.

2. During a turn, a player stands behind the throw line and tosses the bean bag toward the target. If the bean bag does not land on an empty cell in the target, the player gets a second chance to throw the bean bag. If the bean bag still does not land on an empty cell of the target, the player scores zero points for that turn.

3. If the bean bag lands on an empty cell in the target, the player multiplies the number in the horizontal row by the number in the vertical column. The answer to that problem is the player's score for that turn, if the player does the multiplication correctly. If the player does the multiplication incorrectly, the player scores zero points for that turn. If the bean bag lands so that it is on several blank squares simultaneously, the player can choose which problem to solve.

4. Players keep a cumulative record of their scores by adding their scores from each round.

    Winning: The winner is the player with the highest cumulative score after each player has had the same number of turns.

    Playing variations:

- To drill only selected multiplication facts, use a target with fewer rows and columns, and number the rows and columns as desired.

- You can draw the target in a large cardboard box and have players toss a paper clip instead of a bean bag.

- During a turn, players can be allowed to toss the bean bag until it lands on a blank cell on the target.
- Scores can be calculated on a round-by-round basis with the player with the largest product receiving only one point for the round.
- Allow players to use a calculator to check questionable answers.

Skill variations:

Addition: Use an addition table rather than a multiplication table.

Division: Make the target a division table by filling in the answers on the multiplication table and leaving off the numbers in the top row. Players then have to tell what the missing factor is.

Math Jacks

Object: This game is played as a series of ten rounds, one for each of the numbers from 1 to 10. The player throws a small bouncy ball up into the air, moves one or more counters onto a numbered square on a playing board, announces the result of multiplying the number for that round (1 to 10) by the number in the square onto which the counter is being moved, and then catches the ball before it bounces on the ground more than once.

Skills: multiplication

Number of players: 2 to 5

Grades: 3 to 5

Materials: a small bouncy ball about the size of a Ping-Pong ball, a playing board, 10 small counters (such as pebbles or buttons), paper, and pencils

Preparation: Make the playing board, as shown. It can either be drawn with chalk on a floor or playground or drawn on a piece of paper (which can be laminated for repeated use). Each of the small rectangles should be at least two inches on a side. The circles in the diagram show where the counters are placed at the beginning of each round of the game.

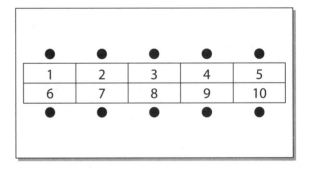

Playing:

1. There are ten rounds in the game. During each round, every player takes a turn. The number for the round is the same as the number that players multiply by during the round (during the first round, they multiply by 1; during the fifth round, they multiply by 5; and so on). To start a turn during each round, a player places the 10 counters around the playing board, as portrayed by the black circles in the illustration.

Math Skill Development Games

2. During a turn, a player holds the ball in one hand, tosses the ball into the air, moves the counter adjacent to the square with the 1 in it into that square using the same hand as the ball was tossed with, calls out the product of the number for the round multiplied by 1 (in the fourth round, for example, the player would call out the answer to 4 × 1), and then catches the ball with the same hand as it was tossed with before it bounces on the ground twice. (Zero or one bounce is allowed.) The player then repeats this sequence of actions using the counter adjacent to the square with a 2 in it (in the fourth round, a player would call out the answer to 4 × 2). The player continues in this manner moving counters onto the squares with 3, 4, 5, 6, 7, 8, 9, and 10 on them, in that sequence. If a player fails to catch the ball before it bounces twice or calls out the wrong answer to a multiplication problem, the player's turn ends, and the player receives as a score for the round the product of the last problem answered correctly. If the player succeeds in completing the sequence of ten problems, the player receives as a score for the round the product of 10 times the number for the round. Note that when a player tosses the ball into the air, it is usually the case that the ball will bounce on the ground once before it is caught.

3. Players record their score from each round and the cumulative sum of their scores from all previous rounds on a piece of paper.

Winning: The player with the highest cumulative score after the ten rounds of the game is the winner.

Playing variation:

- The game can be played for fewer than ten rounds, or for only certain rounds (it could be played for only rounds 5, 6, and 7 if those were the tables being practiced).

Math Marbles

Object: Players take turns shooting marbles at a numbered target. The player with the highest score after a certain number of rounds wins.

Skills: addition

Number of players: 2 to 5

Grades: 1 to 3

Materials: marbles, a shoe box, an X-Acto knife (or other cutting tool), and a marker

Preparation: To make the target, cut a series of arches in the long side of the shoe box with the cutting tool. Four or five arches are adequate, depending on the size of the box, although more can be used if desired. Write numbers above the arches with the marker, as shown. The numbers in the illustration are for children practicing addition facts with the numbers 1, 2, 3, and 4. Other numbers, such as 10, 20, 30, and 40 or 138, 126, 257, and 345, can be used.

Playing:

1. Before beginning to play, put the target box on the floor and mark a shooting line on the floor about five feet in front of the target. (A piece of masking tape or a line drawn with a piece of chalk will work.) Give each player two marbles.

2. The game is played as a series of rounds. During each round, players take turns shooting their two marbles and calculating their score.

3. The marbles must be shot from behind the shooting line. There are many ways of shooting a marble. One popular way is to role the marble out of the palm of the hand. Another popular way is to place the knuckle of the forefinger on the ground, balance the marble on the forefinger, put the thumb behind the forefinger and the marble, and then flick the marble off of the forefinger toward the target.

4. Players shoot their marbles at the target and try to get them to go through the arch that has the largest number above it. Decide on whether or not to apply this rule before the game begins: If a marble misses all the arches, the player can be given a second try at getting it through an arch.

5. A player's score is the sum of the numbers above the arches through which his or her marbles roll. The player with the highest score at the end of each round gets one point.

Winning: The player with the most points after some predetermined time period or number of rounds is the winner.

Playing variations:

- Keep cumulative track of the player's scores, and the player with the highest cumulative score wins.

- Play the game as a single round. More children have a chance to win a game this way.

- Allow players to use five marbles, to have no reshots if they miss the target, and to choose which two marbles' scores they wish to use in calculating their sum.

Skill variation:

Multiplication: Use a shoe box target with eight or nine arches or a circular target with eight or nine concentric circles that are numbered from 1 to 8 or 9. Players multiply together the numbers scored by their two marbles. The winner is the player with the highest cumulative sum of products from the rounds played.

Bounce

Object: A bounce team plays against a guess team. The bounce team is given two numbers from 1 to 9; one player on the team uses a playground ball to bounce their sum; another player on the team uses the ball to bounce their difference. The guess team tries to guess the two numbers.

Skills: addition, subtraction, problem solving

Number of players: 4 or more

Grades: 1 to 4

Materials: a playground ball that can be bounced (such as a basketball, kickball, or soccer ball) and a deck of playing cards

Preparation: Remove the tens and face cards from the deck of cards.

Playing:

1. Divide players into two teams, which will take turns in the role of bouncers and guessers. Have the members of each team line up facing each other. Shuffle the deck of cards and place them between the two teams.

2. Bounce is played as a series of rounds, with each team having one turn as bouncers and guessers during a round.

3. During their turn as bouncers, the first two players in line go to the deck of cards and remove the first two cards. Both players look at the cards. The player who was first in line takes the playground ball and bounces it as many times as is equal to the sum of the two numbers. The player who was second in line bounces the ball as many times as is equal to the difference of the two numbers. (For example, if the numbers chosen were 3 and 5, the first player would bounce the ball 8 times, and the second player would bounce it 2 times.) At the end of the round, these players put the cards on the bottom of the deck and go to the end of the line.

4. During their turn as guessers, the team tries to guess the two numbers drawn from the deck of cards by the bouncers.

5. Scoring: If the guessers guess correctly on the first try, they get one point, if correct on the second try they get two points, if correct on the third try they get three points, and so on. A maximum of five guesses is allowed. If the bouncers bounce the ball an incorrect number of times (for the sum and difference of the two numbers), they get two points for the round, and the guessers get zero points for the round. Teams keep cumulative track of the number of points they acquire as the game progresses.

6. The game ends at the end of a round, after some specified amount of time, or after some specified number of rounds.

Winning: The team with the lowest cumulative score wins.

Playing variations:

- Use a device other than a playground ball to bounce the sum and difference of the numbers. For example, players might jump up and down on one foot the required number of times.

- Have a referee hold the deck of cards, examine them when they are drawn, and check the calculations of the bouncers. The referee could also simply give the bouncers the numbers without using the deck of cards as a randomizing device.

- Play as a noncompetitive game by having players stand in a circle and take turns bouncing the sum and difference of the numbers and let everyone in the circle guess the numbers. In this case, the ball gets passed clockwise to the next person in the circle after two players bounce the ball and everyone guesses.

Skill variation:

Multiplication: Bouncers get two numbers. One player bounces the product. The other player bounces the difference. In bouncing the product of the two numbers, toss the ball up into the air and catch it before it hits the ground to designate a 10, and bounce it on the ground to designate a 1. The number 64 would be acted out by tossing the ball up and catching it 6 times and bouncing it 4 times.

Number Race

Object: Each member of two teams holds a placard with one of the digits from 0 to 9 on it. A leader calls out a problem, and the members of each team holding placards with the digits in the answer race to a staging area to see which team can make the answer first.

Skills: addition, subtraction, multiplication, division

Number of players: two teams for 10 to 20 players, three teams for 21 to 30 players

Grades: 1 to 5

Materials: 20 to 30 placards (sheets of paper or card stock larger than about 5 × 8 inches and smaller than about 9 × 12 inches), markers for writing on the placards, paper, and pencils

Preparation: Make two or three sets of numbered placards (depending on the number of players in the game), each of which contains ten placards with one of the digits from 0 to 9 written on them in a large and bold manner so that the numbers can be easily seen from a distance. Each set of placards should have their numerals written using a specific color of marker so that teams can be easily distinguished. You can write on a sheet of paper the problems that will be used in the game so that children do not have to invent them during play. Problems should not have answers that repeat a digit (for example 323 or 144).

Playing:

1. Form two teams if there are 10 to 20 players, three teams if there are 21 to 30 players. Give each player on each team a placard. If there are fewer than 10 players on a team, give some players two placards. If there are one or two players left over, make them referees to determine the winner of each round or make one of them the leader (if the problems to be solved by the teams are written out ahead of time).

2. The game can be played in a classroom with players sitting at their desks or in a large open area. If it is played in a classroom, establish an "answer display" line for each team at the front of the classroom. If the game is played in a large open area, have players from each team stand behind a starting line with a space of at least ten feet between the starting line and an "answer display" line.

3. The game is played as a series of rounds. At the beginning of each round, players sit at their desks or stand in line with their team. The leader (or teacher) calls out an arithmetic problem (the answer of which does not repeat a digit). Players individually calculate the answer to the problem, and if the answer contains a digit on their placard, they take their placard and run to their "answer display" line as fast as possible. With the members of their team, the players arrange themselves in order so that by holding the placards in front of them they display the answer to the problem given by the leader (23 is not the same as 32). Players are not allowed to call out the answer to the problems. The first team to correctly display the answer to the given problem wins one point. A new round of the game is then begun.

4. The problems given in the game can be of any form that results in two-, three-, or four-digit answers (for example, $8 + 5$, $1234 + 2222$, $432 - 11$, 5×7, 24×35, or $2510 \div 5$ can be used).

Winning: The team with the highest cumulative score after some designated period of time or number of rounds is the winner.

Playing variation:

- Problems can be written on 3×5 index cards and shuffled before the game. A leader can then pick a card, show it to the players, and announce its problem to start a round.

Skill variation:

Place value: Describe two-, three-, four-, or five-digit numbers in words. Players then race to the answer line to display the number with their placards, with all the digits positioned correctly.

Part Two

Problem-Solving Mathematics Puzzles

Chapter Eight

Number Puzzles

Numbers and the relationships among them can be fascinating to children and adults alike, and this interest has led to the creation of many number puzzles. This chapter will focus on two types of number puzzles: magic square puzzles and their relatives, and number patterns on the hundreds chart.

Magic Circles and Squares

Magic squares have been of interest to mathematicians for millennia. By 650 B.C. the Chinese discovered that a set of integers could be arranged in a square so that the sum of the integers in every row, column, and main diagonal is equal to the same constant sum. The Chinese believed that such an array of numbers was magical. It is said that Emperor Yu discovered magic squares by studying the markings on the back of a turtle. The Chinese explored magic squares of many sizes and shapes. Interest in and knowledge of magic squares spread to India and Japan by the first century B.C. and to Europe by about 1600 A.D.

Today we know that numbers can be arranged in many "magic" shapes. It is also possible to use numbers other than integers. The following sets of numbers can be used in the magic cross (Magic Squares Puzzle 1 later in the chapter): $\{-2, -1, 0, +1, +2\}$ have a magic sum of 0; $\{\frac{1}{9}, \frac{2}{9}, \frac{3}{9}, \frac{4}{9}, \frac{5}{9}\}$ have a magic sum of 1; $\{.25, .50, .75, 1, 1.25\}$ have a magic sum of 2.25; and $\{10\%, 20\%, 30\%, 40\%, 50\%\}$ have a magic sum of 90%. To understand what is occurring, explore the number patterns. When using five consecutive numbers, each of which is larger than the last by a fixed amount, the magic sum is the sum of the first, middle, and last numbers. With this observation, you and children should be able to invent many new puzzles.

The Magic Squares section includes two games: Get 15 and Hot. They are designed to show different aspects of magic shapes. Get 15 can be played like Tic-Tac-Toe if the integers from 1 to 9 are arranged in a 3 × 3 magic square summing to 15. With this "magical secret," the game of Get 15 is easy to play, for all possible combinations of its numbers that equal 15 are easily visible and correspond to Tic-Tac-Toe playing positions. Hot works similarly. Its words can be put in a magic square in such a way that every row across, column down, and main diagonal has a word that contains the same letter. Try to figure out how to construct this magic square of words. Hot shows that things other than numbers can be put in magic shapes.

The Magic Circles section has been designed as an introduction to the study of magic squares, as magic circles are easier than magic squares and should be introduced first.

Hundreds Chart Problems and Puzzles

This chapter includes two sets of problems and puzzles on the hundreds chart: Hundreds Chart Explorations and Hundreds Chart Discoveries. Hundreds Chart Explorations are more introductory and can be used to introduce children to the hundreds number chart. Hundreds Chart Discoveries are more advanced and present children with many fascinating number relationships that can be found on the hundreds number chart. Each puzzle in the Hundreds Chart Discoveries section can be turned into a magic trick on the hundreds chart that children can share with friends and parents.

The hundreds chart allows children to see patterns that operate throughout our number system. Normally children learn only about very specific numerical relationships—for example, that 24 + 9 = 33. With the hundreds chart, children see patterns that operate over all numbers simultaneously. For example, they discover that adding 9 to any number results in a number that is one column down and one row to the left, or results in increasing the digit in the tens column by 1 and decreasing the digit in the ones column by 1 (except if there is a 0 in the tens place). Seeing arithmetic as a set of orderly patterns, rather than as a set of numerical triples, is an important perspective for children to acquire.

The activities accompanying each puzzle focus attention on the mathematics underlying the puzzle. Children should discuss the puzzle and accompanying activity in cooperative groups and write down their answers to them. Students can then share written answers with the whole class to help them find language to explain what they have observed and to help them reach higher levels of mathematical generalization.

A reproducible copy of a hundreds chart is included at the end of the chapter. Be sure to provide children with multiple copies of the chart, both for working on the problems and puzzles and for trying experiments and making discoveries on their own.

Many children wonder what happens if you fall off the hundreds chart: what happens if you move to the right of 39 or below 95? The number chart does not stop at its edges. It keeps going. So 40 is just to the right of 39, and 41 just beyond that. There is also a row of numbers below the row containing the number 95—and that row has the numbers from 100 to 109. All we see in the hundreds chart is a snapshot of part of ten number lines stacked one on top of the other, each offset ten squares to the right from the one above it. However, the number lines keep going to the right and the left. In addition, there are more number lines—for numbers in the hundreds and thousands—below those in the chart. The number lines also extend into the negative numbers—above and to the left of what we see in the 0 to 99 hundreds number chart.

The 0 to 99 number chart is used in these activities rather than the 1 to 100 number chart. This is because we believe that it is important to keep all the numbers in a decade together in a single row, rather than having the multiples of 10 in the row with numbers from the previous number decade. However, everything that works on the 0 to 99 chart also works equally well on the 1 to 100 chart. When working with multiples, the 1 to 100 chart is more useful than the 0 to 99 chart, because you do not have to deal with the 0 that is located in the first square.

Magic Circles

Abracadabra!

See if you can solve these "magic" puzzles.

Write each of the numbers **0**, **1**, **2**, **3**, and **4** once in the circles so that the three numbers in each straight line add up to **6**. (This one is done for you.)

Magic Circles Puzzle 1

Write each of the numbers **1**, **2**, **3**, **4**, **5**, **6**, and **7** once in the circles so that the three numbers in each line add up to **12**.

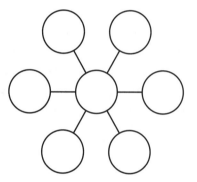

Magic Circles Puzzle 2

Write each of the numbers **1**, **3**, **5**, **7**, **9**, **11**, and **13** once in the circles so that the three numbers in each line add up to **21**.

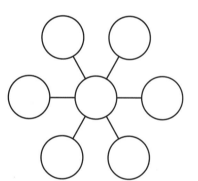

Magic Circles Puzzle 3

Write each of the numbers 2, **4**, **6**, **8**, **10**, **12**, and **14** once in the circles so that the three numbers in each line add up to **24**.

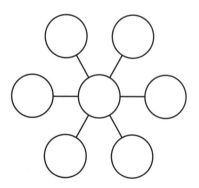

Magic Circles Puzzle 4

Write each of the numbers **1**, **2**, **3**, **4**, **5**, and **6** once in the circles so that the three numbers on each side of the triangle add up to **9**.

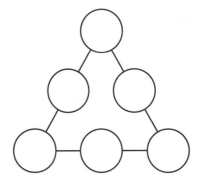

Magic Circles Puzzle 5

Write each of the numbers **1**, **2**, **3**, **4**, **5**, and **6** once in the circles so that the three numbers on each side of the triangle add up to **10**.

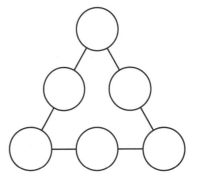

Magic Circles Puzzle 6

Write each of the numbers **1**, **2**, **3**, **4**, **5**, and **6** once in the circles so that the three numbers on each side of the triangle add up to **11**.

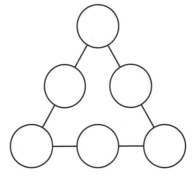

Magic Circles Puzzle 7

Write each of the numbers **1**, **2**, **3**, **4**, **5**, and **6** once in the circles so that the sum of the three numbers on each side of the triangle add up to **12**.

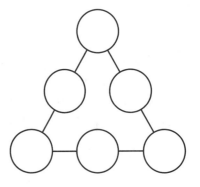

Magic Squares

ZimZamZoom!

　　See if you can solve these "magic" puzzles.

　　Write the numbers **0**, **1**, **2**, **3**, and **4** once in the squares below so that the three numbers in a line add up to **6**. (This one is done for you.)

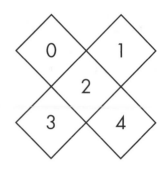

Magic Squares Puzzle 1

Write each of the numbers **1**, **2**, **3**, **4**, and **5** once in the squares of the figure at the right so that the three numbers in the row across and the column down add up to **9**.

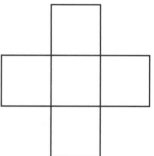

Magic Squares Puzzle 2

Write each of the numbers **2**, **4**, **6**, **8**, and **10** once in the squares so that the three numbers in the row across and the column down add up to **18**.

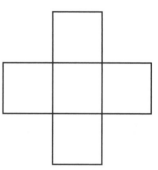

Magic Squares Puzzle 3

Write each of the numbers **1**, **2**, **3**, **4**, **5**, **6**, **7**, and **8** once in the squares so that the three numbers in each row across and column down add up to **12**.

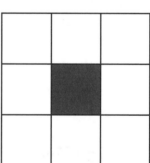

Magic Squares Puzzle 4

Write each of the numbers **1**, **2**, **3**, **4**, **5**, **6**, and **7** once in the squares so that the three numbers in each row across, column down, and main diagonal add up to **12**.

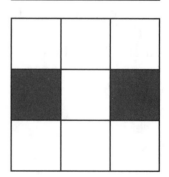

Magic Squares Puzzle 5

Write each of the numbers **1**, **2**, **3**, **4**, **5**, **6**, **7**, **8**, and **9** once in the squares so that the three numbers in each row across, column down, and main diagonal add up to **15**.

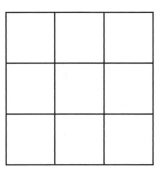

Get 15

Needed: two players, the numbers from 1 to 9 written on a piece of paper, two different colored crayons (or pencils or pens).

Playing:

- Each player uses a different color crayon.
- Players take turns. During a turn, a player circles one of the numbers from 1 to 9. A number can be circled only once.

Winning: The first player to circle three numbers that add up to 15 wins. A player may circle more than three numbers, but three of them must add up to 15. Draws are possible.

Sample game:

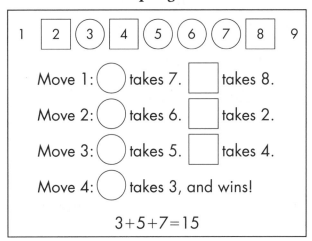

Hot

Needed: two players and nine small cards (such as index cards) with the following words written on them:

hot, hear, tied, form, wasp, brim, tank, ship, woes

Playing:

- Place the cards face up between the players.
- Players take turns. During a turn, a player picks one card and places it face up in front of himself or herself.

Winning: The first player to acquire three cards that contain the same letter (for example, three words with an "s" in their words) wins. Players can acquire more than three words before the game ends. Draws (no winner) are possible.

Hundreds Chart Explorations

Use a hundreds chart to do these activities. One that can be photocopied and enlarged can be found at the end of the Hundreds Chart puzzles.

Arrow Paths

Start with the circled number on the number grid. Follow each arrow path. Write the number you end on in the square.

Tell how these paths relate to addition.

> → Move 1 number to the right.
> ← Move 1 number to the left.
> ↓ Move 1 number down.
> ↑ Move 1 number up.

(13) ↓↓↓↓ ☐

(22) ↓↓↓→→ ☐

(55) ↓↓↓→→→ ☐

(33) →→→ ☐

(65) →→↓↓↓ ☐

(41) →→→→↓↓ ☐

How do these paths relate to subtraction?

(55) ↑↑↑↑ ☐

(45) ↑↑↑←← ☐

(88) ↑↑↑↑←←← ☐

(36) ←←←←← ☐

(77) ←←↑↑↑↑ ☐

(96) ←←↑↑↑↑ ☐

Number Grid Puzzles

Here are parts of a number grid. What number goes in each circle? Can you find out without looking at a complete grid?

Can you find more than one way to do this?

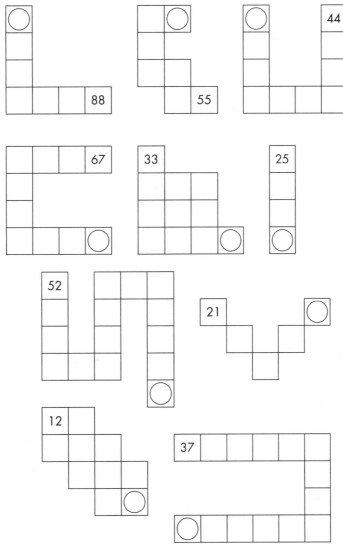

What's My Rule?

Look at the diagonal arrows on the grid at the right. Try each movement on your number grid. What number calculation does each arrow do?

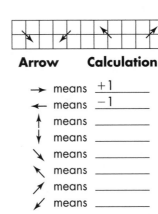

Arrow   **Calculation**

→ means __+1__
← means __−1__
↑ means _____
↓ means _____
↘ means _____
↖ means _____
↗ means _____
↙ means _____

More What's My Rule?

Each arrow describes a number pattern on the grid. Using the shaded squares, find three numbers on the grid to fit each pattern. Extend it for two more numbers. What's the rule?

Make up some problems to share with friends.

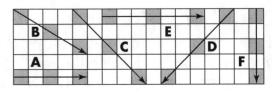

Arrow	Numbers					Rule
A	20	22	24	26	28	+2
B	___	___	___	___	___	___
C	___	___	___	___	___	___
D	___	___	___	___	___	___
E	___	___	___	___	___	___
F	___	___	___	___	___	___

Operational Arrows

Create an arrow path for each problem below. The first two problems are done for you.

Hint: Each problem has more than one solution.

Find five different paths from 62 to 30. Which path is the shortest?

$21 + \boxed{2} = 23$ $\quad 21 \underline{\qquad \rightarrow \rightarrow \qquad} 23$

$21 + \boxed{11} = 32$ $\quad 21 \underline{\;\downarrow\uparrow\downarrow\rightarrow\qquad} 32$

$35 + \boxed{} = 46$ $\quad 35 \underline{\qquad\qquad} 46$

$12 + \boxed{} = 45$ $\quad 12 \underline{\qquad\qquad} 45$

$38 + \boxed{} = 46$ $\quad 38 \underline{\qquad\qquad} 46$

$38 - \boxed{} = 26$ $\quad 38 \underline{\qquad\qquad} 26$

$55 - \boxed{} = 24$ $\quad 55 \underline{\qquad\qquad} 24$

$62 - \boxed{} = 30$ $\quad 62 \underline{\qquad\qquad} 30$

Discoveries

Use a hundreds chart to do these activities. One that can be photocopied and enlarged can be found at the end of the Hundreds Chart puzzles.

Explore some numbers on a hundreds grid.

Discover a number pattern.

Check to see if it works everywhere on the grid.

Describe the number pattern in words.

Explain in words why the pattern works.

Sum of Six Numbers in a Row

Add any six consecutive numbers in a row. Then add the two middle numbers. What do the middle numbers have to be multiplied by to get the sum of the six numbers? Add the two outer numbers. What happens?

Try this with six numbers in a column.

0	1	2	3	4	5	6	7	8	9
10	11	12	13	14	15	16	17	18	19
20	21	22	23	24	25	26	27	28	29
30	31	32	33	34	35	36	37	38	39
40	41	42	43	44	45	46	47	48	49

Sum-Digit Pattern of Numbers on a Main Diagonal

Add the digits in the ones and tens place of numbers in any diagonal that runs from upper right to lower left. (The digit in the tens place of numbers less than 10 is 0.) What do you notice about the sums?

0	1	2	3	4	5	6	7	8	9
10	11	12	13	14	15	16	17	18	19
20	21	22	23	24	25	26	27	28	29
30	31	32	33	34	35	36	37	38	39
40	41	42	43	44	45	46	47	48	49
50	51	52	53	54	55	56	57	58	59
60	61	62	63	64	65	66	67	68	69
70	71	72	73	74	75	76	77	78	79
80	81	82	83	84	85	86	87	88	89
90	91	92	93	94	95	96	97	98	99

Inners and Outers

Pick any four numbers that are an equal distance apart in a single row of the number grid.

Add the two outer numbers.

Add the two inner numbers.

What do you notice about the sums?

Magic trick: Have a friend pick any four numbers that are an equal distance apart on the number grid and add the outer two numbers and inner two numbers. Can you always guess their difference? Can you always guess their quotient?

0	1	2	3	4	5	6	7	8	9
10	11	12	13	14	15	16	17	18	19
20	21	22	23	24	25	26	27	28	29
30	31	32	33	34	35	36	37	38	39
40	41	42	43	44	45	46	47	48	49
50	51	52	53	54	55	56	57	58	59

Three in a Row

Pick any three numbers that are an equal distance apart in single row of the grid. Add the three numbers. Multiply the middle number by 3. What do you notice?

Magic trick: Have a friend pick three numbers an equal distance apart on the grid, add them, and multiply the middle number by 3. Then you guess the difference if he subtracts the sum from the product, and guess the quotient if he divides.

0	1	2	3	4	5	6	7	8	9
10	11	12	13	14	15	16	17	18	19
20	21	22	23	24	25	26	27	28	29
30	31	32	33	34	35	36	37	38	39
40	41	42	43	44	45	46	47	48	49
50	51	52	53	54	55	56	57	58	59

Adding Opposite Corners of Four Small Squares

Find any four small squares that meet in a single corner. Add the numbers in the two pairs of opposite corners. Compare sums.

What happens with any size square? Why?

What happens with any rectangle? Why?

Can you invent a magic trick?

0	1	2	3	4	5	6	7	8	9
10	11	12	13	14	15	16	17	18	19
20	21	22	23	24	25	26	27	28	29
30	31	32	33	34	35	36	37	38	39
40	41	42	43	44	45	46	47	48	49
50	51	52	53	54	55	56	57	58	59

The Great X

Locate any square on the grid that is three numbers high by three numbers wide. Add the three numbers on the two diagonals between each of the corners. Compare.

> What happens with any size square?

> Can you invent a magic trick?

0	1	2	3	4	5	6	7	8	9
10	11	12	13	14	15	16	17	18	19
20	21	22	23	24	25	26	27	28	29
30	31	32	33	34	35	36	37	38	39
40	41	42	43	44	45	46	47	48	49
50	51	52	53	54	55	56	57	58	59
60	61		63	64	65		67	68	69

Multiplying Opposite Corners of Four Small Squares

Find any four small squares that meet in a single corner. Multiply the numbers in the upper left and lower right corners. Multiply the numbers in the upper right and lower left corners.

> What happens with any three-by-three square? Why?

> What happens with any four-by-four square? Why?

0	1	2	3	4	5	6	7	8	9
10	11	12	13	14	15	16	17	18	19
20	21	22	23	24	25	26	27	28	29
30	31	32	33	34	35	36	37	38	39
40	41	42	43	44	45	46	47	48	49
50	51	52	53	54	55	56	57	58	59
60	61	62	63	64	65	66	67	68	69
70	71	72	73	74	75	76	77	78	79

Number Puzzles

Hundreds Chart

0	1	2	3	4	5	6	7	8	9
10	11	12	13	14	15	16	17	18	19
20	21	22	23	24	25	26	27	28	29
30	31	32	33	34	35	36	37	38	39
40	41	42	43	44	45	46	47	48	49
50	51	52	53	54	55	56	57	58	59
60	61	62	63	64	65	66	67	68	69
70	71	72	73	74	75	76	77	78	79
80	81	82	83	84	85	86	87	88	89
90	91	92	93	94	95	96	97	98	99

Problem-Solving Mathematics Puzzles

Chapter Nine

Algebra and Logic Puzzles

The problems and puzzles in this chapter provide children with experiences that require the use of mathematical logic. In addition, the Pockets Full of Pennies and Magic Math puzzles introduce children to algebra. The puzzles in this chapter also help children develop the mathematical skills of problem solving, reasoning and proof, and communication; help them make mathematical connections; and provide the opportunity to use mathematical representation.

Mystery Monsters

The ability to identify the characteristics of objects, compare their attributes, and sort and classify objects into sets according to their attributes is essential to the ability to use mathematical logic. These are particularly important skills for young children to acquire, and Mystery Monsters give children practice in these skills.

Mystery Monsters puzzles are designed to motivate children to identify, discriminate, and compare characteristics of "monsters." In these puzzles, children must focus on the many attributes of two sets of monsters and look for similarities and differences among the monsters in the two sets. They must then identify the characteristics that determine whether something does or does not belong to a particular set. Then, using mathematical logic, they must test their hypotheses. Finally, also using mathematical logic, they must apply their understanding of the attributes of the objects within each set, either to identify which monsters in a third set belong to one of the initial sets, or to draw a monster that has the attributes of those within one of the initial sets.

Mystery Monster puzzles are sequenced in order of difficulty. Initially, one attribute defines a monster, then two, and finally three. In the first two puzzles, children decide if a creature belongs to a particular class of monsters. Remaining puzzles ask children to draw their own version of a monster that exhibits the defining characteristics of a set of monsters and to write how they know it is one of those monsters. They are also invited to create their own mystery monsters to share with friends.

When children examine the sets of monsters in these problems, they must use mathematical problem solving to determine the attributes of each set. But what is critical to these puzzles is that children answer the question, "How do you know it's a ___?" To do this, children must use "logical reasoning" to "prove" to others that they know what the attributes of an object are that make it a member of a particular set. It is important for adults to push children to find the words to describe "why," and use those words in telling why a monster is similar to or different from those in two contrasting sets. This is what mathematical reasoning and mathematical proof consist of when working with children.

Children should not only communicate their reasons "why" to adults but also be encouraged to discuss with other children why certain monsters do or do not meet specific criteria and what those criteria are. In doing so, they develop their skills in mathematical communication.

Penny-in-Pocket Puzzles

These puzzles are a form of pre-algebra problem, accessible to children without the need for formal algebraic notation to solve them or for logical proof to demonstrate that answers are correct. These puzzles also provide a context for the development of a good understanding of what mathematical language means, and what some of the implications of that language are. They involve the use of mathematical problem solving at the intuitive level, as well as the use of logical reasoning and the coordination of mathematical information found in separate statements.

Let's examine the fourth puzzle in Pockets Full of Pennies as an example. It states the following:

> Two pockets have pennies. The sum of the number of pennies in the two pockets is 10. The difference in the number of pennies in the pockets is 0. How many pennies are in each pocket?

This puzzle is easy to solve if you know how to translate each verbal statement into a formal algebraic statement and solve simultaneous linear equations.

Let x and y stand for the number of pennies in each pocket.

x + y = 10 and x − y = 0
Solve for x and y.

Getting elementary school-age children to use formal algebraic notation and algorithms is not the intention of these problems. All that is needed to solve these problems are some simple problem-solving skills, in addition to skill in the use of mathematical language.

Mathematical communication is at the heart of these puzzles. What children must determine is what it means when we say such things as "The difference in the number of pennies in the pockets is 0." To do so, they must explore such questions as "What does the word 'difference' mean?" "Does the word 'difference' mean the same as 'subtract'?" and "If the difference is 0, is one number larger than the other, or are they the same size?"

All the penny-in-pocket puzzles use such words as "difference," "sum," "most," and "fewest." Children will need to discuss the language to understand the problems, and adults will need to help clarify the meaning of many mathematical terms. Discussions can lead to a rich exchange of mathematical ideas and much clarifying of meaning that children may not have fully constructed. When children begin making up their own puzzles—as they should do—they will need to be able to find mathematical words to express their mathematical ideas. Penny-in-pocket puzzles are also excellent in helping children whose first language is not English clarify the meaning of English-language mathematical terms.

Underlying penny-in-pocket puzzles is the use of algebraic reasoning and mathematical proof. Therefore, you should ask children to use such reasoning and proof, but do not require them to provide formal mathematical proofs to demonstrate why their answers to the puzzles are correct. All they need to do is demonstrate using language, visual images, or mathematics manipulatives that their solutions meet the specifications of the puzzles. And they should always tell or show why their solution to a puzzle actually solves the puzzle. Mathematics manipulatives, such as coins, number rods, and color cubes, can be particularly helpful in demonstrating why a solution to a puzzle fulfills the mathematical requirements of the puzzle (as demonstrated in the next section).

Mathematical Magic Tricks

The Magical Math puzzles introduce children to algebra, for underlying most tricks is a simple algebraic equation. The magic tricks also require a good deal of mathematical communication, for children need to learn how to use the language and ideas required by the tricks if they are to perform them. In addition, the magic tricks require that children engage in mathematical problem solving (to figure out how a trick works) and in mathematical reasoning and proof (to explain why a trick works—and you should always ask children to do this to the best of their ability).

Let us take a look at one of the magic tricks, Magic Sub 5, to see what is occurring in it.

SAY THIS TO A FRIEND:	EXAMPLE
Write down a counting number—remember, no 0s!	8
Add 4 to it.	$8 + 4 = 12$
Multiply the sum by 4.	$12 \times 4 = 48$
Add 4 to the product.	$48 + 4 = 52$
Divide the sum by 4.	$52 \div 4 = 13$
Tell me the answer.	13
Here's the magic: To find your friend's original number, subtract 5 from the answer he or she gives you!	$13 - 5 = 8$

Underlying this magic trick is the simple algebraic equation $[4(x + 4) + 4] \div 4 = x + 5$, where x is the number chosen by a friend or a member of the audience. If you know that an equivalent way of writing this equation is $x + 5$, and you know what your friend's answer is, then you need only solve the simple equation $x + 5 =$ friend's answer. No matter what counting number x your friend chooses, $x =$ (friend's answer to the trick) $- 5$.

Underlying this magic trick is also a lot of mathematical language and the ability to verbally state a complex set of mathematical instructions in the correct order. When children tell these tricks to their friends and family—and they should do so—they must meaningfully use the language in the trick and be able to correctly order the mathematical instructions. Children will need to explore what mathematical terms and concepts mean, practice sequencing a set of mathematical statements, and practice public speaking. They can do this during instruction in class in small groups and whole-class work, and outside the classroom with friends and family.

When children explore why the magic tricks work, they are engaging in mathematical problem solving. When children attempt to explain to you and to each other why the tricks work—and you must ask them to do this, or they will miss much of the value of these exercises—children are engaging in mathematical reasoning and proof. There is no need for children to use algebraic symbols or equations when explaining why and how the magic tricks work (although if adults are comfortable using them in a way that can be understood by young children, they help clarify the tricks' magic). All that children need to do is explain what is going on in the tricks using their own everyday language. Such statements as "You multiply by a number and then divide by it, and the division undoes the multiplication, so you are left where you started" or "The subtraction undoes the addition" suffice. Children also can use manipulatives, such as number rods, to help clarify ideas, as shown here.

VERBALIZATION	NUMBER ROD REPRESENTATION	EQUATION
Write down a counting number—remember, no 0s!	Let [ ] be the number	x
	Let [ ] equal 1	
Add 4 to it.	[ ] □□□□	$x + 4$
Multiply the sum by 4.	[ ] □□□□ [ ] □□□□ [ ] □□□□ [ ] □□□□	$4(x + 4)$
Add 4 to the product.	[ ] □□□□□ [ ] □□□□□ [ ] □□□□□ [ ] □□□□□	$4(x + 4) + 4$
Divide the sum by 4.	[ ] □□□□□	$[4(x + 4) + 4] \div 4$
Tell me the answer.	[ ] □□□□□	$x + 5$
Here's the magic: To find your friend's original number, subtract 5 from the answer he or she gives you!	[ ]	$(x + 5) - 5 = x$

These tricks are not designed simply for an adult to tell to children. You can demonstrate a trick to children as an introduction to it, but the purpose of the exercise is to have children learn to tell the tricks, to explore how they work, and to be able to tell the tricks to others and to explain to others (whether an adult or another child) why the tricks work. Have children practice and explore the tricks in cooperative groups. Once they learn a trick, encourage them to try it on parents, siblings, or friends from other classes—these are the people to trick.

Once children learn how a trick works, encourage them to create their own variations. For example, in Magic Sub 5, if the number 7 were used in all calculations, then the trick would be called Magic Sub 8.

In describing the magic tricks, I have taken the liberty of using the word "number" when the term "counting number" would have been more accurate. Whenever the word "number" is used, it should be understood that the counting numbers are being referred to.

Following are six suggestions for helping children use these magic tricks:

- When magicians do tricks, they talk a lot to distract the audience from a trick's essence. Encourage children to develop the ability to "ham it up" with distracting statements. Learning to talk in front of an audience is important.

- Magicians do not repeat a trick many times on the same person, or else the person will figure it out. Encourage children to develop magic shows—a series of tricks.

- The magic tricks provide children with a lot of arithmetic practice. The difficulty of the arithmetic increases as one proceeds through the tricks.

- Try not to let children "race through" one trick after another. The tricks are to be savored, and discussions need to take place about why each trick works and to clearly explain its mathematics. Introducing one trick every other day is fine. Introducing one trick a week, perhaps on a Friday afternoon, also works well.

- The inability to do a trick's calculations can ruin it. When a child is performing a trick in front of an audience, have the person who chooses a number share it with others so that they can check all calculations.

- If children have difficulty doing the arithmetic, allow them to use a calculator to check their work.

Mystery Monsters

Can you spot the Mystery Monsters? Figure out the characteristics that each monster group shares. Then find more monsters.

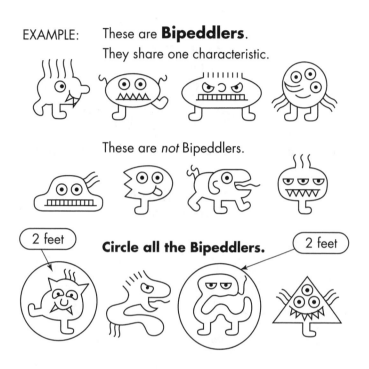

EXAMPLE: These are **Bipeddlers**.
They share one characteristic.

These are *not* Bipeddlers.

2 feet

Circle all the Bipeddlers.

2 feet

These are **Liats**.
They share one characteristic.

These are *not* Liats.

Circle all the Liats.

These are **Biojos**.
They share one characteristic.

These are *not* Biojos.

Circle all the Biojos.

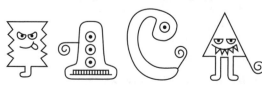

These are **Taileroos**.
They share two characteristics.

These are *not* Taileroos.

Draw a Taileroo. How do you know it's a Taileroo?

These are **Snailies**.
They share two characteristics.

None of these are Snailies.

Draw a Snailie. How do you know it's a Snailie?

These are **Hatterworts**.
They share two characteristics.

None of these are Hatterworts.

Draw a Hatterwork. How do you know it's a Hatterwort?

These are **Rhinobeaks**.
They share three characteristics.

None of these are Rhinobeaks.

Draw a Rhinobeak. How do you know it's a Rhinobeak?

These are **Polypods**.
They share three characteristics.

None of these are Polypods.

Draw a Polypod. How do you know it's a Polypod?

Pockets Full of Pennies

In each of the following puzzles, a child has pennies in one, two, three, or four pockets of his or her clothes. Your task is to guess how many pennies are in each pocket.

Puzzle 1

Four pockets have pennies.
There are a different number of pennies in each pocket.
No pocket has more than 4 pennies.
How many pennies are in each pocket?

Puzzle 2

Four pockets have pennies.
There are a different number of pennies in each pocket.
The sum of all the pennies is less than 11.
How many pennies are in each pocket?

Puzzle 3

Four pockets have pennies.
The sum of the number of pennies in all four pockets is 5.
How many pennies are in each pocket?

Puzzle 4

Two pockets have pennies.
The sum of the number of pennies in the two pockets is 10.
The difference in the number of pennies in the pockets is 0.
How many pennies are in each pocket?

Puzzle 5

Two pockets have pennies.
The right pocket has 2 more pennies than the left pocket.
The right pocket has 2 times as many pennies as the left pocket.
The number of pennies in the left pocket times itself equals the number of pennies in the right pocket.
How many pennies are in each pocket?

Puzzle 6

Three pockets have pennies.

There are a different number of pennies in each pocket.

The difference in the number of pennies in the pocket with the most pennies and the pocket with the fewest pennies is 2.

The sum of the number of pennies in the three pockets is 12.

How many pennies are in each pocket?

Puzzle 7

Four pockets have pennies.

There is the same number of pennies in each pocket.

The sum of the number of pennies in all four pockets is more than 16 and less than 24.

How many pennies are in each pocket?

More Pockets, More Pennies

In each of the following puzzles, a child has pennies in one, two, three, or four pockets of his or her clothes. Your task is to guess how many pennies are in each pocket.

Puzzle 1

Two pockets have pennies.
There are a different number of pennies in each pocket.
The difference in the number of pennies in the pockets is 4.
The sum of the number of pennies in the two pockets is 10.
How many pennies are in each pocket?

Puzzle 2

Three pockets have pennies.
There are a different number of pennies in each pocket.
The difference in the number of pennies in the pockets with the most pennies and the fewest pennies is 2.
The sum of the number of pennies in all three pockets is 15.
How many pennies are in each pocket?

Puzzle 3

Four pockets have pennies.
There are a different number of pennies in each pocket.
The pocket with the most pennies contains fewer then 7 pennies.
The sum of the number of pennies in all four pockets is 18.
How many pennies are in each pocket?

Puzzle 4

One pocket has pennies.
It has more than 5 pennies in it.
The number of pennies in the pocket times itself is less than 50.
There are an odd number of pennies in the pocket.
How many pennies are in each pocket?

Puzzle 5

Two pockets have pennies.

There are a different number of pennies in each pocket.

The number of pennies in each pocket is an even number.

The sum of the number of pennies in both pockets is 14.

The pocket that contains the fewest number of pennies has more than 5 pennies in it.

How many pennies are in each pocket?

Puzzle 6

Four pockets have pennies.

Three pockets have the same number of pennies.

One pocket has 1 more penny than the others.

The sum of the number of pennies in the four pockets is 21.

How many pennies are in each pocket?

Puzzle 7

Four pockets have pennies.

There are a different number of pennies in each pocket.

The number of pennies in one pocket is equal to 24 ÷ 4.

The number of pennies in another pocket is equal to 35 ÷ 5.

The number of pennies in another pocket is equal to 48 ÷ 6.

The sum of the number of pennies in all four pockets is 26.

How many pennies are in each pocket?

Magical Math!

Try these magic tricks on friends. Follow the steps below. Who knows—you may become a great magician. Examples of how to do the magic tricks, using randomly chosen numbers, are provided at the end of each line of instruction in italic type, next to the right margin.

- Practice a trick several times before trying it on someone. This will also help you discover how the trick works.
- An example of the trick appears next to the steps of each trick.
- If you need a calculator or paper and pencil for a trick, have them ready to use.
- Do not do the same trick for someone over and over again—or he or she will figure out how it works.

Two Number Magic

Say this to a friend: Pick two one-digit counting numbers (not 0). DO NOT show them to me. I'll ask you to do some calculations. Then I'll tell you what your numbers are!

1. Write down your two numbers. *3, 2*
2. Multiply the first number by 10. *3 × 10 = 30*
3. Add the second number to the product. *30 + 2 = 32*
4. Tell me the sum. *32*

Here's the magic: Your friend's original two numbers are the digits in the tens and ones places of the sum!

After you figure out how this trick works, can you do the trick with three numbers? Multiply the first number by 100, the second number by 10, and the third number by 1. Then add the three products.

Two-Digit Number Magic

Say this to friend: Pick a two-digit counting number and a one-digit counting number (not 0). DO NOT tell me what they are. I'll ask you to do some calculations. Then I'll tell you what your numbers are!

1. Write down your two numbers. *35, 7*
2. Multiply the two-digit number by 10. *35 × 10 = 350*
3. Add the one-digit number to the product. *350 + 7 = 357*
4. Tell me the sum. *357*

Here's the magic: Your friend's original two-digit number appears in the hundreds and tens places of the sum, and the one-digit number is the number in the ones place of the sum!

Two Number Magic 2

Say this to a friend: Pick two one-digit counting numbers (not 0). DO NOT show them to me. I'll ask you to do some calculations. Then I'll tell you what your numbers are!

1. Write down your two numbers.	*3, 5*
2. Multiply the first number by 5.	*3 × 5 =15*
3. Add 2 to the product.	*15 + 2 = 17*
4. Multiply the sum by 2.	*17 × 2 = 34*
5. Subtract 4 from the product.	*34 − 4 = 30*
6. Add the second number to the difference.	*30 + 5 = 35*
7. Tell me the sum.	*35*

Here's the magic: Your friend's original two numbers appear in the tens and ones places of the sum!

Even I Win, Odd I Win

Say this to a friend: We each secretly write down a counting number (not 0). I'll tell you if the sum of our numbers is even or odd—without looking at your number!

1. Your friend writes down a number.	*12*
2. You always write down any odd number.	*5*

3. Say, "If your number is even and we add our numbers, the sum will be an odd number. If your number is odd, and we add our numbers, the sum will be an even number."

4. Show your numbers to each other and then add them.	*12 + 5 = 17*

Here's the magic: Your friend picked an even number. You picked an odd number. The sum is odd.

The trick is that you must always pick an odd number:

$$\text{even} + \text{odd} = \text{odd, and odd} + \text{odd} = \text{even}$$

Even I Win, Odd You Lose

Magician (that's you): Here's an amazing magic trick. You pick a number. DO NOT tell me what it is. I'll ask you to do some calculations. If the answer is even, I win. If the answer is odd, you lose.

Friend: Hey! That's not fair!

Magician: OK. Even I win. Odd you win.

1. Pick a number.	*21*
2. Add 4 to it.	*21 + 4 = 25*
3. Multiply the sum by 4.	*25 × 4 = 100*
4. Subtract 4 from the product.	*100 − 4 = 96*
5. Divide by 2.	
6. What is the quotient?	*96 ÷ 2 = 48*

Here's the magic: The answer is even; the answer will *always* by even, so you *always* win.

Penny, Nickel, and Dime Magic

1. Hide a penny, nickel, and dime in one of your hands. Don't tell what you have hidden.

2. Find a friend who has a penny and say, "Guess what will happen when you add your penny to my money. Here's what can happen: If you guess even and the total amount is even, you win. If you guess odd and the total amount is odd, you win. Otherwise, I win."

3. Have your friend guess odd or even.

4. If your friend guesses even, here's what you do: Put his or her penny with your penny, nickel, and dime, and add the amount of money. The sum is 17¢, which is an odd number, so you win!

   If your friend guesses odd, put his or her penny with your penny, nickel, and dime, and count the number of coins. You have four coins, which is an even number, so you win! Magic!

5. Give the penny back to your friend.

Penny and Dime Magic

Say to a friend: If you hide a penny in one hand and a dime in the other hand, I can tell you where each coin is hidden.

1. Hide a penny in one hand and a dime in the other hand —without letting me see in which hands the coins are hidden.

   left hand = penny
   right hand = dime

2. Multiply the value of the coin in the left hand by 2, 4, 6, or 8.   *1¢ × 6 = 6¢*

3. Multiply the value of the coin in the right hand by 1, 3, 5, 7, or 9.   *10¢ × 3 = 30¢*

4. Add the two products together and tell me the sum.   *6¢ + 30¢ = 36¢*

5. The penny is in your left hand.

Here's the magic: If the sum is odd, the penny is in the right hand. If the sum is even, the penny is in the left hand. The dime is in the other hand.

More Magical Math!

Amaze your friends with these magic tricks. Examples of how to do the magic tricks, using randomly chosen numbers, are provided at the end of each line of instruction in italic type, next to the right margin.

- Practice, practice, practice! This will help you discover how the tricks work.
- An example of the trick appears next to each trick.
- If a calculator or paper and pencil are needed, have these things ready to use.
- Do not do the same trick for someone over and over again—or he or she'll will figure out how it works.
- Try these things to discover how the tricks work: Use different numbers each time you do the trick; explain to a friend why you think the trick works.

Descend and Reverse

Write the number 198 on a piece of paper. Hide it in your pocket.

Say this to a friend: Pick a three-digit number. DO NOT tell me what it is. I'll ask you to do some calculations. Then I'll tell you the number.

1. Write down a three-digit number that has no 0s. Its digits should decrease by 1 from left to right. *543*
2. Reverse the order of the digits, and write down the new number below the original number. *345*
3. Subtract the smaller number from the larger number. *543 − 345 = 198*

   Slap your pocket two times. Pull out the piece of paper with the answer 198 on it. Amazing!

You can do the same trick with a four-digit number. The answer will always be 3087.

Double Reverse

Say this to a friend: Pick a three-digit number. DO NOT tell what it is. I'll ask you to do some calculations. Then I'll tell you the number.

1. Write down any three-digit number that doesn't contain any 0s. *527*
2. Reverse the order of the digits and write down the new number. *725*
3. Subtract the smaller number from the larger number. *725 − 527 = 198*
4. Reverse the order of the digits in the difference. Write that new number below the answer to the previous subtraction problem. *891*
5. Add the numbers. *198 + 891 = 1089*

Here's the magic: Without seeing any of the calculations, you know that the sum is 1089! Use magic to check the subtraction: Have your friend add the first and last digits of the difference in step 3. They will equal the middle digit. Magic! In this example, 1 + 8 = 9.

Magic Sub 5
Say this to a friend: If you think of a number that is not 0, I can guess it. Try it!

1. Secretly write down a number—remember, no 0s!	8
2. Add 4 to it.	8 + 4 = 12
3. Multiply the sum by 4.	12 × 4 = 48
4. Add 4 to the product.	48 + 4 = 52
5. Divide the sum by 4.	52 ÷ 4 = 13
6. Tell me the answer.	13

Here's the magic: To find your friend's original number, subtract 5 from the answer he or she gives you!

A Fantastic Two-Person Trick
You will need two people to do this trick. Tell them that if they do some math together without telling you what they are doing, you can tell them the result of their efforts.

1. Write the number 12 on a piece of paper. Put it in your pocket.
2. Have Person A pick a number between 10 and 20 and record it.
   Person A picks 15
3. Have Person B double Person A's number and record it.
   Person B: 15 + 15 = 30
4. Have Person A subtract 4 from his or her number. Have Person B add 4 to his or her number.   *Person A: 15 − 4 = 11*
   Person B: 30 + 4 = 34
5. Have Person A multiply the difference obtained in the last calculation by 2. Then have Person A add this product to his or her difference from the calculation obtained in step 4. Now have Person B subtract the product Person A just obtained from the sum he or she calculated in step 4.
   Person A: 11 × 2 = 22; 11 + 22 = 33
   Person B: 34 − 22 = 12

Here's the magic: Slap your pocket two times. Remove the piece of paper with the number 12—Person B's final number!

This Trick Is About 1

Say this to a friend: Think of a number and then follow my instructions, and I will show you something magic.

1. Secretly write down a counting number.	5
2. Add 2 to the number.	5 + 2 = 7
3. Multiply the sum by 2.	7 × 2 = 14
4. Add 2 to the product.	14 + 2 = 16
5. Multiply the sum by 2.	16 × 2 = 32
6. Divide the product by 2.	32 ÷ 2 = 16
7. Subtract 2 from the quotient.	16 − 2 = 14
8. Divide the difference by 2.	14 ÷ 2 = 7
9. Subtract your original number.	7 − 5 = 2
10. Divide the difference by 2.	2 ÷ 2 = 1

Here's the magic: This trick is about the number 1. The answer is *always* 1! Can you change the trick so that a friend adds, subtracts, multiplies, and divides by a number other than 2—and still ends up with an answer of 1?

More Two Number Magic

Challenge a friend to do the following:

1. Secretly write down two one-digit numbers (not 0).	2, 8
2. Add 2 to the first number.	2 + 2 = 4
3. Multiply the sum by 5.	4 × 5 = 20
4. Add 2 to the product.	20 + 2 = 22
5. Multiply the sum by 2.	22 × 2 = 44
6. Subtract 4 from the product.	44 − 4 = 40
7. Add the second number to the result.	40 + 8 = 48
8. Subtract 20 from the sum.	48 − 20 = 28
9. Ask your friend to tell you the result.	28

Here's the magic: Your friend's original numbers are the digits in the tens and the ones places of the final difference! Hmm—where have you seen this magic trick before?

Speed-Add with Two Friends

Find two friends who will to try to add faster than you.

1. Have the first friend write down a counting number (not 0).   *2*

2. Ask the second friend to write down a larger counting number under the first number.   *3*

3. Tell the first friend to add the two numbers and write the sum underneath the second number.   *2 + 3 = 5*

4. Instruct your friends to take turns adding the last two numbers in the list and writing the sum at the bottom of the list. They repeat this until there are a total of ten numbers in the list.   *2, 3, 5, 8, 13, 21, 34, 55, 89, 144*

5. Have your friends show the list to you. Challenge them to add the column of numbers faster than you. They can even use a calculator.   *374*

Here's the magic: The sum is 11 times the seventh number on the list! (In this example, 34 × 11 = 374)

Chapter Ten

Geometry Puzzles

Geometry is one of the major areas of the school mathematics curriculum and one of the content standards of the National Council of Teachers of Mathematics. This chapter presents three different types of puzzles involving geometry. Visual Estimation puzzles use the medium of visual illusions to raise issues about how we can use the tools of mathematics, such as calipers and straightedges, to verify what we think is true on first sight. Line Designs and Shape Designs introduce children to the field of analytic geometry. Analytic geometry is that part of mathematics where algebra (and its subfield of arithmetic) intersects with geometry, allowing us to provide a visual picture of an algebraic equation or table of numerical data. Triangle Trouble and the Magic Tile use the medium of the tangram to present puzzles that help develop part-to-whole skills and spatial relations skills. Both are foundational to doing mathematics, whether it is geometry or arithmetic.

Visual Estimation

This set of puzzles presents a number of visual illusions and asks children questions about them. It is about things that we perceive through our eyesight that do not correspond to what is reality in our world. Visual illusions have existed for thousands of years, yet they still baffle and delight us. The purpose of these puzzles is not to offer or ask children for technical explanations of visual illusions, but to inquire into how mathematics can help distinguish illusion from reality.

The puzzles in this set are called Visual Estimation because the intent is to have children first examine each illusion and make an estimation about "what appears to be" and then use mathematics to determine "what really is." To decide "what really is," children choose math tools that might be helpful in determining the nature of reality. Children should use tools other than just rulers to check hypotheses. They can create a simple caliper by making two marks on the side of a piece of paper for one length and then moving the paper to check that length elsewhere. A straight edge exists on the edge of every sheet of paper.

The puzzles have six parts. The first part involves looking at a visual illusion and trying to make a decision about it. We call this estimating. The second part involves having children choose a tool of geometry, such as a caliper or straightedge, that might help them verify if their estimate was or was not accurate, and actually using that tool to verify the estimate. The third part involves mathematical communication: discussing what was discovered with a classmate or friend. The topic is not just about what the child measured, but also about why things look as they do. The fifth part of each puzzle involves speculating about why things look different from what one would expect. This involves the endeavors of mathematical problem solving and mathematical reasoning and proof.

Finally, there is a saying on each page. For example, one puzzle contains this saying: "Not everything is as it seems." Children should reflect on, discuss, and attempt to explain the saying for each puzzle. Explanations can reference many things in children's lives. These saying are designed to prompt children to engage in mathematical communication, to discuss mathematical connections that relate measurement to their everyday life, and to participate in some of the types of philosophical discussions in which mathematicians engage.

Line Designs and Shape Designs

Line Designs and Shape Designs combine algebra and geometry. Each design consists of an equivalent numerical table, equation, and geometrical construction. Understanding the equivalence that can exist among these different representations of a function is at the heart of analytic geometry—which, as I mentioned earlier, is that area of mathematics where algebra and geometry intersect.

While students are working on designs, ask them to explain how the equation, table, and geometric construction relate to each other. After the fourth problem in Line Designs, students must start to see the relationships in order to complete the designs. A class discussion that allows children to verbalize the relationships among the equation, table, and geometric construction can be very helpful, for it allows children to present their verbalizations (and thus bring ideas that are sometimes held at the intuitive level to a more objective verbal level), hear other children's explanations (and perhaps learn from those explanations), and compare their ideas to those of their peers (and in the process perhaps correct any misconceptions that they might have).

The question asked by the last problem in Line Designs is crucial: Why do straight lines make curves? There is no one correct answer, but children should be able to describe how an "offset saddle" creates the illusion of a curve. This way of making curves underlies much architecture, as can be seen in many buildings with curved arches or roofs. Children can be asked to look for curves in their daily lives and report back to the class on their findings.

Use Line Designs before Shape Designs. Their equations are simpler. After children have created designs, you can ask them to complete a map-coloring problem: color the spaces between the lines with two different colored pencils in such a way that no two spaces sharing an edge are the same color. (Yes, there is an area of mathematics concerned with the coloring of designs such as these. In case children ask, it is possible to color all of the designs in this set of puzzles in the way specified with two different colored pencils. However, it is not possible for all designs.) The curves created by most of the designs are called parabolas. The curve in the second Shape Design is called a cardioid.

Three reproducible design frames are included following the puzzles; you can duplicate these for children so that they can experiment with creating their own designs. A good deal of problem solving is involved in creating an original design. Many exist that are not presented here.

Using line designs in education is not new. Edith Somervell wrote *A Rhythmic Approach to Mathematics* about line designs and curve stitching in 1906. Teacher trainees at the beginning of this century were required to create line designs with needle and thread by sewing them on cardboard as part of their teacher training programs. They often made books that displayed their creations.

Displaying student work is important. Display on bulletin boards children's line and shape designs to illustrate and highlight the effects of neatness, accuracy, imagination, and understanding of geometry, particularly when children create their own designs.

You can find many articles on line design on the Internet. Search on the words *line design* or *curve stitching*.

Triangle Trouble and the Magic Tile

Triangle Trouble and the Magic Tile are both based on the tangram puzzle. Triangle Trouble uses five of the seven traditional tangram pieces, and each puzzle includes the two small triangles. Children should be encouraged to think about why these triangles, with the addition of one of the other pieces, can be used to form so many different shapes. The Magic Tile uses all seven pieces of the traditional tangram. Templates for Triangle Trouble and the Magic Tile accompany the puzzles. You can photocopy them onto heavy paper or card stock. The template for Triangle Trouble matches the size of the puzzles so that children can manipulate the pieces and record answers on each page. The Magic Tile puzzles use the traditional seven-piece tangram to make animal shapes. Children can use the reproducible tangram template that accompanies the Magic Tile, a standard classroom tangram, or any other tangram to assemble puzzles adjacent to the shapes. Children should also be encouraged to create and share their own animal puzzles. Many more shapes that can be made from tangrams are available on the Internet; search on the word *tangram*.

Tangrams are said to have originated in China. The following fictional story is a variation on the original legend. Tell it to children just before they begin Triangle Trouble.

The Tangram Story

Many years ago, the emperor of China hired a Chinese potter named Tan to make a special tile to replace a broken one in a corner of a very old tile table. It took Tan many weeks to make the tile, using lengthy secret processes, and clay found only in a remote part of China.

While delivering his tile to the emperor, Tan tripped over a rock and dropped his triangular tile. It broke into five pieces. Tan sat down and wept. It would be weeks before he could make another. He tried to put the tile back together, and as he did, he noticed that it had broken into two small triangles, one medium-size triangle, one square, and one parallelogram. As he tried to reconstruct his original triangle, he discovered he could make many different shapes. But he did not have the single triangular tile that the emperor requested that he make.

Tan stared up at the sky with a look of desperation on his face. A magic dragon flew down to Tan and, to his amazement, began to speak. He told Tan not to be upset, for the emperor of China loved puzzles, and he would be thrilled to have a puzzle tile that he could take out of his table and use to make pictures. Before Tan could thank the dragon, it disappeared. Tan joyfully continued on to the palace.

As the dragon predicted, the emperor of China was delighted with his puzzle. He was so pleased that he paid Tan twice the amount that he was supposed to for the tile and asked Tan to make him another tile puzzle with more pieces. The puzzle Tan created is called the tangram.

The mathematics involved in Triangle Trouble and the Magic Tile go beyond just learning the names of different geometric shapes and how certain geometrical shapes can be assembled to make other shapes.

These puzzles can help children develop their ability to work at the intuitive level in the branch of geometry that is called transformational geometry, which is presented in the next chapter. Transformational geometry involves the ability to move objects about in space by using the mathematical operations of translations (slides), rotations (turns), and reflections (flips). Using transformational geometry at the intuitive level involves being able to see how to slide a tangram piece into location, rotate and then slide a piece into location, or flip a piece over and then slide it into location to produce various effects.

The puzzles used in Triangle Trouble and the Magic Tile also help children develop part-to-whole skills and spatial relations skills. Both are critical to the development of children's mathematical abilities. Watching children work on tangram puzzles can help adults determine whether a child has well- or poorly developed skills, which can lead to a child's receiving remedial help if needed.

Part-to-Whole Skills

Part-to-whole skills are those skills that allow a person to see how the parts of an interconnected set of geometric shapes relate to the whole set and how the whole relates to its parts. Without well developed part-to-whole skills, children have difficulty seeing how two separate shapes might be put together to make another shape—how, for example, two triangles might be put together to make a rectangle, or how seven tangram pieces might be assembled to make a fish. The ability to construct tangram objects involves the ability to see how individual shapes might relate to an overall geometric construction. These are the same skills that are needed to be able to meaningfully add numbers (to see how two parts can be joined to make a whole) or subtract numbers (to understand how a whole can be broken into separate subsets).

Spatial Relations Skills

Spatial relations skills are those skills that allow one to see the locations of objects in space and the relationships among objects in space. They are the skills that allow a child to see how to rotate, slide, or flip a triangle to fit into a missing position in a tangram construction—for example, that a right triangle might need to be rotated 180 degrees so that its right angle moves from pointing to the left to pointing to the right, or to flip a parallelogram so that its acute angle moves from lower right to upper right. These are the same skills that are needed when solving a multidigit multiplication or division problem, in which a series of numbers must be properly lined up with respect to each other in order to get a correct answer (which is why we sometime have children do their work on graph paper, to enable them to line up numbers correctly).

Visual Estimation

Visual Estimation Puzzle 1

Which is the lowest step?   **Estimate.**

Can math tools help you find out? **Try it.**

Share your answers with a friend. **Discuss it.**

And always wonder . . .   **Why?**

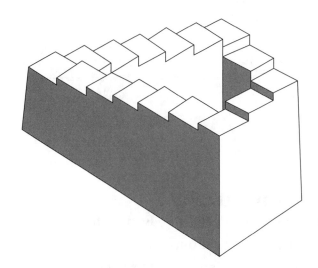

Visual Estimation Puzzle 2

Are the smiles the same length?   **Estimate.**

Which math tools help you find out?   **Try it.**

Share your answers with a friend.   **Discuss it.**

And always wonder . . .   **Why?**

Not everything is as it seems.

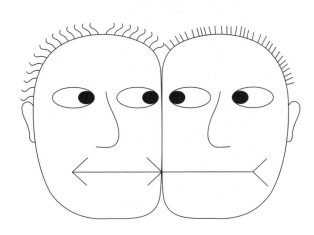

Visual Estimation Puzzle 3

Which box top is the largest?   **Estimate.**

Which math tools help you find out?   **Try it.**

Share your answers with a friend.   **Discuss it.**

And always wonder . . .   **Why?**

Seeing is believing—or is it?

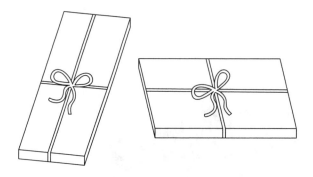

Visual Estimation Puzzle 4

Are the sides of the square straight?   **Estimate.**

Which math tools help you find out?   **Try it.**

Share your answers with a friend.   **Discuss it.**

And always wonder . . .   **Why?**

**The setting in which things are observed
influences how you see them.**

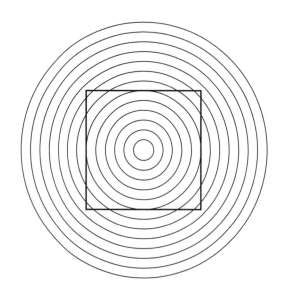

Visual Estimation Puzzle 5

Is line AB longer than line BC? | Estimate.
Which math tools can help you find out? | Try it.
Share your answers with a friend. | Discuss it.
And always wonder . . . | Why?

Measure before you leap.

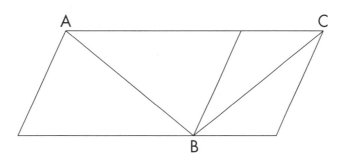

Visual Estimation Puzzle 6

Will line A or line B extend to line C? | Estimate.
Which math tools can help you find out? | Try it.
Share your answers with a friend. | Discuss it.
And always wonder . . . | Why?

Not everything in mathematics is obvious.

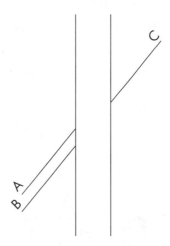

Visual Estimation Puzzle 7

Which arc comes from the largest circle?   **Estimate.**

Which math tools help you Find out?   **Try it.**

Share your answers with a friend.   **Discuss it.**

And always wonder . . .   **Why?**

Let not your eyes be the only window to your world.

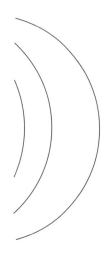

Visual Estimation Puzzle 8

Are the men different sizes?   **Estimate.**

Which math tools help you find out?   **Try it.**

Share your answers with a friend.   **Discuss it.**

And always wonder . . .   **Why?**

I see and I believe; I measure and I know.

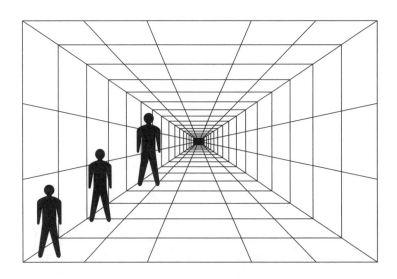

Line Designs: From Straight to Curved

Use a straightedge to draw a line segment that connects numbers on the △ side of the angle with numbers on the □ side of the angle. The point connection table and equation tell how to connect the points. (This one is done for you.)

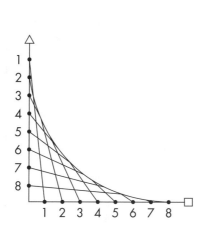

□	△
1	1
2	2
3	3
4	4
5	5
6	6
7	7
8	8
□ = △	

Line Designs Puzzle 1

Use a straightedge. Draw line segments that connect the numbers on the △ side of the angle with the numbers on the □ side of the angle. The point connection table and equation tell how to connect the points. The first line is drawn for you.

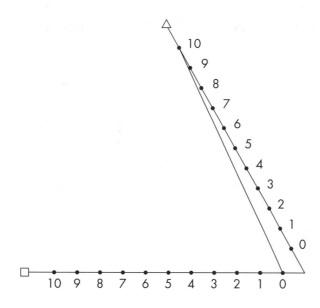

□	△
0	10
1	9
2	8
3	7
4	6
5	5
6	4
7	3
8	2
9	1
10	0
□ + △ = 10	

Line Designs Puzzle 2

Use a straightedge. Draw line segments that connect the numbers on the △ side of the angle with the numbers on the □ side of the angle. The point connection table and equation tell how to connect the points.

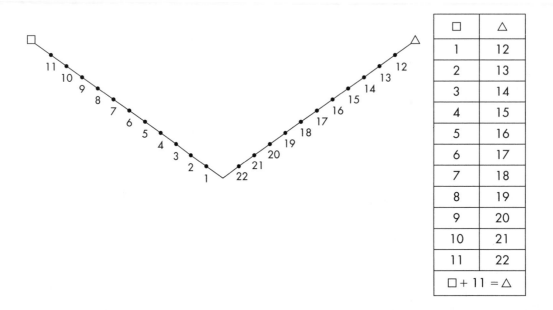

□	△
1	12
2	13
3	14
4	15
5	16
6	17
7	18
8	19
9	20
10	21
11	22
□ + 11 = △	

Line Designs Puzzle 3

Use a straightedge to draw line segments that connect the numbers on the △ side of the angle with the numbers on the □ side of the angle. The point connection table and equation tell how to connect the points.

Color in spaces between the lines to make an interesting design.

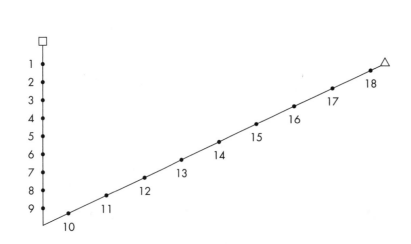

□	△
1	10
2	11
3	12
4	13
5	14
6	15
7	16
8	17
9	18
□ + 9 = △	

Line Designs Puzzle 4

Fill in the missing numbers in the table. Connect numbers on the □ line to numbers on the △ line. The table and equation tell how to connect points.

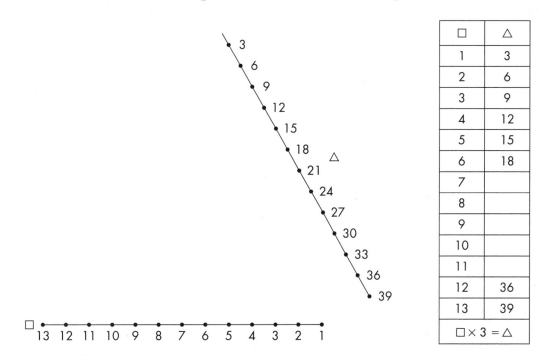

□	△
1	3
2	6
3	9
4	12
5	15
6	18
7	
8	
9	
10	
11	
12	36
13	39
□ × 3 = △	

Line Designs Puzzle 5

Calculate to find the missing numbers in the table. Complete the table on a separate piece of paper. Connect points on the zigzag line. *Hint: Each number in the middle line will be connected to two other numbers.*

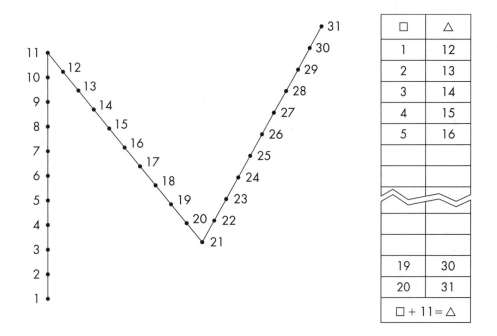

□	△
1	12
2	13
3	14
4	15
5	16
19	30
20	31
□ + 11 = △	

Geometry Puzzles

223

Line Designs Puzzle 6

Calculate to find the missing numbers in the table. Complete the table on a separate piece of paper. Use a straightedge to connect numbers around the perimeter of the triangle. The table and equation tell how to connect the points.

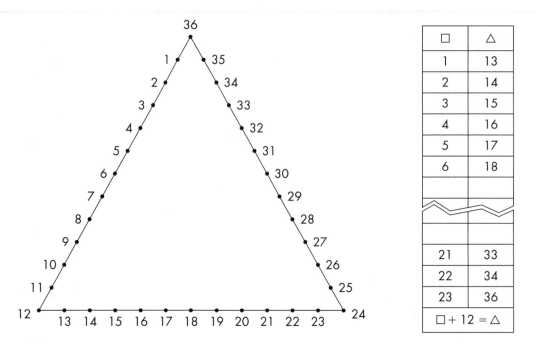

□	△
1	13
2	14
3	15
4	16
5	17
6	18
21	33
22	34
23	36
□ + 12 = △	

Line Designs Puzzle 7

On each of the pairs of lines below, connect

1 to 1, 2 to 2, 3 to 3, 4 to 4, 5 to 5, 6 to 6, 7 to 7, 8 to 8, and 9 to 9 (□ = △).
Why do straight lines make curves?

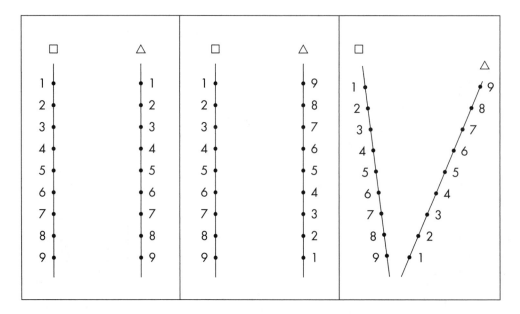

Shape Designs: From Straight to Curved

Use a straightedge to draw a line segment that connects numbers on the angle's □ side with numbers on the angle's △ side. The point connection table and equation tell how to connect the points. (This one is done for you.)

How do you stay in shape? By exercising your mind!

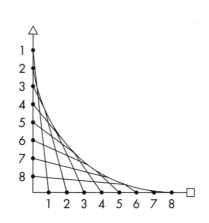

□	△
1	1
2	2
3	3
4	4
5	5
6	6
7	7
8	8
□ = △	

Shape Designs Puzzle 1

Draw line segments that connect □ numbers with △ numbers around the circle. The table and equation tell how to connect the points. On a separate sheet of paper, calculate the numbers missing from the table. Add additional numbers around the circle as you need them.

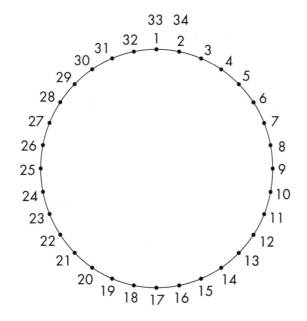

□	△
1	7
2	8
3	9
4	10
5	11
6	12
〜	〜
30	36
31	37
32	38
□ + 6 = △	

Shape Designs Puzzle 2

Draw line segments that connect □ numbers with △ numbers around the circle. The table and equation tell how to connect the points. On a separate sheet of paper, calculate the numbers missing from the table. Add additional numbers around the circle as you need them.

Now invent your own design using the circle design template.

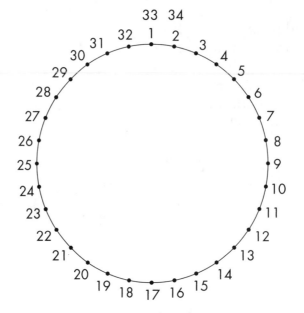

□	△
1	2
2	4
3	6
4	8
5	10
6	12
~	~
29	58
30	60
31	62
$2 \times \square = \triangle$	

Shape Designs Puzzle 3

Connect the points in each small square according to the equation and the numbers in the table.

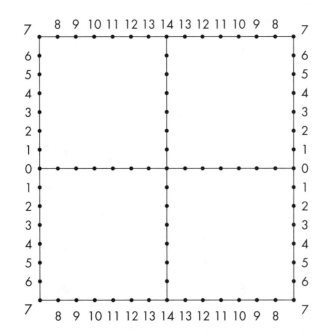

□	△
0	8
1	9
2	10
3	11
4	12
5	13
6	14
$\square + 8 = \triangle$	

Shape Designs Puzzle 4

Look at the pattern in the upper right quadrant of the square.

Continue the same pattern in the other three quadrants of the square.

Color in the spaces between the lines to make an interesting design. Then invent your own design using the square design template.

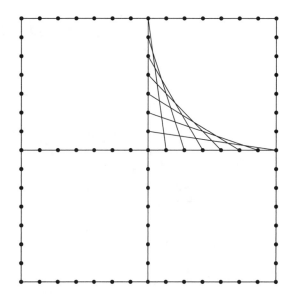

Shape Designs Puzzle 5

Draw line segments that connect □ numbers with △ numbers in each inscribed triangle in the hexagon. The table and equation tell how to connect the points.

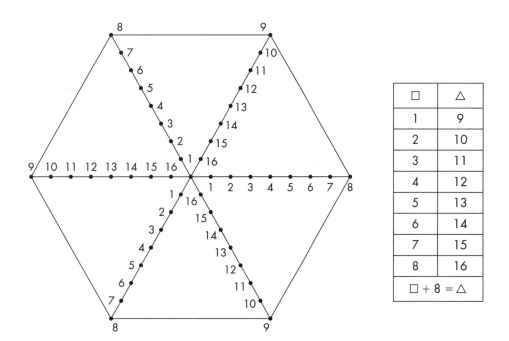

□	△
1	9
2	10
3	11
4	12
5	13
6	14
7	15
8	16
□ + 8 = △	

Now invent your own design using the hexagon design template. Color in the spaces between the lines to make an interesting design.

Circle Design Template

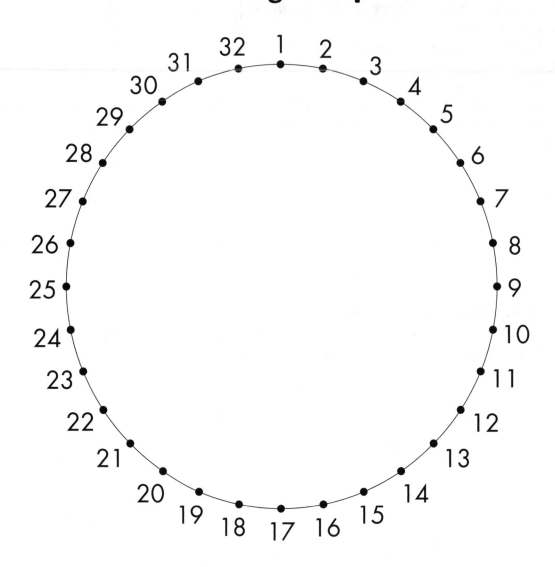

Problem-Solving Mathematics Puzzles

Square Design Template

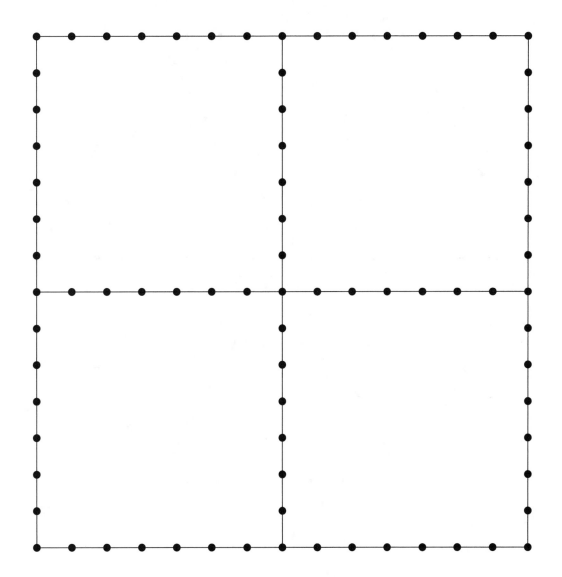

Hexagon Design Template

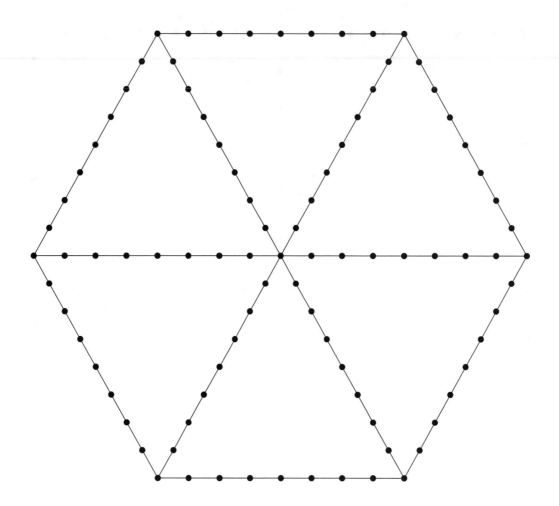

Problem-Solving Mathematics Puzzles

Triangle Trouble!

Tan accidentally dropped his triangle-shaped tile. It broke into five pieces: two small triangles, one medium-size triangle, one square, and one parallelogram. This is how he put the triangle back together.

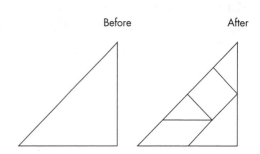

Before   After

Tan discovered that he could put the pieces together to make different shapes. These puzzles show some of the shapes Tan made. A Triangle Trouble Template that you can copy and then cut out to use in solving these puzzles exists at the end of this set of puzzles. Cut out your pieces and use them to solve these puzzles. Use the shaded pieces shown in the diagram at the top of each puzzle. You can put the pieces on each puzzle to solve it.

Triangle Trouble Puzzle 1

Make a square. Use only the two shaded pieces shown in the diagram to the right. Draw lines to show your solution. (This one is done for you.)

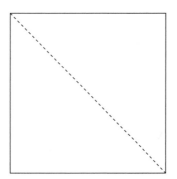

Triangle Trouble Puzzle 2

Make a parallelogram out of the two shaded pieces shown to the right. Draw lines to show your solution.

Now make a triangle out of the same two pieces. Draw lines to show your solution.

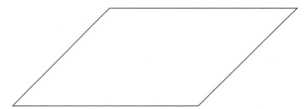

Triangle Trouble Puzzle 3

Make the large triangle using the shaded pieces shown to the right. Draw lines to show your solution.

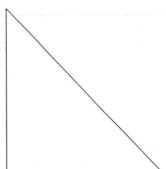

Triangle Trouble Puzzle 4

Make the large triangle using the shaded pieces shown to the right. Draw lines to show your solution.

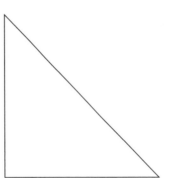

Triangle Trouble Puzzle 5

Use the three shaded pieces shown to the right to make this rectangle. Draw lines to show your solution.

Triangle Trouble Puzzle 6

Use the three shaded pieces shown to the right to make this rectangle. Draw lines to show your solution.

Triangle Trouble Template

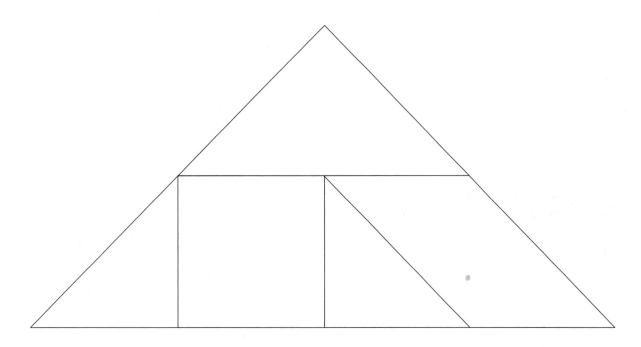

The Magic Tile

This is a tangram. What's magic about its pieces? Do these puzzles and find out. A Magic Tile Tangram Template that you can copy and then cut out to use in solving these puzzles exists at the end of this set of puzzles. Cut out the pieces and use them to solve these puzzles.

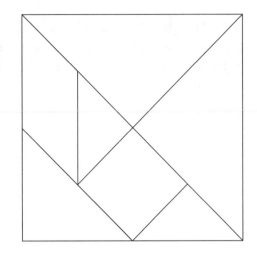

Magic Tile Puzzle 1

Use your tangram pieces to make the owl. Draw lines to show your solution.

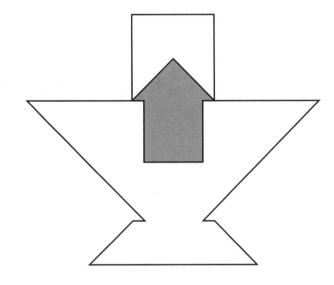

Magic Tile Puzzle 2

Use your tangram pieces to make the lion. Draw lines to show your solution.

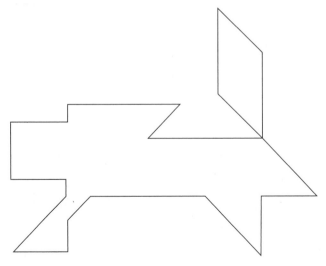

Magic Tile Puzzle 3

Use your tangram pieces to make the bear. Draw lines to show your solution.

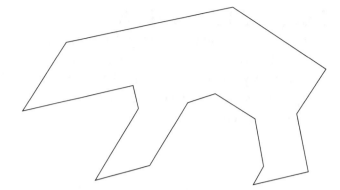

Magic Tile Puzzle 4

Construct the rabbit with your tangram pieces. Draw lines to show your solution.

Create your own creature. Outline the shape on a piece of paper. Give it to a friend to solve.

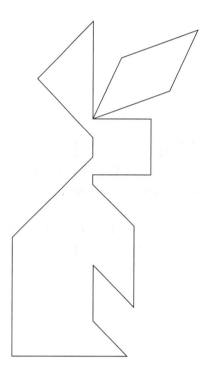

Magic Tile Puzzle 5

Construct the fox using your tangram pieces. Draw lines to show your solution.

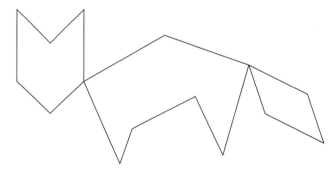

Magic Tile Puzzle 6

Construct the swan using your tangram pieces. Draw lines to show your solution.

Create your own swan. Outline the shape on a piece of paper. Give it to a friend to solve.

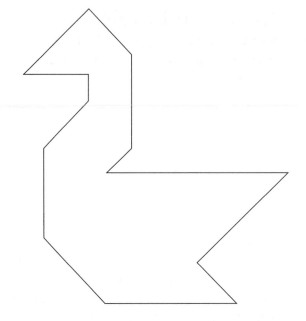

Magic Tile Puzzle 7

Construct the skunk using your tangram pieces. Draw lines to show your solution.

Create your own creature. Outline the shape on a piece of paper. Give it to a friend to solve.

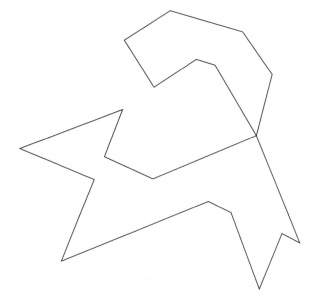

Magic Tile Tangram Template

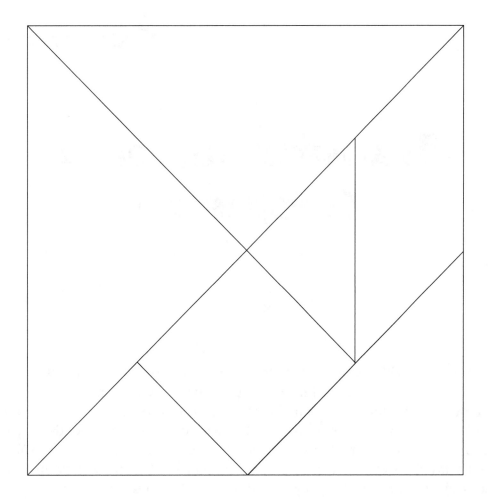

Chapter Eleven

Transformational Geometry

Geometry is a subject that has interested people for thousands of years. The ancient Egyptians calculated the circumference of the Earth to within a few hundred miles. The ancient Chinese and Indians had extremely accurate calculations for the value of pi. And the ancient Greeks founded what we now know as Euclidean geometry. Today people are still interested in geometry, as mathematicians study such topics as fractals. And children experience geometry all around them as they encounter the shapes of objects in their everyday world and as they navigate through the spaces in which they travel.

There are many different branches of geometry. We often teach measurement in elementary and middle school. Another branch of geometry is concerned with the attributes of geometric figures (such as their shapes) and the comparison of those attributes. And one branch of geometry is concerned with how the orientation and location of objects in space relate to those of other objects. This type of geometry is called transformational geometry, which is the topic of the puzzles in this chapter.

For our purposes, there are three mathematical operations that help us answer the question, "How can the location and orientation of one object be compared to those of another by moving the first object so that it achieves the same location and orientation as that of the second object?" The three operations are called translations, rotations, and reflections. In the informal language of children, they are called slides, turns, and flips.

Translations involve sliding objects through space without changing their orientation. Rotations involve turning objects without otherwise changing their location.

238

Reflections involve flipping objects over without changing their location—as you might do with a mirror when studying reflective symmetry.

Crayon Digits and Crayon Constructions present puzzles that use translations and rotations, but not reflections. Coin Challenges involve translations, but neither rotations nor reflections. Mirror Puzzlers involve reflections, but neither translations nor rotations. All these types of puzzles involve mathematical problem solving (to figure out their answers), mathematical reasoning and proof (to explain how the answers were achieved and why they satisfy the requirements of the puzzle), and mathematical representation (to draw or otherwise describe how to transform one geometrical situation into another with a series of slides, turns, and flips). When children share their answers and thinking processes, they engage in mathematical communication. And as they relate the crayon, coin, and mirror puzzles to objects in their lives and to the way in which they move their bodies through space, children will see connections between mathematical processes and daily real-world experiences.

Crayon Digits and Crayon Constructions

These puzzles use a familiar material, crayons, in an unfamiliar way. The puzzles may also be constructed of other materials, such as toothpicks with blunt tips, coffee stirrers that have been cut in half, or straws that have been cut in small pieces of equal length.

Central to the puzzles in Crayon Digits and Crayon Constructions are issues of how to change one configuration of crayons into another by sliding one or more crayons from one position to another, rotating a crayon around itself, or doing some combination of turns and rotations. Children do not need to use the formal symbolism and language of transformational geometry to describe what they are doing, but as they complete the puzzles, do have them draw their solutions. This is a critical part of the activity, for by inventing a notation to explain what they have done, children develop intuitive primitive concepts related to translations and rotations. Children should also share their drawings and explanations with their classmates. As they progress through the puzzles, their explanations and diagrams will become increasingly sophisticated.

In addition to introducing transformational geometry, these puzzles require the use of arithmetic concepts and skills. Crayon Digits uses numbers that have been constructed in the same style as the digits on digital clocks, microwaves, and calculators. The structure of these numerals allows them to be turned into other numbers by making minor changes. The first five puzzles help children understand how the numerals are constructed. Then children apply this knowledge as they think about different ways of making number sentences true. They also become involved in analyzing number relationships and operations using whole numbers.

As children complete the crayon puzzles, they should be encouraged to create their own number sentence puzzles and crayon constructions to share with friends and family.

Coin Challenges

Coin Challenges use coins or other round objects, such as buttons, bottle tops, or bingo chips. Many of the problems can be worked on the puzzle pages; others require more space. Critical to all the puzzles is that children draw or otherwise describe how they solved them. Much of the mathematical benefit of these puzzles relates to developing notation and language that describe how one initial state is transformed into another ending state as a result of using a series of translations. In addition, the mathematical process skills of reasoning and proof, communication, and representation are all linked to having children record and explain how they achieved their solutions to the puzzles.

Mirror Puzzlers

Mirror Puzzlers involve the use of reflections (flips). When acquiring mirrors to use with this activity, try to get inexpensive rectangular plastic or metal mirrors. Avoid glass mirrors (which can break) or mirrors with a frame around them (the frame interferes with the images that can be created). The page that introduces Mirror Puzzlers should be cut in half so that the Pencil Match Card is separate from the instructions.

As children work on the Mirror Puzzlers, introduce them to the concept of a line of symmetry. Children's attempting to determine where a line of symmetry might be placed on a puzzle in order to create a particular image, before ever actually placing a mirror on that line to try to create an image, is an important step to helping them understand reflective symmetry.

Always ask children to guess whether or not they can make a particular image. If they think that they can, they should explain where they would place the mirror (where the line of symmetry is) before using a mirror to find out for sure. If they think it is impossible to create the image, ask them to answer the question "Why not?" Making hypotheses, justifying those hypotheses with the use of mathematical reasoning (and a first intuitive attempt at mathematical proof), and then testing to see if the hypotheses are correct or incorrect, introduce children to an important kind of mathematical and scientific thinking about our world.

Let children make their own sets of Mirror Puzzlers. Take any simple picture from a book or a piece of clip art from the Web, give a student a mirror, and see what the student can create. Make multiple copies of the picture or clip art on a copying machine; give children scissors, paper, and glue sticks; and have them make possible and impossible mirror puzzles for others to solve. It is possible to get some very interesting results using two mirrors that are hinged at their edges with a piece of tape.

Many interesting activities are available that can expand the encounters children have with reflective symmetry. Young children can readily work on reflective symmetry using pattern blocks. Jill Britton's Web site (http://britton.disted.camosun.bc.ca/jbsymteslk.htm) offers many activities that expand the ideas on reflective symmetry. You can also search the Web for sites that offer activities that expand on these mirror puzzles and others presented in this chapter.

Crayon Digits

Digital numerals can be found on calculators, watches, clocks, and microwaves. In these puzzles, the digital numerals will look like this:

Use crayons to make the digital numerals in these puzzles.

Add one crayon to change the 4 into a 9. (This one is done for you.)

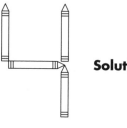

Solution: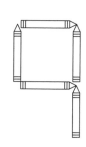

Crayon Digits Puzzle 1

Use crayons to make a 9. Now move one crayon to change the 9 to a 5.

Draw your solution.

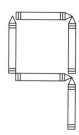

Crayon Digits Puzzle 2

Use crayons to make a 5. Then move one crayon to turn the 5 into a 3.

Draw your solution.

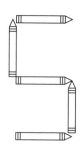

Crayon Digits Puzzle 3

Use crayons to make a 3. Move one crayon
to turn the 3 into a 2.
  Draw your solution.

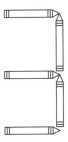

Crayon Digits Puzzle 4

Use crayons to make a 5. Move one crayon
to turn the 5 into a 6.
  Draw your solution.

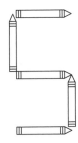

Crayon Digits Puzzle 5

The number sentence below is false. Move one crayon to make it true.

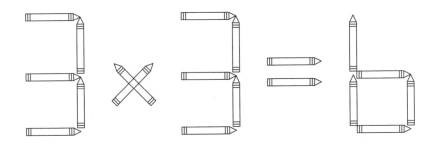

Draw your solution.

Crayon Digits Puzzle 6

The number sentence below is false. Move one crayon to make it true.

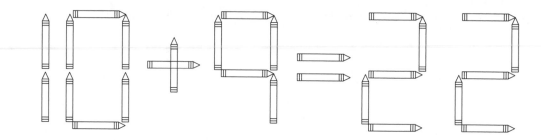

Draw your solution.

Crayon Digits Puzzle 7

The number sentence below is false. Move one crayon to make true.

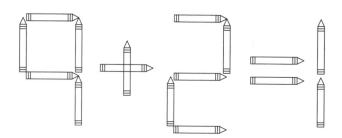

Draw your solution.

Crayon Constructions

In each of these puzzles you will rearrange, add, or remove crayons to make new shapes. You can also use toothpicks, straws, or coffee stirrers. There may be more than one way to solve a puzzle.

Remove two crayons and leave exactly three squares. (This one is done for you.)

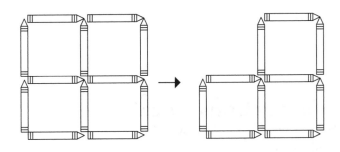

Crayon Constructions Puzzle 1

Use crayons to make this house. Make two houses by moving one crayon.

Draw your solution.

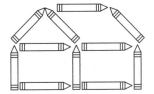

Crayon Constructions Puzzle 2

Make this crayon creature. Move one crayon to turn the creature around.

Draw your solution.

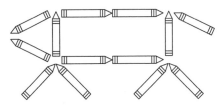

Crayon Constructions Puzzle 3

Change these two rectangles into two squares. Move only two crayons.

   Draw your solution.

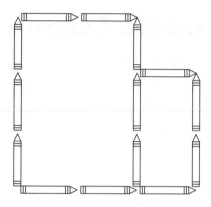

Crayon Constructions Puzzle 4

Create this goblet. Turn it upside down by moving only two crayons.

   Draw your solution.

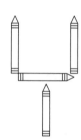

Crayon Constructions Puzzle 5

Make this fish swim in the opposite direction. Move only three crayons.

   Draw your solution.

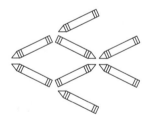

Crayon Constructions Puzzle 6

Use 16 crayons to make this construction. Move 4 crayons and turn it upside down.
　　Draw your solution.

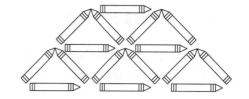

Crayon Constructions Puzzle 7

Use 24 crayons to make this construction. Remove 4 crayons and leave five equal squares.
　　Draw your solution.

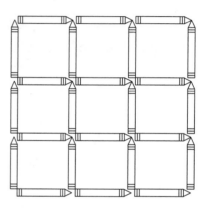

Transformational Geometry

Coin Challenges

Here's your first challenge. Can you arrange 6 coins in two rows? You think that was easy?

    Think again—each row must contain 4 coins.

    See? The middle of each row has 2 coins stacked on top of each other.

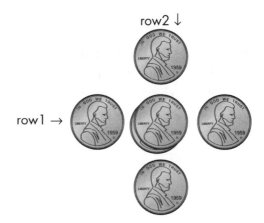

Coin Circle

Arrange 6 coins as shown in the diagram. Rearrange the coins into a circle by moving 2 coins.

    What coins did you move? Draw pictures to show how you solved the puzzle.

Coin Lineup

Use the line below. Place 3 coins so that there are two heads on one side of the line and two tails on the other side of the line.

Draw or write your solution.

Coin Pyramid

Arrange 10 coins in a pyramid, as shown. Move just 3 coins to turn the pyramid upside down.

Draw your solution.

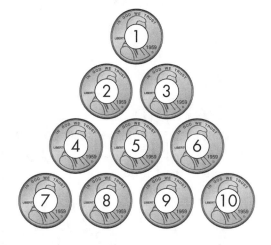

Puzzling H

Arrange 7 coins to form an H pattern. Counting horizontal, diagonal and vertical lines, there are 5 rows with 3 coins in each row. Add 2 coins to create a new pattern that has 10 rows with 3 coins in each row. Draw the coins in the illustration to show where you would place them.

Odd Coins

Take 12 coins and arrange them in a pattern that contains three straight lines with an odd number of coins in each line.

Draw your solution.

Coin Jump

Arrange 8 pennies in a line, as shown. Now make four stacks of penny pairs in four moves. Do this by picking up 1 penny at a time and jumping over 2 others until you make the four stacks.

Draw your solution.

Coin Cover-Up

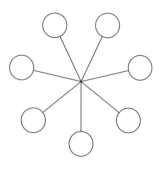

Put your finger in any circle in the drawing below. From there count 1, 2, 3 as you move your finger around the drawing, either clockwise or counterclockwise. Place a penny on the circle you land on at 3. Continue doing this until all the circles have pennies—except one. You can start from any empty circle each time.

Can you figure out how to solve the coin cover-up puzzle no matter which circle you start from?

Mirror Puzzlers

Place a mirror on the Pencil Match Card. Can you make what is on the Pencil Match Card and in the mirror look like what is on each Pencil Image Card? Can you figure out how to do it before you try it with the mirror?

Sample Problem   **Possible Solution**

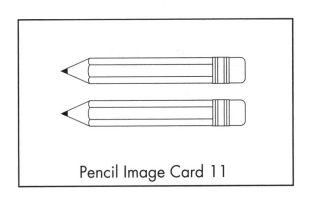

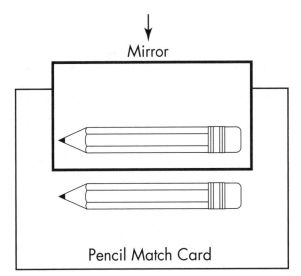

These puzzles are best solved if the Pencil Match Card is near the Pencil Image Cards and can be physically moved around. To accomplish this, photo copy this page and cut out the Pencil Match Card. It can then be placed next to the Pencil Image Cards and moved about as desired. The pages with Pencil Image Cards can also be photocopied and the individual cards cut out of the photocopy.

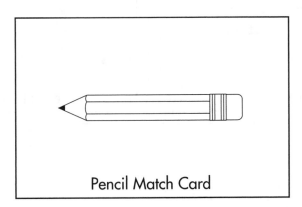

Transformational Geometry

Mirror Puzzlers

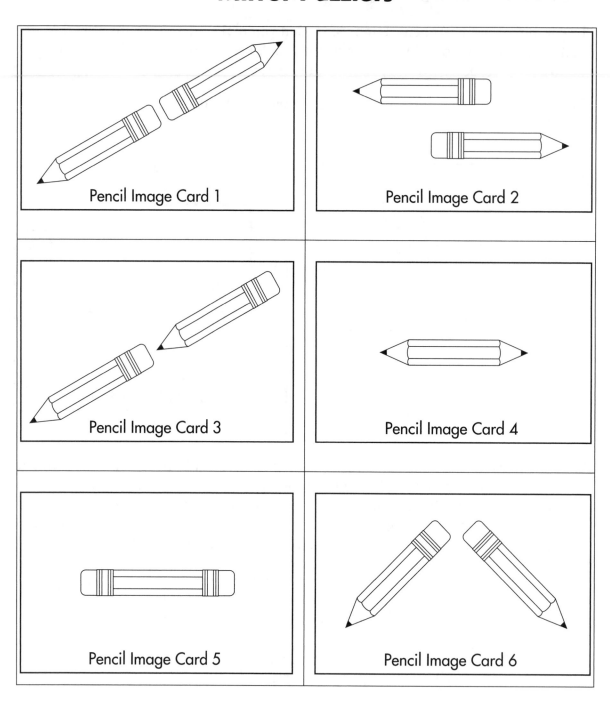

Pencil Image Card 1

Pencil Image Card 2

Pencil Image Card 3

Pencil Image Card 4

Pencil Image Card 5

Pencil Image Card 6

Mirror Puzzlers

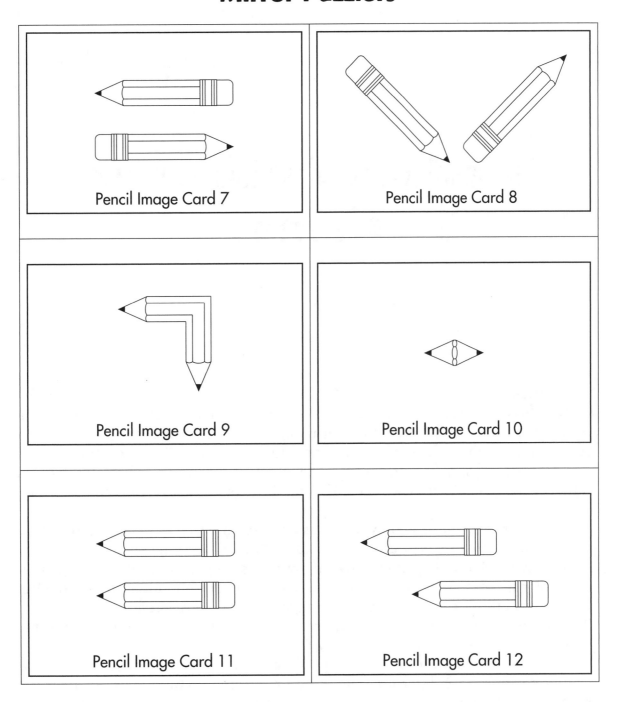

Pencil Image Card 7

Pencil Image Card 8

Pencil Image Card 9

Pencil Image Card 10

Pencil Image Card 11

Pencil Image Card 12

Chapter Twelve

Modular Arithmetic Games

The games of Count Up, Pick Up, Calculator Countdown, Fill Up, and Run the Track all have the same underlying mathematical structure. Dicey Count Up is a similar game except that players determine a winning number by throwing dice (doing so helps them generalize winning strategies). What is important for children to discover is the underlying mathematical structure of these games, as well as that these games that look very different on the surface can be mathematically identical.

These games are governed by three features: the number of objects in the game (which are counted, picked up, subtracted, colored in, or moved on a racetrack), a choice rule (that tells players how many items they can count, pick up, subtract, color in, or move on a racetrack), and a winning position (that tells if the last player to count, pick up, subtract, color in, or move on a racetrack wins or loses). These three things, taken together, determine a set of winning numbers or playing positions.

I will analyze the game of Count Up to illustrate how the winning numbers (or playing positions) are determined and the underlying mathematical structure of these games. This information also applies to Pick Up, Calculator Countdown, Fill Up, Run the Track, and Dicey Count Up. The game of Odds has a very different mathematical structure.

Mathematical Structure and Strategy

In Count Up, a player can say one or two numbers in succession, beginning from where the last player left off counting. The choice rule is saying one or two numbers. In Count Up, players count from 1 to 21. There are thus 21 objects in this game. The player who says 21 loses. As children will quickly discover, this means that the player who says 20 (and stops counting at 20) wins, for that player forces the other player to say 21.

Using mathematical problem solving (and lots of trial-and-error experimentation), children will discover that the next winning number before 20 is 17. Their reasoning for why 17 is the next winning number might go something like this: if you say 17 and your opponent says 18, then you can say 19, 20 and get the last winning number of 20; if you say 17 and your opponent says 18, 19, then you can say 20 and get the last winning number of 20. Because of the size of the choice rule, no choices are available other than saying one or two numbers, and thus the player who says 17 can get 20 and force his or her opponent to say 21. Numbers such as 19 are often called one less than a winning number. Numbers such as 18 and 21 are often called one more than a winning number.

This process of reasoning can be extended backward to the beginning of the game, as children discover that to get 17 they must say 14, that to get 14 they must acquire 11, and so on. The winning numbers for Count Up are thus discovered to be 20, 17, 14, 11, 8, 5, and 2. This is illustrated in the next figure.

1 ②3 4 ⑤6 7 ⑧9 10 ⑪ 12 13 ⑭ 15 16 ⑰ 18 19 ⑳ 21

From this analysis of Count Up, children will also discover several other things. They will discover that the winning numbers are one more apart than the size of the choice rule. In Count Up, the choice rule is two (because players can only count one or two numbers beyond where their opponent stopped counting), and thus the winning numbers are three numbers apart.

Children will discover that the first player in Count Up will always win if that player counts wisely.

Children will discover a winning strategy (for the first player) for playing Count Up that does not require that the player constantly think through the ramifications of every choice that is made. This winning strategy is described by the following flow chart.

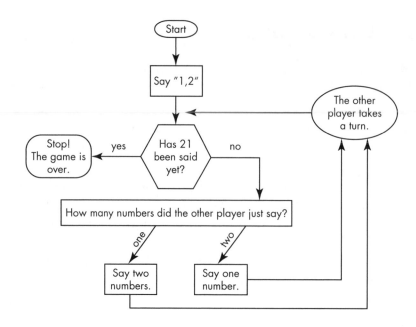

The Mathematics Underlying the Games

Children will also discover that there are three different types of numbers in the game: the winning numbers (the circled numbers in the first figure), the numbers one less than winning numbers, and the numbers one more than winning numbers. These numbers can be delineated using set notation, as follows:

winning numbers = {20, 17, 14, 11, 8, 5, 2}
winning numbers − 1 = {19, 16, 13, 10, 7, 4, 1}
winning numbers + 1 = {21, 18, 15, 12, 9, 6, 3}

Using set notation, where {x| x = 20, 17, . . .} is read "the set of numbers x such that x = 20, 17, and so on," we can rewrite these sets as follows:

winning numbers = {x| x = 20, 17, 14, 11, 8, 5, 2}
winning numbers − 1 = {x| x = 19, 16, 13, 10, 7, 4, 1}
winning numbers + 1 = {x| x = 21, 18, 15, 12, 9, 6, 3}

These sets are defined by a mathematical structure used in the fields of study of linear algebra, number theory, and discrete mathematics that is called modular arithmetic. Notice in the above sets that the numbers are a multiple of 3 different from any other number in the set (that is, the winning numbers of 20, 17, 14, 11, 8, 5, and 2 can be expressed as $20 − 0 \times 3$, $20 − 1 \times 3$, $20 − 2 \times 3$, $20 − 3 \times 3$, $20 − 4 \times 3$, $20 − 5 \times 3$, and $20 − 6 \times 3$). In the language of modular arithmetic, the phrase "20 (mod 3)" is read "twenty mod three" and means those numbers that are a multiple of 3 different from 20. Using the notation of modular arithmetic, where {x| x ≡ 20 (mod 3)} means the set of numbers x such that x is a multiple of 3 different from 20, or in the language of mathematics that x is congruent to 20 (mod 3), we can rewrite these sets as follows:

winning numbers = {x| x ≡ 20 (mod 3)}

winning numbers − 1 = {x| x ≡ 19 (mod 3)}

winning numbers + 1 = {x| x ≡ 21 (mod 3)}

Note that we write ≡ and not =, and say "congruent" and not "equal," because the numbers in each set are similar in their function in the game but not equal to each other.

Some children might notice that this modular arithmetic is similar to what is used in telling nautical and conventional time, where 3 P.M. in conventional time is the same as 15 hours in nautical time, or in mathematical terms that 3 P.M. ≡ 15 hours.

To generalize the specifics of the game of Count Up thus far discussed, we need to return to an observation that we started with. Three things govern these games: the number of objects in the game (the range of numbers that are counted), a choice rule (that tells players how many items they can count), and a winning position (that tells if the last player to count wins or loses). If we vary each of these things, we can create a generalized game of Count Up.

To help children intuitively discover the essence of the mathematics involved, you should vary the game of Count Up in the following three ways. First, ask children to play the game counting up to different numbers (for example, they might count from 1 to 25). This is the purpose of the game Dicey Count Up. Second, vary whether saying the last number produces a win or loss. Third, vary the choice rule—that is, in different games, players should be able to count a different number of counting numbers (perhaps three, four, or five numbers on a turn). If children first learn how to win at Count Up and can describe their winning strategy, then learn how to win at these different variations of Count Up and develop the ability to describe a winning strategy for each variation they play, then they will be well on their way to understanding the games in this chapter.

The games of Pick Up, Calculator Countdown, Fill Up, and Run the Track all have the same underlying mathematical structure as Count Up. All that has been varied is the type of action taken in the game and the type of object acted on, as described in the following chart. These games are just disguised variations on Count Up, and using the language of mathematics we can say that they are isomorphic to each other (when the number of objects in each game and the choice rules are the same), meaning that they have the same underlying mathematical structure and the same winning strategy as the game of Count Up.

Modular Arithmetic Games

	Action	Objects Acted On
Count Up	Count numbers	Numbers
Fill Up	Color squares	Squares
Pick Up	Pick up objects	Objects
Run the Track	Move spaces	Playing positions
Calculator Countdown	Count backward	Calculator numbers
Dicey Count Up	Count numbers	Numbers

The game of Odds is not the same as the other games in this chapter. It is included as a distracter, in order to help children discover the essential elements and relationships of the other games. I discuss Odds as part of the next section.

Instructional Considerations

Children should work in pairs. Their goal is to figure out a winning strategy, understand it, and be able to describe it to others in words, diagrams, actions, or a combination of these modes of expression. Children can test strategies and explanations for why strategies work by playing classmates and friends. When most class members discover winning strategies, share the different ways of describing the strategy in large-group discussions.

Some children will discover winning strategies quickly. Others will need more time. Give them the time they need, and allow children to learn from and teach each other. Once children discover a strategy for Count Up and explore reasons for why it works, strategies for the other games will surface more quickly.

These games have been successfully played and analyzed by children from grade 1 through grade 6 (and far beyond that). We must expect, however, different things from first graders than from third or sixth graders. First graders can learn to play the games, intuitively figure out winning strategies, and appreciate diagrams such as the first figure in this chapter. Third graders can go beyond this to provide primitive descriptions and drawings of winning strategies. By sixth grade, students can comprehend the mathematics, flow chart, diagrams, and some of the mathematical symbolism presented in this chapter—as they relate to the games in this chapter and other everyday phenomena such as writing clock time.

Discovering the winning numbers in Count Up requires that children engage in mathematical problem solving. Explaining why certain numbers are winning numbers requires that children engage in mathematical reasoning and proof, and they should always be asked to describe in words, actions, or pictures why certain numbers are winning numbers. Doing so requires that children engage in mathematical communication. While playing these games, continually ask children to engage in all three of these mathematical processes.

When you are presenting these games to children, I suggest that you demonstrate how to play them rather than simply offer children verbal descriptions. I often play against myself (using a high voice for one opponent and a low voice for the other) to illustrate how to play Count Up, and then after the demonstration describe the rules of the game.

As I suggested earlier, once children learn the winning strategies of the games, you should vary the elements in the games. Not everyone in a class has to be playing the same variation, so when a first group figures out how to play 1 to 21 Count Up, you can have them play 1 to 25 Count Up; the second group finished can play 1 to 15 Count Up. Remember to vary the number of objects in the game, the choice rule, and whether the last position in the game produces a win or loss.

I suggest that you begin with Count Up and follow with Dicey Count Up. One or two of the games of Pick Up, Calculator Countdown, Fill Up, and Run the Track can be the next games you introduce. Introduce Odds after these, and when children try to apply the strategy they have learned for the other games, you can have a discussion about how Odds might be different from the others. At this point, you can introduce the remaining games isomorphic to Count Up. How you time the introduction of the various games is flexible: you can introduce them to your class in close time proximity to each other or months apart. One advantage of allowing a longer interval between games is that it facilitates children's process of rediscovery and reconceptualization of the mathematics underlying the games. Each time children rediscover the strategy for playing a game and verbalize the strategy, they are likely to do so in a slightly different way that leads them to new insights.

The game of Odds is different from the other games in this chapter in several ways. First, the criterion which states that "the player who has an odd number of objects at the end of the game is the winner" is very different from the criterion which states that "the player who picks up the last object loses." Second, most of the games in this chapter can be played with any number of objects, and ties are impossible. In contrast, Odds needs to be played with an odd number of objects; otherwise every game will produce a tie (because odd + odd = even, because even + even = even, and because if there is an even number of objects, you cannot divide it into two groups with an odd number in one and an even number in the other). Third, there is a simple winning strategy for Odds, but in using the strategy, the winner does not predictably respond to the opponent the same way on every move. For example, if the other player picks up two markers, you respond differently if it is the first or third time this happens than if this is the second time the other player does so.

Varying one of the rules of Fill Up can create another game that is similar to but different from the rest of the games in this chapter. Instead of "coloring in either one or two empty spaces on the game board," players must "color in one or two empty spaces on the game board that share an edge." This can create isolated spaces, so that as the end of the game approaches, it is sometimes not possible to color in two spaces, even though more than two spaces may be available to be colored in. This variation of Fill Up can help children understand the underlying structure of the games in this chapter.

Modular Arithmetic Games for Two Players

Play each game several times until you discover a winning strategy. Then move on to the next game.

Count Up

Object: to force your opponent to say the number 21, while counting from 1 to 21 together

    Materials: none

    Preparation: none

    Playing:

- Players alternate turns while counting from 1 to 21.
- Each player may say one or two numbers in succession, starting where the other player left off.

Winning: The player who says 21 loses. The other player wins.

Here is a sample game in which the circle player loses and the square player wins.

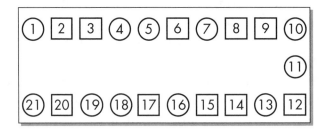

Dicey Count Up

Object: to be the first to say a target number, while counting from 1 to that number

    Materials: pair of dice

    Preparation: none

    Playing:

- Before beginning the game, each player rolls one die. The two numbers are added to 20 to get the target number (the number to play to). The player with the higher roll goes first.

- Players alternate turns counting from 1 to the target number.
- Each player may say one, two, or three numbers in succession, starting where the other player ended.

Winning: The player who says the target number loses. The other player wins.

Fill Up

Object: to be the player who colors in the last space on a grid

Materials: colored pencils or crayons, a 3 × 6 rectangle that contains eighteen smaller rectangular spaces drawn on graph paper or a game board

Preparation: Have players draw a rectangle that is three spaces high and six spaces wide on graph paper or prepare a game board, as shown.

Playing:
- Players take turns coloring in either one or two empty spaces on the game board.
- The spaces do not have to be next to each other.

Winning: The player who colors in the last space is the winner.

Pick Up

Object: to force your opponent to pick up the last object

Materials: 16 small objects (such as pebbles, buttons, beans, pennies, or cubes)

Preparation: none

Playing:
- Players put all 16 objects between them.
- Players take turns picking up 1, 2, or 3 objects at a time.

Winning: The player who picks up the last object loses. The other player wins.

Run the Track

Object: to be the first to reach the last space on a racetrack

Materials: racetrack with 35 resting places and a start line and a finish space, as shown; one playing piece (a bean, pebble, or button) that will fit in the spaces of the racetrack

Preparation: Photocopy the accompanying racetrack for players or draw on a piece of paper a racetrack with 35 spaces, the first of which is labeled Start and the last of which is labeled Finish.

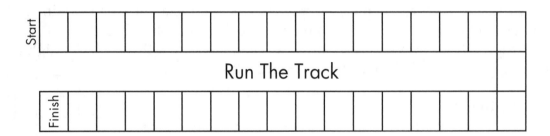

Playing:

- Put the playing piece on Start.
- Players take turns moving the playing piece one, two, three, or four spaces along the racetrack toward Finish.

Winning: The player who moves onto Finish wins.

Calculator Countdown

Object: to be the first to get 0 to show in a calculator display

 Materials: calculator

 Preparation: none

 Playing:

- One of the players enters the number 35 into the calculator.
- Players take turns subtracting 1, 2, or 3 from the number showing in the calculator display. (Example: The first player might subtract 2 by pressing the calculator − key, then the calculator 2 key, and then the calculator = key. The display should then read 33.)

Winning: The player who gets 0 to show in the calculator display is the winner.

Odds

Object: to pick up objects so that you have an odd number of them at the end of the game

    Materials: 15 small objects (such as pebbles, buttons, beans, pennies, or cubes)

    Preparation: none

    Playing:

- Players put all 15 objects between them.

- Players take turns picking up 1, 2, or 3 objects at a time until all of them are gone.

    Winning: The player who has an odd number of objects at the end of the game is the winner.

Chapter Thirteen

Network Puzzles

Bridge crossing puzzles, bug house problems, tracing puzzles, line crossing problems, and geometric travel problems all belong to a branch of mathematics called topology, and more specifically to an area of specialty called network theory. These puzzles are presented in a very anthropomorphic format that is designed to encourage children to imagine that they are actors in the puzzles. The anthropomorphic act of putting yourself in a situation you are trying to understand or of identifying with someone in that situation is helpful to many children. Where appropriate, you can ask, "What would you do if you were in this situation [as a bug in a bug house puzzle, person in a bridge crossing problem, or a pencil in the tracing puzzles]?" With young children, it is appropriate to have them walk through imaginary situations, such as bug houses, that are drawn on a floor or playground blacktop. Or they can move a toy bug through an enlarged diagram of a puzzle. And when children are explaining why things are possible or impossible—that is, when they are using mathematical reasoning and proof to explain their thinking—they should be allowed to speak in the first person, and present things from the perspective of "If I were a bug in that situation, then..."

History of Network Theory

The inventor of topology and network theory, Leonhard Euler, was born in Basel, Switzerland, in 1707 and died in St. Petersburg, Russia, in 1783. He invented network theory as a result of solving a well-known real bridge crossing problem in Koenigsberg, Germany.

Koenigsberg, which is now called Kaliningrad, was in the old kingdom of Prussia, which is now Germany. The city was built where the Pragel River formed an island just after two rivers joined to form a single river. There were seven bridges in the city, arranged in the same way as in the third problem in More Bridge Crossing Puzzles. On Sundays, after church, it was the custom of the people of Koenigsberg to stroll about their city and try to walk across each of the seven bridges once and only once. The people of Koenigsberg could not find a way to do this. In time, the problem of crossing the seven bridges became famous, and people from all over Europe came to Koenigsberg to see if they could walk about the city in such a way as to cross each bridge only once. No one succeeded. Leonhard Euler heard about the problem and started thinking about it. He considered an idea that for some reason had never been seriously considered: that it was impossible to cross the seven bridges only once on a single trip through the city. In 1736, he published a mathematical paper about the bridges of Koenigsberg, in which he proved that the problem was impossible, and in which he generalized the results of his thinking to all problems like the ones found in this chapter. The birth of network theory and topology is dated from the writing of that paper.

Euler proved that the only bridge problems that can be solved are those with two or fewer land masses with an odd number of bridges. To come up with this conclusion, he had to figure out that the essential mathematical elements in the problem are the land masses, which include both the land on the sides of the river and the islands. He also had to conclude that the essential mathematical relationships in the problem are the bridges that connected the land masses. What he first discovered is that the existence of land masses with an even number of bridges leading to or from them make no difference to the ability to solve this type of problem: it is easy just to pass through these land masses or, if there are several of them, to begin in one, pass through the others, and end up where one started. What does make a difference is the number of land masses with an odd number of bridges leading to or from them. Euler's proof went something like this:

- If a bridge crossing problem has one land mass with an odd number of bridges, you must start or end your travels on that land mass.

- If a problem has two land masses with an odd number of bridges, you must start your travels on one of those land masses and end it on the other land mass.

- If a bridge crossing problem has three or more land masses with an odd number of bridges, you must start your travels on one of the land masses and end your travels on *each* of the other two land masses. But it is impossible to end your travels in two different places. Therefore, the Bridges of Koenigsberg Problem is impossible to solve.

These conclusions about bridge problems apply to all other network problems that are isomorphic to bridge problems—that is, that are basically the same as bridge problems even though they may be hiding under surface disguises that make them look different. The bridge crossing, tracing, line crossing, and bug house puzzles are designed to help children discover which network puzzles are impossible, how to solve those that are possible, and how these different types of puzzles are similar.

The first set of bridge crossing puzzles, I'll Cross That Bridge When I Get to It, are possible to solve. Children should discover where to start and end a trip in order to complete a puzzle. In the second set of bridge crossing puzzles, More Bridge Crossing Puzzles, students should discover that if a problem has three or more land masses with an odd number of bridges, then it is impossible. The bug house puzzles reemphasize these two ideas: where to start and end a trip, and that if a puzzle has three or more bug houses with an odd number of doors, then it is impossible. Both of these types of problems are anthropomorphic—that is, they allow children to project themselves into the puzzles as actors in them. Line crossing problems become more abstract. Tracing problems are still more abstract and provide the mathematical structure that allows students to generalize and compare network problems most easily.

Geometric Travels are different from the rest of the puzzles in this chapter because the beginning and end points are predetermined. These puzzles are included to emphasize how small differences in assumptions can produce major differences in conclusions—or how we need to be sensitive to the fact that in mathematics, things can look similar and yet be very different.

The Isomorphism

Bridge crossing, bug house, line crossing, and tracing puzzles are all basically the same, even though the disguises they wear make them look different. Underlying each type of puzzle are essential elements and relationships. The following table presents these essential components.

Puzzle	Essential Elements	Essential Relationships	Actions
Tracing	Vertices	Edges	Tracing
Bridge Crossing	Land	Bridges	Crossing
Bug House	Spaces	Doors	Traveling
Line Crossing	Spaces	Line segments	Drawing

Speaking in terms of tracing puzzles, the essential elements are vertices (or corners), and the essential relationships are the edges (or lines). It makes no difference whether an edge (line) connecting two vertices (corners) is straight or curved, so long as it begins in one vertex and ends in another without crossing any other edges. Thus no special distinction needs to be made between the right-hand edges of the two shapes in the first figure. However, it is necessary to distinguish between the number of edges that meet in a vertex.

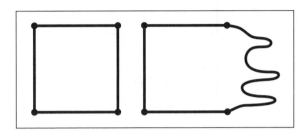

Even though the two shapes in the second figure have four vertices, the number of edges that meet in their upper right corners are different. Two edges meet in the upper right corner vertex in the shape on the left. Three edges meet in the upper right corner vertex in the shape on the right.

In network theory, we say that if an even number of edges meet in a vertex, then it is an even vertex. Similarly we say that if an odd number of edges meet in a vertex, then it is an odd vertex. In addition, when an edge ends without connecting to any other edge, its "dangling" end is still called a vertex. Thus the following figure has five vertices and four edges.

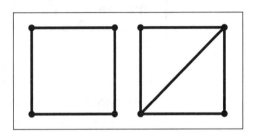

To determine if a figure can be traced, we first count the number of edges that meet in each vertex, and then determine how many vertices are odd and even. If the figure has more than two odd vertices, it cannot be traced. If it has one odd vertex, the tracing must begin or end in the odd vertex. If the figure has two odd vertices, the tracing must begin at one odd vertex and end at the other odd vertex. The number of even vertices is irrelevant to the ability to trace a figure. This is what Euler discovered, and this is what children should discover.

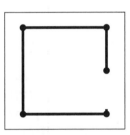

The process for transforming bridge crossing problems into tracing problems is shown in the next figure. Transforming a tracing problem into a bridge crossing problem simply involves reversing the process. The process for transforming tracing, bridge crossing, bug house, or line crossing puzzles into each other is similar.

Network Puzzles

Flow Chart of Process　　　**Illustration of Process**

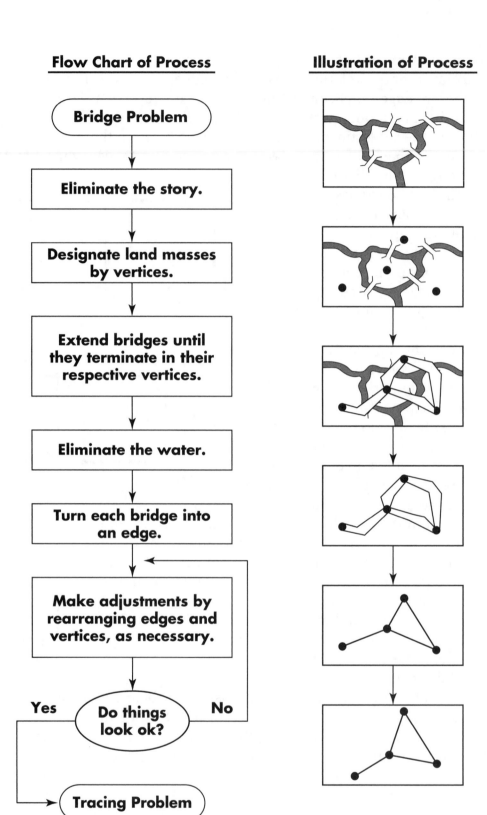

Bridge Problem

Eliminate the story.

Designate land masses
by vertices.

Extend bridges until
they terminate in their
respective vertices.

Eliminate the water.

Turn each bridge into
an edge.

Make adjustments by
rearranging edges and
vertices, as necessary.

Yes　　Do things
look ok?　　No

Tracing Problem

Instructional Considerations

Bridge crossing puzzles are about people who like to cross bridges; who insist on crossing every bridge available without ever crossing any bridge twice; and who never jump over water, swim in water, or get into boats. Children will want to find ways of getting between land masses without using bridges. Remind them that boats and other such alternatives are not allowed.

To help children determine if a puzzle can be solved, first have them count the number of bridges that give access to each land mass. Then have them label each land mass with an E if it has an even number of bridges, or with an O if it has an odd number of bridges. The figure illustrates how to label a bridge crossing puzzle. Children can then proceed by following these rules. If the puzzle has more than two land masses with an odd number of bridges, it is impossible to solve. If the puzzle has exactly one land mass with an odd number of bridges, begin or end the trip in that land mass. If the puzzle has exactly two land masses with an odd number of bridges, begin the trip in one of the land masses with an odd number of bridges and end the trip in the other land mass with an odd number of bridges.

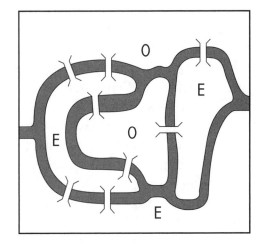

Bug house puzzles highlight the need to count the number of doors that spaces have to determine which puzzles can be solved. Remind children not to forget to count the number of doors that the outside space has. When transforming other types of network puzzles into bug house puzzles, if there is not an outside of a house, as a last step eliminate one or two of the adjacent outside walls of one room, so that there is an outside of the house. The method for determining which puzzles can be solved, which are impossible, and how to solve puzzles is the same as for bridge crossing puzzles.

Tracing puzzles are drawn with a pencil, without lifting the pencil off the paper and by tracing each of its line segments only once. Emphasize that no line segment may be traced twice, even though vertices may be passed through as many times as desired. To help children keep track of how they have solved tracing puzzles, ask them to number the line segments in the order in which they are traced. Unless children do this, they will frequently redraw an edge multiple times. The numbered edges also help children explain to each other their thoughts, using mathematical reasoning and proof. The method for determining which puzzles can be solved, which are impossible, and how to solve puzzles is the same as the one already described.

Line crossing puzzles require that students understand the mathematical difference between a line and a line segment. Mathematically, lines continue indefinitely in both directions. In contrast, line segments terminate in identifiable end points. In line crossing puzzles, the line segments we are concerned with are the shortest ones between two vertices. Thus if the points A, B, and C are on the same line, with B between A and C, and with another line segment ending in B, then what the puzzles are concerned with are the shorter line segments AB and BC, and not longer line segment AC. The method for analyzing and solving puzzles is the same as for tracing puzzles.

As I noted earlier, Geometric Travels are different from the rest of the puzzles in this chapter, because the starting and ending points are specified. Have children make a table that compares the number of sides of a geometric figure with whether or not the puzzle is possible. If the number of sides of a geometric figure is an odd number, the puzzle can be solved. If the number of sides is even, the puzzle is impossible.

I suggest that you first present bridge crossing problems and then bug house problems. Present the bug house problems at least one week but not more than one month after working on the bridge crossing problems. When children have hypotheses about which problems can be solved and which cannot, push them to describe in words (to help them develop communication skills) why they think that this is the case (to help them develop skills in mathematical reasoning and proof). To help children discover the relationship between the different types of problems, have them work on tracing problems after working on bridge crossing and bug house problems. When they conclude that all three types of problems are similar, ask them to clarify what the similarities and relationships between the problems are—while highlighting the essential elements and relationships of each type of problem. Always try to start with children's hypotheses and have children attempt to refine those hypotheses and describe their reasons for believing them, rather than presenting a lecture that conveys the critical information.

I'll Cross That Bridge When I Get to It

This map shows a river with land on the outside, an island in the middle, and four bridges. The line shows how to cross each of the bridges once and only once, without swimming, jumping, boating, or flying over the river. See if you can solve some bridge crossing puzzles.

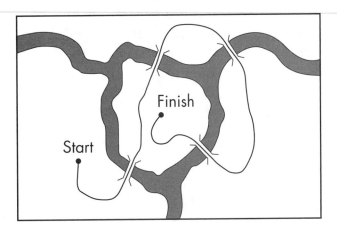

Bridge Crossing Puzzle 1

The village of Four Islands sits in the middle of the Red River. Wendy visits Four Islands every day to deliver bread. As she delivers bread, she walks across each bridge only once. Find and draw Wendy's route from start to finish.

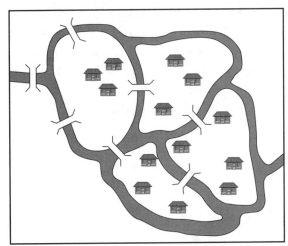

Bridge Crossing Puzzle 2

Juan is trapped inside a house in the middle island! Zelda must save him! To save him she must cross each of the bridges over Zany River once and only once. Find and draw a route for her to follow.

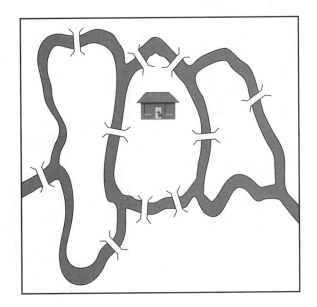

Bridge Crossing Puzzle 3

Rose Ann drives the school bus. While picking up all the children in her town, she crosses over every bridge in the town exactly once. Find and draw a route for her to follow.

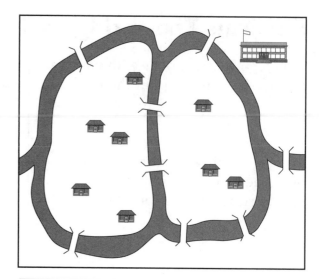

Bridge Crossing Puzzle 4

Karla delivers the mail. Karla's delivery route is between Purpleville and Greensboro. Find and draw how she can cross each bridge once and only once while delivering the mail.

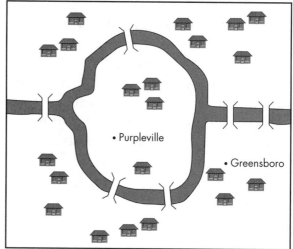

Bridge Crossing Puzzle 5

Mr. Chips delivers potato chips to all the islands in Munchy River. On his deliveries, he drives across each bridge once and only once. (No wonder Mr. Chips lives in his truck!) Find and draw his route.

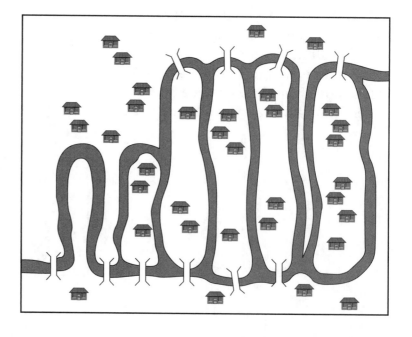

Problem-Solving Mathematics Puzzles

Bridge Crossing Puzzle 6

Jaren and Brooke just finished eating at Three Island Pizza Palace. Jared says it's impossible for them to walk across all of Three Island's bridges once and only once. Brooke says she can. Find and draw her route.

Now it is your turn. Create, draw, and write your own bridge crossing problem.

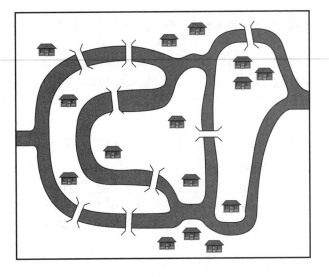

More Bridge Crossing Puzzles

Here are more bridge crossing puzzles to solve. Remember, you must cross each bridge only once. For each puzzle, find and draw the route. No swimming, jumping, boating, or flying across the river.

More Bridge Crossing Puzzles 1

The town of Eyes on the Ball River has ten bridges. After school, the children go to the park. They cross each bridge once and only once on the way to the park. Can you find and draw their route? Draw where you think the school and the park are located.

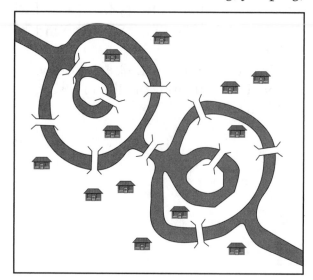

More Bridge Crossing Puzzles 2

Flip Flop Jones owns two homes on the river. He wanders up and down and across and along the river selling apples. Can you draw how Flip Flop can do this every day while crossing every bridge once and only once? Draw where you think his homes are located.

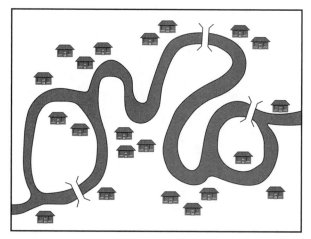

More Bridge Crossing Puzzles 3

Every Sunday afternoon, Maria walks around her town and crosses its bridges. Can you draw how she might cross each bridge once and only once?

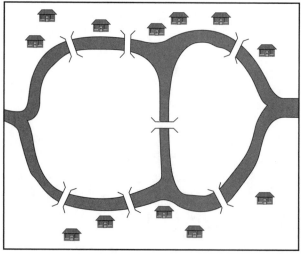

Problem-Solving Mathematics Puzzles

More Bridge Crossing Puzzles 4

Walter collects money from the city's parking meters. On his route, he tries to cross each bridge over the Straight River only once. Can you draw how Walter could do this?

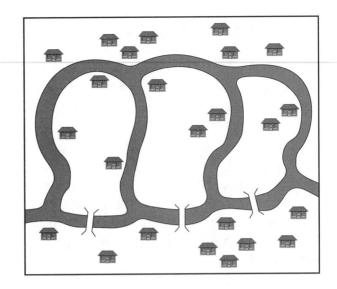

More Bridge Crossing Puzzles 5

An ice cream store in Twelve Bridges is holding a contest. Whoever can cross each of the town's bridges exactly once to get to the store wins twelve free ice cream cones. Can you find and draw a way? Draw where you think the store is located.

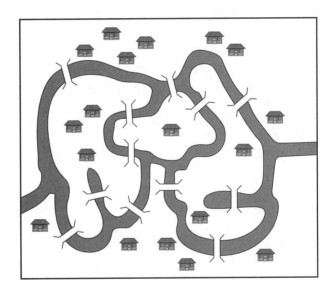

More Bridge Crossing Puzzles 6

Roberto is locked in school by a teacher on an island in the Palomino River. To get out of school, he must draw a map that shows how to cross each bridge once and only once. Can you draw him a map that will get him out of school?

Now it is your turn. Create, draw, and write your own bridge crossing problem.

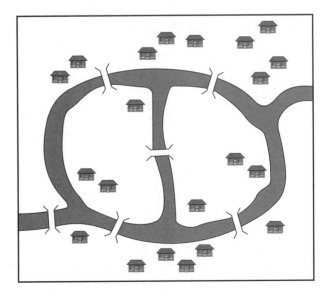

Bug Problems

Door bugs are strange creatures. They like to walk through the doors of bug houses and bug apartment buildings. They also always try to walk through every available door they can find exactly once and only once. In addition, they never jump over or burrow under or through a bug house wall.

The only parts of bug houses and bug apartment buildings are their walls and doors.

In these bug problems, you are shown bug villages that contain bug houses and bug apartment buildings. See if you can travel through all the doors in the bug village exactly once.

Record your solutions by drawing a continuous line that passes through every door in a village exactly once. This will show the path a door bug might travel. The bug can start anywhere. It can travel through the houses and doors in any order.

Here is an example of a Bug Problem puzzle:

Solution:

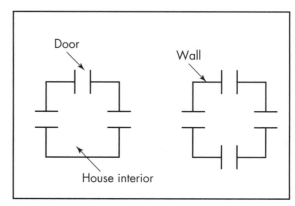

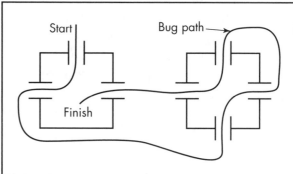

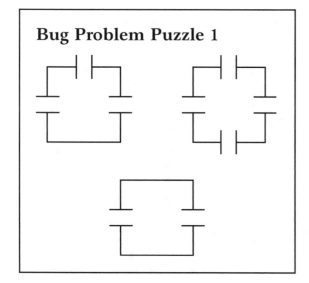

Bug Problem Puzzle 1

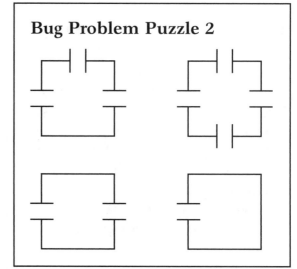

Bug Problem Puzzle 2

Problem-Solving Mathematics Puzzles

Bug Problem Puzzle 3

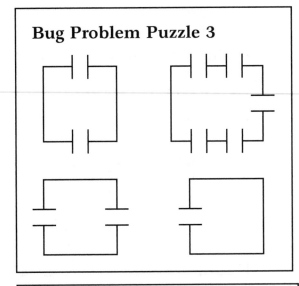

Bug Problem Puzzle 6

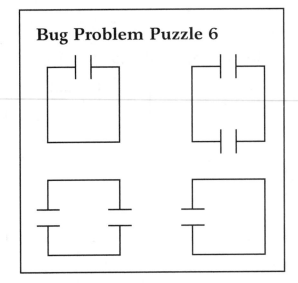

Bug Problem Puzzle 4

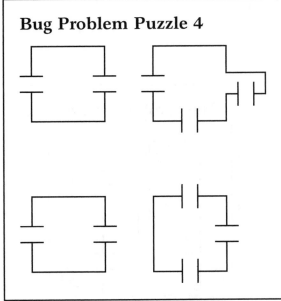

Bug Problem Puzzle 7

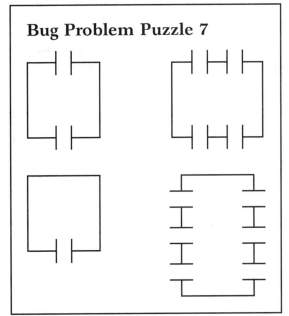

Bug Problem Puzzle 5

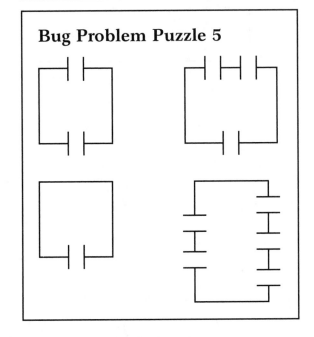

Bug Problem Puzzle 8

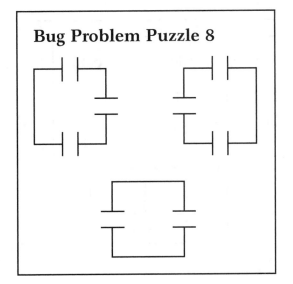

Bug Problem Puzzle 9

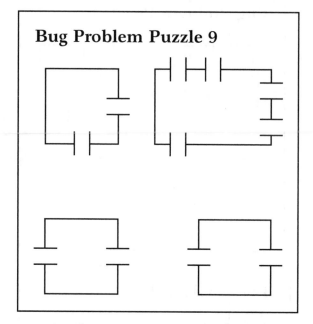

Bug Problem Puzzle 12

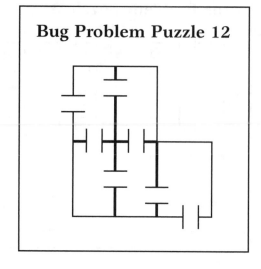

Bug Problem Puzzle 10

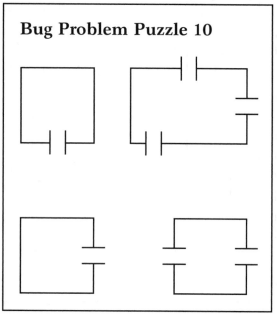

Bug Problem Puzzle 13

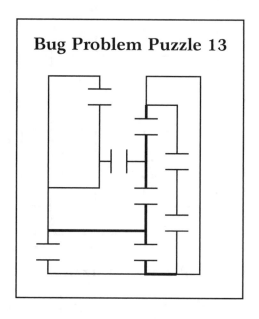

Bug Problem Puzzle 11

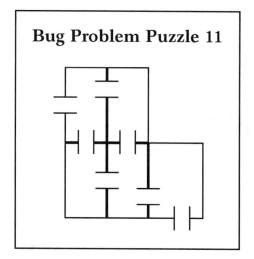

Problem-Solving Mathematics Puzzles

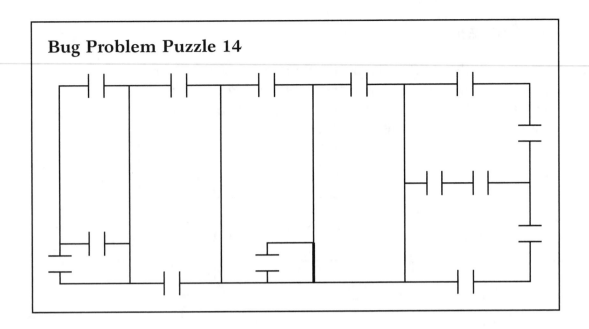

Tracing Puzzles

Draw each figure without lifting your pencil point from the paper and by tracing each line segment once and only once. You may not go back over a line. You may go through corners more than once. Number the line segments in the order that you drew them.

Puzzle

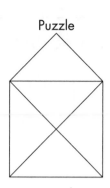

Solution:

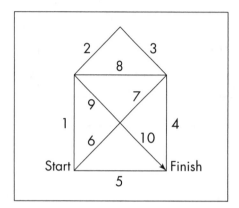

Tracing Puzzle 1

Tracing Puzzle 3

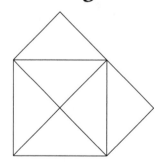

Tracing Puzzle 2

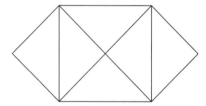

Tracing Puzzle 4

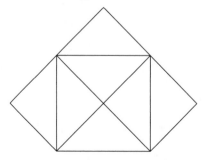

Problem-Solving Mathematics Puzzles

Tracing Puzzle 5

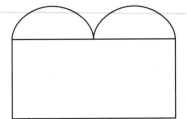

Tracing Puzzle 6

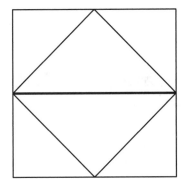

Tracing Puzzle 7

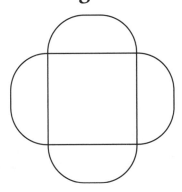

Tracing Puzzle 8

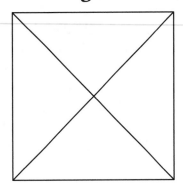

Tracing Puzzle 9

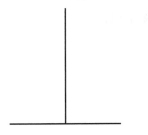

Tracing Puzzle 10

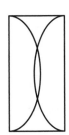

Geometric Travels

There are many geometric shapes. Some have straight lines for their sides. Some have curved lines for their sides.

In these problems, try to connect point A, which is **inside** the shape, with point B, which is **outside** the shape, with a continuous line that crosses each side of the figure exactly once and only once.

This triangle problem is done as an example.

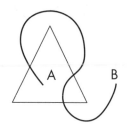

Geometric Travels Puzzle 1
Square = 4 sides

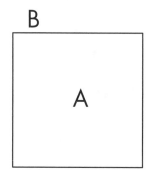

Geometric Travels Puzzle 3
Hexagon = 6 sides

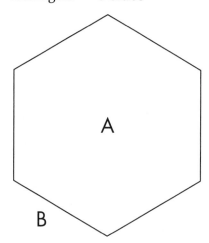

Geometric Travels Puzzle 2
Pentagon = 5 sides

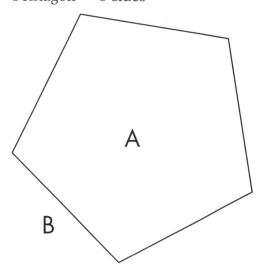

Geometric Travels Puzzle 4
Heptagon = 7 sides

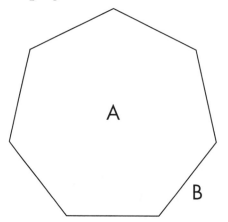

Problem-Solving Mathematics Puzzles

Geometric Travels Puzzle 5
Octagon = 8 sides

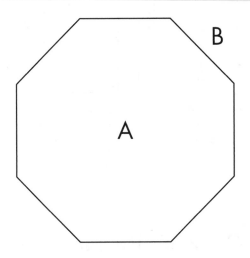

Geometric Travels Puzzle 7
2 sides

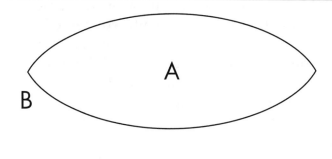

Geometric Travels Puzzle 6
Circle = 1 side

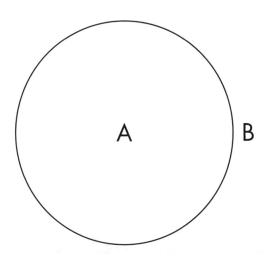

Line Crossing Puzzles

In these puzzles, you are given a geometric shape that consists of interconnected line segments. In the following figures, draw a continuous line that crosses each unbroken line segment exactly once and only once.

Here is an example:

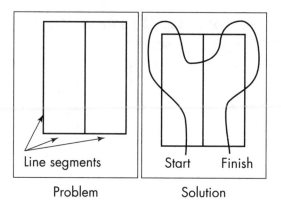

Line segments Start Finish

Problem Solution

Line Crossing Puzzle 1

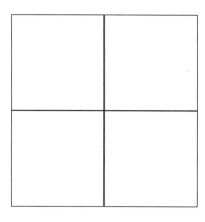

Line Crossing Puzzle 3

Line Crossing Puzzle 2

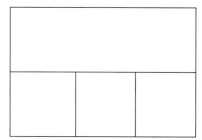

Line Crossing Puzzle 4

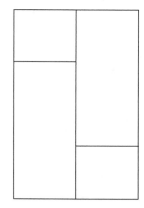

Line Crossing Puzzle 5

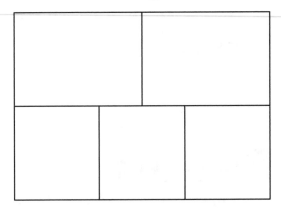

Line Crossing Puzzle 7

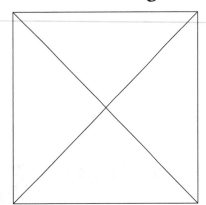

Line Crossing Puzzle 6

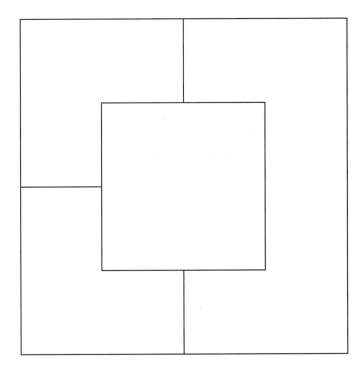

Chapter Fourteen

Topology Puzzles

Scissors, household, and people puzzles are topology puzzles that involve the manipulation of knots, seeing through the disguises that distracting elements can present, and seeing the similarities among geometric structures. The type of topology involved in these puzzles is called rubber sheet geometry. It involves the study of geometric shapes, structures, and constructions whose essential properties are preserved when they are distorted.

Puzzle Structure

The branch of topology that these puzzles belong to is knot theory. There are only a few structures from knot theory that we need to be concerned with, in particular loops and beads.

Loops

In a puzzle, a loop is a geometric structure that has one or more openings. Three basic types of loops are open loops, closed loops, and end loops, illustrated in the first figure. A closed loop has no openings in it and a hole in the middle. An open loop has one or more openings in it. An end loop consists of a closed loop at the end of a piece of rope, wire, plastic, or wood.

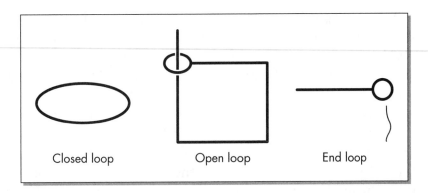

Closed loop   Open loop   End loop

The most basic loop puzzle consists of a closed loop that encircles part of an open loop that is formed out of wood, wire, plastic, or rope and that incorporates an end loop.

This is illustrated in the next figure. Here the task is to remove the open loop from the closed loop. It is assumed that the open loop is a rigid static structure that cannot change its shape, whereas the closed loop is a flexible structure that can be moved about and that can be deformed in a variety of ways, including scrunching it into a small ball, collapsing it into a narrow loop, or deforming it so it can be pulled thorough the small end loop of the larger open loop.

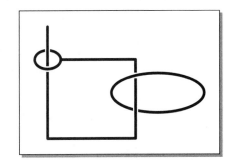

Beads

Rigid beads that can be attached to either an open or a closed loop are another important part of these puzzles. Two such beads are illustrated in the following figure. Both are portrayed as larger than the small end loop that forms part of the open loop. The goal in this basic puzzle is to remove the flexible open loop from the rigid closed loop. What makes this puzzle difficult is that the bead on the closed loop is so large that it will not pass through the closed end loop that is part of the open loop. Beads can take the form of washers of various sizes, nuts, scissors, chairs, and even people's hands or heads.

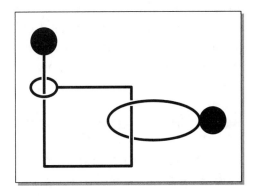

Puzzle Configurations

Most of the scissors, household, and people puzzles consist of open loops, closed loops, some rigid loops, some flexible loops, and a variety of inflexible beads that are so large that they cannot fit through the holes in one or more of the loops. The puzzles involve freeing one loop from another loop, untying a twisted loop (a knot), or moving one part of a puzzle to another part of the puzzle.

Topology Puzzles

Let us examine People Puzzle 1, illustrated on the left in the next figure. This consists of two people tied together with two ropes that loosely encircle their arms at their wrists. Each rope has an end loop at both ends. The people's hands are portrayed by the large black dots. Each hand functions as a bead at the end of an arm, a bead that is sufficiently large that the end loops of the ropes around the people's arms will not fit over the beads. From the perspective of topology, the question we must ask is, "What is essential about the people in the puzzle?" The heads, necks, and legs of the people are unimportant in this puzzle. The only thing that is important about the bodies of the people is that they connect the people's arms, so their bodies could be shrunk to become simply extensions of the arms. If we get rid of the heads, legs, and necks, and shrink the bodies so that they become simply connectors to the arms, we end up with the puzzle portrayed on the right side of the figure. The goal of this puzzle is to separate the ropes.

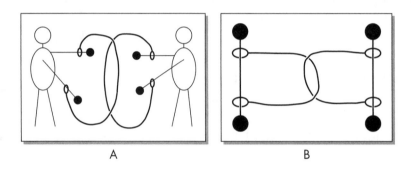

The puzzles in this chapter involve (1) determining the essential components of a puzzle; (2) thinking about a puzzle in terms of beads and open loops, closed loops, and end loops that are either flexible or rigid; and (3) figuring out how to manipulate these components to transform a puzzle from some initial state to some end state (as, for example, in the people puzzle just discussed).

Solutions and Issues Related to Solving Problems

The puzzles in this chapter can be classified into three sets, which are determined by the manner in which they are solved. The three sets are called open loop puzzles, knot manipulation puzzles (which are often called knot equivalence puzzles), and untying knot puzzles.

Open Loop Puzzles

This type of puzzle has two essential components. One is an open loop. The other is something that is entangled in the open loop. The object is to disentangle the two items. The figure shown in the Beads section illustrated the essence of this type of puzzle. The scissors puzzle portrayed in the following figure is another example of this type of puzzle. Here the scissors must be freed from rope A, which is tied to something large, such as a desk or chair.

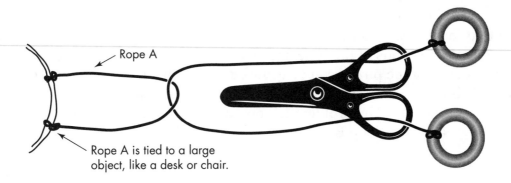

Rope A

Rope A is tied to a large
object, like a desk or chair.

To see more clearly what is occurring in this puzzle, let us redraw it in such a way as to eliminate some of the visual distractions. The next figure portrays the essence of this puzzle. It consists of two parts. One part is an open loop that is portrayed on the right-hand side of the figure. The other part consists of closed loop A, which is portrayed on the left-hand side of the figure.

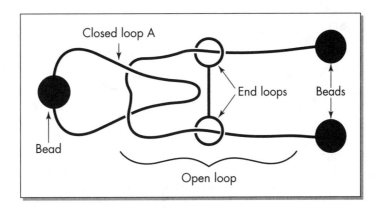

Closed loop A

End loops

Beads

Bead

Open loop

To free the two parts of the puzzle from each other, manipulate part of loop A through the inside of one of the end loops, move it around the free end of the bead, and then pull it back through the other side of the end loop. The two parts of the puzzle (the open and the closed loop part) will then be separate.

All open loop puzzles are solved in this same way: locate the puzzle's open loop, locate the puzzle's closed loop, figure out how to navigate the closed loop around the puzzle's distractions (such as washers, beads, people's heads, and clothing), push the closed loop through the end loop that forms part of the open loop, manipulate it around something, and then pull it back through the other side of the end loop.

Knot Equivalence Puzzles

This type of puzzle has three essential parts: a central knot that is tied to a closed loop, the closed loop around which the central knot is tied, and some object that must relocate its position with respect to the position of the central knot. Image A in the next figure illustrates this type of puzzle. In this potato masher puzzle, the two washers must be moved next to each other on the same loop of rope on one side of the central knot. Image B portrays more of the essence of this puzzle by replacing the potato masher with an inflexible plastic, wood, or leather structure with three holes. Because the ends of the rope are tied to its holes, the holes become irrelevant, and the essence of the puzzle can be reduced to the illustration in image C, in which the rope is linked at its ends to the inflexible structure that consists of two arms that contain a closed loop. The problem is now to move washer A from loop A so that it is next to washer B on loop B.

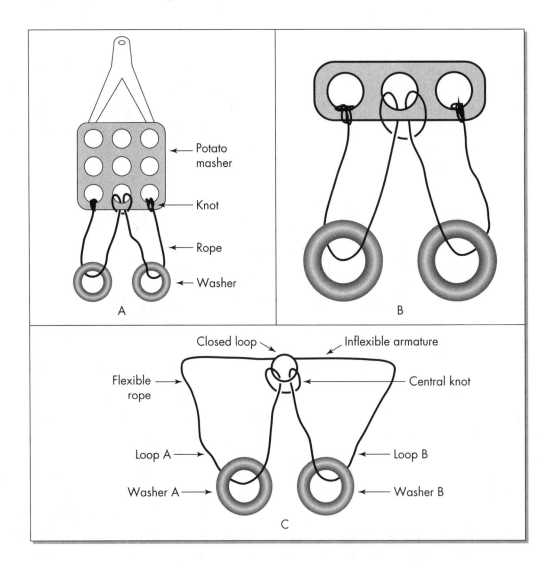

This is accomplished by enlarging the central knot, moving washer A into the left side of the central knot, pulling the central knot through the closed loop from front to back, moving washer A to the right side of the central knot, pulling the central knot back through the closed loop from back to front, moving washer A out of the central knot so it is located next to washer B, and then tightening up the central knot so that it looks like it did initially, except that the two washers are next to each other.

All knot equivalent puzzles are solved in basically the same way. They are called knot equivalent puzzles because even though the central knot is enlarged, twisted, scrunched, and turned, and even though a washer is passed through it several times, the knot itself remains equivalent in structure to its initial state.

Untying Knot Puzzles

Most untying knot puzzles have three components: a knot that needs to be untied, an open loop, and some distractions. The two puzzles in the next figure are examples of untying knot puzzles. In the puzzle on the left, the main knot needs to be untied. In the puzzle on the right, the knot around the upper finger hole in the scissors needs to be untied so that the rope and washer can be separated from the scissors. Both puzzles can be treated as open loop puzzles. To untie the knot in the potato masher puzzle, pull the upper left portion of the knot through the left side of the masher hole on the bottom right, around the washer, and back through the other side of the masher hole. To solve the scissors puzzle, pull the inner horizontal portion of the knot (around the scissors' upper finger hole) down along the rope, through the scissors' lower finger hole, along the rope, around the washer, back along the other side of the rope, through the lower finger hole of the scissors, and then through the upper finger hole of the scissors. The knot will now be untied, and the rope can be pulled away from the scissors.

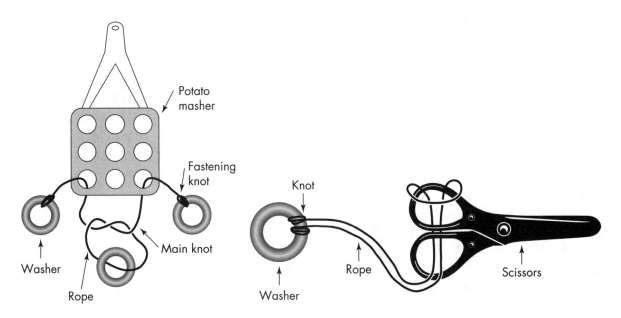

Return to Original State

Puzzles have two parts: solving them and then putting them back into their original states. Returning a solved puzzle to its original state can be as challenging as solving the original puzzle. Be ready to return puzzles to their original state many times for children.

Puzzle Invention and Sharing

As children begin to figure out the principles that underlie how the puzzles can be solved, and which puzzles are disguised versions of each other, they will want to invent their own puzzles and share their discoveries with peers and families. Encourage them to do so. Have puzzles that can be taken home, and have materials with which children can invent their own puzzles.

Possible and Impossible Puzzles

It is important to note that not all topological puzzles can be solved. If children invent their own puzzles, they are likely to invent ones that cannot be solved. In addition, many of these puzzles have two different solutions. As children discover different solutions, have them compare the solutions.

Historical Perspective

Scissors puzzles are of ancient origin. They are often called rope, string, sailor, or tailor's puzzles. The Gordian Knot—tied by King Gordius of Phrygia, which an ancient oracle proclaimed could be undone only by the future master of Asia, and which Alexander the Great is reputed to have cut with his sword in frustration with failing to untie it—was an ancient, and possibly mythical, member of this class of puzzles. Sailors and tailors, reputed to be the masters of knot tying, are often said to have created these types of puzzles in their spare time. Today the study of such puzzles is considered to fall within the subfield of topology called knot theory.

Puzzle Construction

Scissors puzzles are easy and inexpensive to construct. The main ingredient is a pair of scissors. If possible, use round-tipped metal school scissors. Avoid scissors with sharp blades or sharp pointed tips.

Another component of the scissors puzzles are metal washers that are larger than the finger holes in the scissors. Large washers can be purchased inexpensively in most hardware stores. Large hex nuts (as in nuts and bolts), inexpensive plastic curtain rings, inexpensive napkin rings, or any object with a hole in it that is sufficiently large that it will not fit through the finger holes in the scissors can be used instead of washers.

You can use either nylon or cotton rope. The best rope is nylon traverse cord number 3.5, which is $\frac{7}{64}$ inches in diameter. Cotton traverse cord number 3.5 ($\frac{7}{64}$ inches), is an excellent cotton rope. Long shoelaces can also be used.

When preparing nylon rope for use, melt the ends of the rope over a candle flame (or with a match) so that they will not fray. Melt the ends of the rope outdoors or in a well-ventilated area, for the fumes are strong and might be toxic. The ends of cotton rope can be kept from unraveling by wrapping tape, such as black electrician's tape, around them.

When tying the two ends of a piece of cotton rope together, the most useful knot is the square knot. When tying the two ends of a piece of nylon rope together, the most useful knot is the over-and-under knot. To tie a piece of rope to an object, such as a washer, use the double half hitch. These knots are illustrated in the next figure.

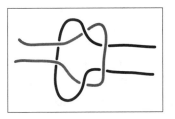

Square knot

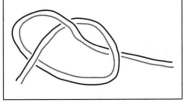

Over and under knot

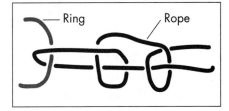

Double half hitch

When measuring out rope to make a puzzle, it is always better to have too much rather than too little rope. The proportions of rope needed are the same as in the puzzle diagrams in relation to the size of scissors and washers. It is usually necessary to leave about an extra foot of rope to cover the waste in making knots.

Household puzzles have three components: a household implement, a rope, and a washer. Numerous household implements can be used to make these puzzles. Potato mashers are my favorite, for they have numerous holes that are a nice size through which to string rope. Spatulas with holes or slits in them also work well, although if you are using a spatula with slits, you need to use hex nuts, for washers easily slip through the slits. The aforementioned information about rope and washers also applies to household puzzles.

People puzzles require clothing and rope. I suggest that the clothing used be large compared to the size of the person who will be working the puzzle, in order to minimize stretching or ripping the clothing. Adult T-shirts and sweatshirts work well for children. Once children figure out how to solve the puzzles, they can then use their own clothing. Short-sleeve shirts, sweaters, and vests are recommended over long-sleeve ones if you want to make the puzzles a bit easier to solve. Information about rope is discussed earlier, except that for people puzzles, larger-size rope should be used, at least $\frac{5}{32}$ inch in diameter.

Topology Puzzles   **293**

People Puzzles

People Puzzle 1

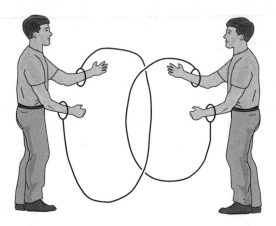

Tie loops at the ends of two pieces of rope that are each about five feet long. Put the loops of one rope over one person's wrists and loosely tighten the loops. Put one loop of the other rope around the second person's wrist, put the free end of the rope around the first person's rope, put the other loop around the second person's other wrist, and loosely tighten the loops.

Now separate the two people, without removing the loops from the people's wrists.

People Puzzle 2

Have a person put on a vest or sweater with pockets. Tie a piece of rope about five feet long into a loop. Put an arm through the loop and then into one of the pockets in the vest.

Now separate the rope from the person without removing the hand from the pocket and without slipping the rope around the person's hand.

People Puzzle 3

Have a person put on a large vest or sweatshirt. Have the person clasp his or her two hands together.

Now turn the sweater inside out without having the person unclasp his or her hands.

People Puzzle 4

Have a person put on a large sweatshirt or sweater. Tie loops at the ends of a piece of rope that is about four feet long. Put the loops of the rope over the person's wrist and loosely tighten the loops.

Now have the person turn the sweater inside out without removing the rope from his or her wrists.

People Puzzle 5

Have a person put on a loose-fitting T-shirt (or large vest). Have the person put on a large sweatshirt (or sweater) over the T-shirt.

Now have the person take off the T-shirt without removing the sweatshirt.

People Puzzle 6

Have a person put on a loose-fitting sweatshirt (or sweater). Give the person a loose-fitting T-shirt.

Now have the person put on the T-shirt so that it is under the sweatshirt, without removing the sweatshirt.

Problem-Solving Mathematics Puzzles

Scissors Puzzles

Scissors Puzzle 1

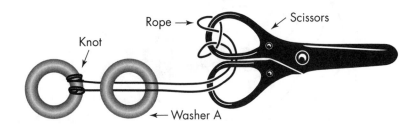

Free washer A from the puzzle.

Scissors Puzzle 2

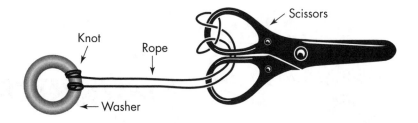

Free the rope and washer from the scissors.

Scissors Puzzle 3

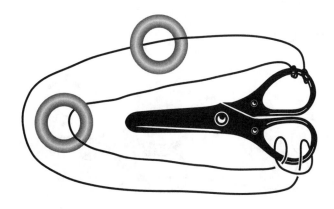

Get the two washers on the same segment (or loop) of the rope.

Scissors Puzzle 4

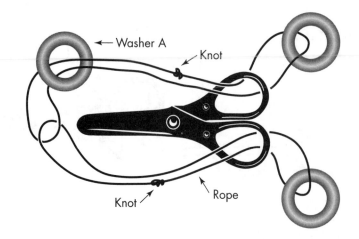

Free washer A from the rope.

Scissors Puzzle 5

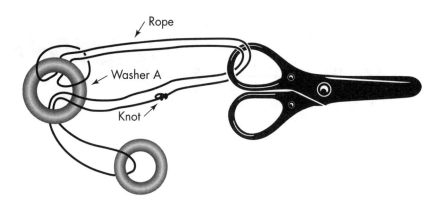

Remove washer A from the rope.

Scissors Puzzle 6

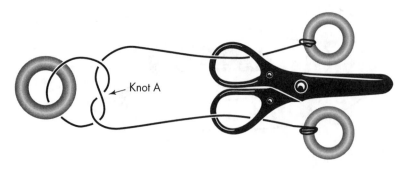

Untie knot A from the scissors.

Scissors Puzzle 7

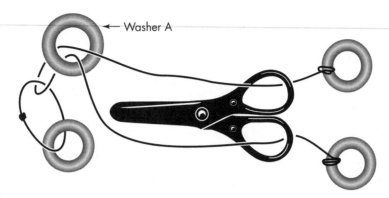

Free washer A from the rope.

Scissors Puzzle 8

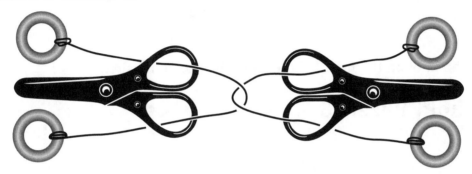

Separate the scissors.

Household Puzzles

Household Puzzle 1

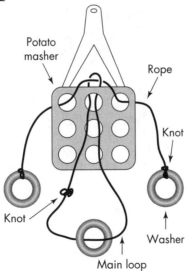

Remove the main loop from the potato masher.

Household Puzzle 2

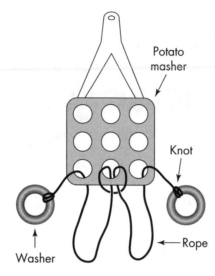

Untie the knot on the middle hole from the potato masher.

Household Puzzle 3

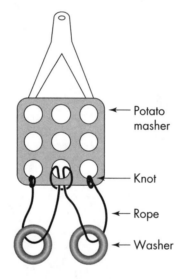

Get the two washers next to each other on the same loop of the rope.

Problem-Solving Mathematics Puzzles

Household Puzzle 4

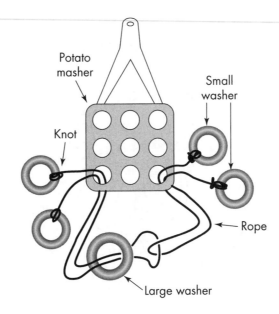

Remove the large washer from the ropes.

Household Puzzle 5

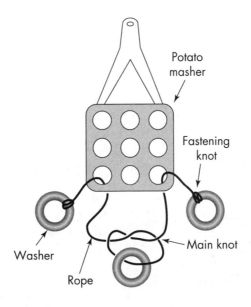

Remove the main knot from the rope.

Household Puzzle 6

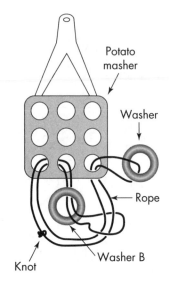

Remove washer B from the rope.

Household Puzzle 7

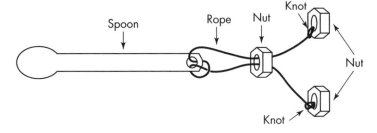

Remove the spoon from the rope.

Household Puzzle 8

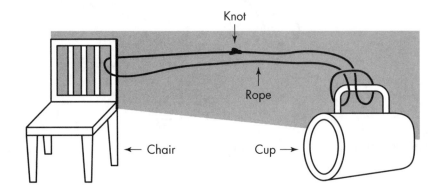

Free the mug from the rope.

Selected Solutions

Hundreds Chart Explorations

Arrow Paths: 53, 44, 88, 36, 97, 65

Remember: 15, 13, 45, 31, 35, 54

Number Grid Puzzles: 55, 24, 41, 97, 66, 55

More Grid Puzzles: 96, 25, 45, 67

What's My Rule? -10, $+10$, $+11$, -11, -9, $+9$

More What's My Rule? B $= +12$, C $= +22$, D $= +18$, E $= +3$, F $= +20$

Operational Arrows: Multiple solutions exist.

Hundreds Chart Discoveries

Sum of Six Numbers in a Row: Three times the sum of the inner two numbers or the outer two numbers equals the sum of all six numbers.

Sum-Digit Pattern of Numbers on a Main Diagonal: The sum of the digits is always the same because you are adding 9 by increasing to the tens row by one 10 and decreasing in the ones row by 1.

Inners and Outers: The sums are always the same. This relates to finding averages.

Three in a Row: The sum always equals the product. The equation for relating the sum and the product is $a + (a + 1) + (a + 2) = 3a + 3 = 3(a + 1)$, where a is the number in the upper left corner.

Adding Opposite Corners of Four Small Squares: The sums equal each other. The sums on one diagonal equal the sums on the other diagonal: $[a + (a + 11)] = (a + 1) + (a + 10) = 2a$, where a is the number in the upper left corner.

The Great X: The sums are equal to each other. The sums are the same as in the previous puzzle, except that you add the central number to both sides.

Multiplying Opposite Corners of Four Small Squares: One product is always 10 more than the other product. The product of one diagonal is $a(a + 11) = a^2 + 11a$. The product of the other diagonal is $(a + 10)(a + 1) = a^2 + 11a + 10$. Here a is the number in the upper left corner.

Pockets Full of Pennies

pz. 1: 1, 2, 3, 4; **pz. 2:** 1, 2, 3, 4; **pz. 3:** 1, 1, 1, 2; **pz. 4:** 5, 5; **pz. 5:** 2, 4; **pz. 6:** 3, 4, 5; **pz. 7:** 5, 5, 5, 5

More Pockets, More Pennies

pz. 1: 7, 3; **pz. 2:** 4, 5, 6; **pz. 3:** 3, 4, 5, 6; **pz. 4:** 7; **pz. 5:** 6, 8; **pz. 6:** 5, 5, 5, 6; **pz. 7:** 5, 6, 7, 8

Tracing Puzzles

Tracing Puzzles 1 through 7 are possible; puzzles 8 through 10 are impossible.

People Puzzles

People Puzzle 2 is an open loop puzzle, with multiple open loops that need to be navigated. To solve it: Push the rope through the vest armhole. Loop one side over the head, down through the vest, out of the other armhole, around the arm and hand, and then back up through the vest armhole. Now just pull the rope to the floor and step out of the loop.

People Puzzles 3 and 4 are solved in the same way. The difference between them is that in puzzle 3, the person with the clothing on cannot do the puzzle. Someone else has to do it on the person. In contrast, the person tied up in the puzzle 4 can do it. To solve it: Lift the sweatshirt over the head from the back so it hangs over the arms. Turn it inside out by pulling one armhole through itself and out of the other armhole, with the rest of the sweatshirt following the armhole. Then slide the sweatshirt back over the head.

People Puzzles 5 and 6 are basically the same. One involves putting on the inner garment; the other involves removing it. Two solutions exist. This is one: Pull the bottom of one side of the inner garment up to the outer garment armpit. Stuff it down the inside of the arm of the outer garment, pull it around the hand and arm, and then pull it back up the inside of the arm hole of the outer garment. Then put that side of the inner garment through the neck hole of the outer garment, over the head, and back through the neck hole. Next stuff the entire inner garment down the other armhole of the outer garment and pull it free from the person's arm.

Line Designs

Shape Designs

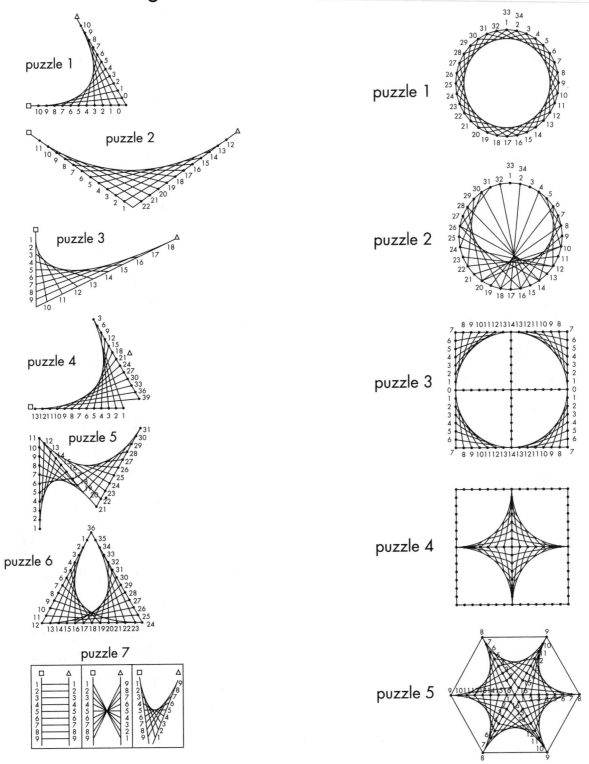

Magic Circles
Answers vary. Possible answers.

puzzle 1

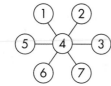

puzzle 2

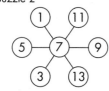

puzzle 3

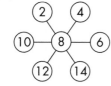

puzzle 4

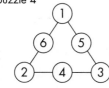

puzzle 5

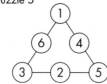

puzzle 6

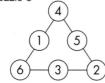

puzzle 7

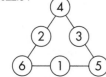

Magic Squares
Answers vary. Possible answers.

puzzle 1

	1	
2	3	4
	5	

puzzle 2

	2	
4	6	8
	10	

puzzle 3

3	7	2
8	■	4
1	5	6

puzzle 4

2	3	7
	4	
1	5	6

puzzle 5

2	9	4
7	5	3
6	1	8

puzzle 6

2	9	4
7	5	3
6	1	8

All possible Get 15 sums are laid out in this magic square.

puzzle 7

hot	form	woes
tank	hear	wasp
tied	brim	ship

All possible Hot sums are laid out in this magic square.

Coin Challenges

Coin Circle: Move coin 1 so that it touches coins 4 and 5. Slide coin 5 out of the middle to between coins 1 and 6.

Coin Line-Up: Place one coin heads up on one side of the line. Place a second coin tails up on the other side of the line. Stand a third coin on its edge on the line with the heads side facing the heads up coin and the tails side facing the tails up coin.

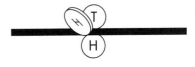

Coin Pyramid: Move coin 1 below coins 8 and 9. Move coin 10 beside coin 3 and above coin 6. Move coin 7 beside coin 2 and above coin 4.

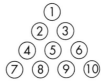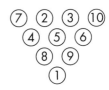

Puzzling H: Put the two additional coins slightly above and below the middle coin.

Odd Coins: Form a pyramid with five coins on each side.
Coin Jump: A. Move coin 4 on top of coin 7. B. Move coin 6 on top of coin 2. C. Move coin 1 on top of coin 3. D. Move coin 8 on top of coin 5.

Coin Cover-Up: Start in any circle. Put your finger on that circle and count three clockwise from there. Place a coin on the circle. Then count three counterclockwise to the circle you started from. Place a coin on the circle. Then continue counting three in any direction that lands you on an empty circle, and place a coin each time you finish counting.

① ② ③ ④ ⑤ ⑥ ⑦ ⑧

A. ① ② ③   ⑤ ⑥ ④ ⑧
B. ① ⑥ ③   ⑤   ④ ⑧
C.   ⑥ ①   ⑤   ④ ⑧
D.   ⑥ ①   ⑧   ④

Mirror Puzzlers

These Pencil Image Cards are possible: 1, 4, 5, 6, 10, 11. These cards are impossible: 2, 3, 7, 8, 9, 12.

Selected Solutions

References

Bright, G., Harvey, J., and Wheeler, M. *Learning and Mathematics Games*. Journal for Research in Mathematics Education Monograph, vol. 1. Reston, Va.: National Council of Teachers of Mathematics, 1985.

Kamii, C., and Livingston, S. *Young Children Continue to Reinvent Arithmetic: Implications of Piaget's Theory*. New York: Teachers College Press, 1994.

Kamii, C., and Housman, L. *Young Children Reinvent Arithmetic: Implications of Piaget's Theory*. (2nd ed.) New York: Teachers College Press, 2000.

Kamii, C., Rummelsburg, J., and Kari, A. "Teaching Arithmetic to Low-Performing, Low-SES First Graders." *Journal of Mathematical Behavior*, 2005, *24*, 23–50.

Kaye, P. *Games for Math*. New York: Random House, 1987.

Kliman, M. "Math out of School: Families' Math Game Playing at Home." *School Community Journal*, 2006, *16*(2), 69–90.

National Council of Teacher of Mathematics. *Principles and Standards for School Mathematics*. Reston, Va.: National Council of Teachers of Mathematics, 2000.

Polya, G. *How to Solve It*. Princeton, N.J.: Princeton University Press, 1957.

Schiro, M. *Mega-Fun Math Games*. New York: Scholastic, 1995.

Schiro, M. *Oral Storytelling and Teaching Mathematics: Pedagogical and Multicultural Perspectives*. Thousand Oaks, Calif.: Sage, 2004.

Somervell, E. *A Rhythmic Approach to Mathematics*. London: George Philip & Son, 1906.